The Latin Passion Play:
Its Origins and Development

Jesus' Trial and Judas's Repentence

From *Codex Purpureus Rossanensis*, Fol. 8,
Bibliothèque Nationale, Paris, 19207 Fac. Sim. 200.

The Latin Passion Play: Its Origins and Development

Sandro Sticca

State University of New York Press

Albany

PUBLISHED BY STATE UNIVERSITY OF NEW YORK PRESS
THURLOW TERRACE, ALBANY, NEW YORK 12201

COPYRIGHT © 1970 BY THE RESEARCH FOUNDATION OF
STATE UNIVERSITY OF NEW YORK. ALL RIGHTS RESERVED

CHAPTER V,
"THE *Planctus Mariae* AND THE PASSION PLAYS,"
ORIGINALLY APPEARED IN *Symposium*, © 1961
BY SYRACUSE UNIVERSITY PRESS
AND IS REPRINTED BY PERMISSION OF THE PUBLISHER

STANDARD BOOK NUMBER 87395-045-3
LIBRARY OF CONGRESS CATALOG CARD NUMBER 69-11318
MANUFACTURED IN THE UNITED STATES OF AMERICA
DESIGNED BY RHODA C. CURLEY

To My Parents and to Mimi and Jennifer

Ne putetis, fratres, quod sine spectaculis nos dimisit Dominus Deus noster . . . Et magnum est hoc spectare per totum orbem terrarum, victum leonem sanguine Agni.

St. Augustine, *In Joannis Evangelium*

Table of Contents

Foreword

L'aventure de Sandro Sticca nous amène à réfléchir sur les aléas de la recherche scientifique. L'ambition de tout *scholar* n'est-elle pas de faire une découverte, de prouver qu'on s'était trompé jusqu'alors et qu'une part de mystère se dissipe? Sans doute, les moins modestes des confrères prétendront toujours qu'on pressentait depuis longtemps l'existence de ce que l'on vient d'exposer au grand jour.

Ils n'avaient rien soupçonné pourtant, les historiens du théâtre, lorsque D. M. Inguanez révéla la *Passion* du Mont-Cassin en 1936, dans les *Miscellanea Cassinese*. C'était une découverte que rien n'annonçait et on se le dit en Italie et en Angleterre, tout de suite après. Mais il semble que les historiens du théâtre n'aient pas été touchés par ce qu'en ont écrit F. Neri dans le *Giornale storico della letteratura italiana* et P. Toschi dans l'*Archivum Romanicum* en 1937, C. S. Gutkind dans les *Modern Language Studies* en 1938. La guerre de 39–45 ne suffit pas à expliquer ce long silence.

Grâce à Sandro Sticca, la découverte de 1936 ne fut pas un avortement. Dans la revue belge *Latomus,* le professeur de Binghamton republia le texte de la *Passion* et en souligna l'originalité. C'était en 1961 et notre auteur s'adressait aux latinistes. J'ignore quel profit ceux-ci en ont retiré et où ils ont logé la fiche qu'ils ont pu établir. Je me défends à peine de croire que les spécialistes de l'Antiquité ont dédaigné ce texte du bas moyen âge et que les rares historiens de la littérature latine tardive ont fait la petite bouche: fi de la littérature populaire, hors du sillon de la tradition savante!

Ils nous auraient dit leur plaisir de compter une oeuvre de plus qu'ils eussent été loin d'apprécier toute la portée de la découverte. Sandro Sticca a peut-être mal choisi son public. Mais quelle est la revue internationale qui convenait à son message? C'est qu'il eût fallu toucher à la fois les historiens du théâtre médiéval en langue vulgaire et les spécialistes du drame liturgique. Pour ma part, le hasard m'ayant mis sous les yeux l'article de Sandro Sticca paru dans mon pays, j'ai tenté, en 1964, de lui donner quelque publicité en le célébrant devant la Classe des Lettres de l'Académie Royale de Belgique; grâce aux tirages à part de cette communication, j'ai pu en informer les meilleures revues de philologie romane.

J'ignorais alors qui était Sandro Sticca, mais le poids de ce qu'il m'apprenait me contraignait assez à ne pas le laisser ignorer autant.

Quoi qu'il en soit, il me semble que, jusqu'à present, on n'ait jamais parlé de la *Passion* du Mont-Cassin *in the right place* et c'est ce que je voulais dire lorsque j'ai parlé des aléas de la recherche scientifique. Une découverte risque d'être sans effets, l'enfant mourra dans ses langes si, pour le faire connaître, on n'utilise pas la longueur d'onde appropriée ou si l'événement surgit dans le brouhaha de faits d'autre nature.

Aujourd'hui, Sandro Sticca nous donne tout un livre sur le sujet. Pendant plus de dix ans, il a médité sur le drame liturgique et sur la place que la Passion de 1160 occupe dans cet ensemble où l'on s'étonnait de ne pas trouver un *ludus* sur la Rédemption. On avait dit bien des choses—et des erreurs aussi—sur les premières *Passions* en langue vulgaire: Sandro Sticca, aujourd'hui, peut condamner certaines hypothèses qui, à force d'être répétées, sont devenues des assertions. En somme, notre auteur a démoli, puis a reconstruit tout un mur de l'histoire du premier théâtre occidental.

On goûtera la pertinence de ses analyses, la largeur de son horizon et l'acuité de sa pensée. Cette fois, grâce au livre, fruit d'une lente étude et d'une exploitation personnelle et complète, la découverte du Mont-Cassin ne sera pas passée inaperçue.

Omer Jodogne, Louvain

Preface

In the past fifty years a great deal of scholarly writing has been done on the origin of the religious drama. Speculations on this subject have been varied and at times stimulating. There are those, for instance, who believe that the origin of this religious drama was provided by the Church's liturgy with its abundance of antiphons and responses of all sorts, and the symbolical action, gesture, and movement inherent in the allocation of parts or roles in the services, especially the Mass. There are those, however, who believe that these services cannot be considered drama in an exact sense until they have been cast into a dramatic form, that is until they have mimetic action, impersonation and dialogue.

Recent studies have definitely proven that the plays of the Church did not arise directly from the fundamental liturgy used *in Christian worship, but from additions to it called tropes. In broadest definition, tropes are Latin passages in addition to, amplification of, or interpolation in the authorized liturgy. The recognition of the Easter and Christmas tropes as the original germ of later Latin Easter and Christmas liturgical dramatic plays is unquestioned. Performed within the confines of Christian worship and subservient to the end of that worship, they exhibit dramatic action and liturgical rite in the closest conjunction. Spanning many centuries, the plays are testimony of the growth of the liturgical dramatic form and of the dramatic movement and temper of the liturgy in which they find their origin.*

The liturgical drama, like the Church that produced it, was international. As such, from its earliest beginnings in the tenth-century Quem quaeritis *to the thirteenth-century* Ludi Paschales *and Latin Passion plays, it exhibits a cultural and thematic unity binding the various plays: a thematic unity from the fabric of Christian thought, and a cultural unity from the fact that these productions, at least up to the end of the thirteenth century, generally share a technical-philological medium: the Latin language.*

Although aspects of the liturgical drama of the Middle Ages have already been treated by competent scholars, no formal discussion exists of the Latin Passion play, since very few of these dramas have survived and also because the full development of the vernacular plays belongs to the late Middle Ages. It must be given fresh consideration, though, in the light of the discovery of a Latin Passion play at Montecassino, which precedes by one hundred years what scholars have traditionally considered to be the earliest extant Latin Passion plays, the two Latin dramas from the Carmina Burana *collection. The specific purpose of this study will be apparent both from the title and the thematic structure of the Table of Contents.*

Any scholar writing on the Middle Ages deeply realizes the debt he owes his predecessors and teachers, for they are both custodians of a tradition and the fresh arrows pointing to new discoveries. It is with gratitude, therefore, that I acknowledge my indebtedness to Prof. Mary H. Marshall, of Syracuse University, whose stimulating lectures first initiated me in the subject of the medieval religious drama and to Prof. Albert D. Menut, of Syracuse University, for the privilege of sharing in the fruits of his erudition. I am also grateful for the guidance provided me by the scholarly acumen of Prof. Lawton G. Peckham, of Columbia University. I am particularly indebted to the National Foundation on the Arts and Humanities, for their fellowship allowed me to organize and evaluate material. To my colleague, Prof. Frederick Garber, a personal thanks for reading the manuscript. I could not fail to express my gratitude to my wife who, as sponsa et amica, *has provided counsel and comprehension.*

Illustrations

xix

The Latin Passion Play:
Its Origins and Development

Abbreviations Used
In Notes and Bibliography

CSEL   *Corpus Scriptorum Ecclesiasticorum Latinorum*
JEGP   *Journal of English and Germanic Philology*
MLN   *Modern Language Notes*
P.G.   *Patrologia Graeca*
P.L.   *Patrologia Latina*
PMLA   *Publications of the Modern Language Association of America*
RR   *Romanic Review*

1. Classical Heritage and the Liturgical Drama

N ORDER TO PLACE the origin of the Latin Passion play in its proper historical, liturgical, and dramatic perspectives, it is necessary to consider the problem of the origin and development of liturgical drama. Although much has been written on the subject by competent scholars, my own research suggests that a reappraisal of certain traditional views is needed. I shall study specifically the rise of the Latin Passion play, showing that it developed as the continuation and expansion of themes already present in the liturgical rites of Easter week.

The theory of the ecclesiastical origin of modern European drama has won wide acceptance. Learned studies by Toschi, Franceschini and de Bartholomaeis in Italian; [1] Knudsen, Vey, Kindermann, Hartl and Froning in German;[2] Hamelin, Pignarre, Moussinac and Cohen in French; [3] Gardiner, Frank,

Craig, Donovan, Speaight and Hardison in English; [4] all based on the foundation provided by Karl Young's monumental liturgical corpus,[5] have seriously weakened the thesis that surviving pagan representations, theatrical in essence, such as mimes, determined the rise of liturgical drama, as Magnin, Du Méril, Reich, and Chambers maintained.[6] Yet similar views are found in more recent studies, such as the *Storia del teatro drammatico* by Silvio D'Amico,[7] *The Origin of the Theater* by B. Hunningher,[8] and W. Bridges-Adams' *The Irresistible Theater*.[9] D'Amico, for example, while agreeing that modern drama derives from the liturgical, insists on the continued existence in the Middle Ages of a pagan Latin theater. Yet he considers the medieval *mimus* and the scholastic *comoedia elegiaca*, often cited as the main link between medieval and classic drama, as literary exercises not destined for representation.[10]

HROTSWITHA

The most important evidence for the existence of a preliturgical theater is found by D'Amico in the six "dramatic" pieces in Latin prose written in the tenth century by the Benedictine nun of Gandersheim.[11] Opinion remains divided on their theatricality. Scholarly commentaries range from categorical assertions that Hrotswitha's writings have nothing to do with theater [12] to claims supporting the potentiality for performance apparent in her dramas.[13] If the actual performance of these "plays" could be ascertained, the discovery

> would have serious consequences. It would bring with it the necessity of rewriting much of the history of the early European (not only German) drama between the tenth and the twelfth centuries because that history as now written does not take proper account of Hrotswitha's dramas as acting plays, and therefore ignores them in their possible relationship to other dramatic activity during the period from about 960 on.[14]

English [15] and American [16] writers on medieval religious drama have expressed doubt that her plays were intended for representation, and German [17] scholars on the whole have attributed little significance to them as drama. French scholars, however, give them more importance. The French thesis is based almost solely on the fragment of Froumond of Tegernsee. A monk and teacher, this contemporary of Hrotswitha alludes to scenic representations in the schools of the time:

> Si facerem mihi pendentes per cingula caudas Gesticulans
> manibus, lubrice stans pedibus, Si lupus aut ursus vel vellem
> fingere vulpem, Si larvas facerem furciferis manibus, Dulcifer
> aut fabulas nossem componere mendax, Orpheus ut cantans
> Euridicen revocat, Si canerem multos dulci modulamine leudos
> Undique currentes cum trepidis pedibus, Gauderet mihi qui pro-
> prior visurus adesset, Ridiculus cunctos concuteret pueros.[18]

The value of this fragment is relatively negligible since it alludes to mimetic performance by means of dance and gesture and not to representation by actors assuming the roles of characters.

As to Hrotswitha, Ricaumont states categorically that her plays are "le plus ancien monument non seulement du théâtre allemand mais du théâtre européen." [19] Sprague [20] and Jones are confident that her works were performed. Ermini [21] points to an inherent dramatic pathos in them resulting from the conflict between the *pia devotio* and the *mundana pravitas*. It seems to me, however, that the notion that Hrotswitha's pious legends were performed is based primarily on the belief that a potentially dramatic milieu existed at the time. Scholars point to the influence of Plautus and Terence, to a dramatic instinct preserved by the *mimi* and the incipient Latin liturgical drama. In refutation, one can cite Young, Frank, and Franceschini, who assert that in the tenth century the Western world had no understanding of an acted classical drama.[22] The existence of a secular dramatic activity by the twelfth and thirteenth centuries has, however, been suggested [23] and richly attested for religious drama. We need mention only the twelfth-century Montecassino Latin Passion play and the French *Jeu d'Adam*, both truly stageworthy.

The existence of a dramatic milieu as early as the tenth century would not, however, solve the problem of Hrotswitha's plays, for it is apparent they were intended for recitation, declamation, or private reading and not for actual production.[24] There is no mention in her writings of such terms as *comoedia* and *tragoedia*, and she fails to mention *drama* in describing the works of Terence. The preface to her plays reveals her motivation:

> Plures inveniuntur catholici, cuius nos penitus expurgare nequimus facti, qui pro cultioris facundia sermonis gentilium vanitatem librorum utilitati praeferunt sacrarum scripturarum. Sunt etiam alii, sacris inhaerentes paginis, qui licet alia gentilium spernant, Terentii tamen fingmenta frequentius lectitant et, dum dulcedine sermonis delectantur, nefandarum notitia rerum maculantur. Unde ego, Clamor Validus Gandeshemensis, non recusavi illum imitari dictando, dum alii colunt legendo, quo eodem genere, quo turpia lascivarum incesta feminarum recitabantur, laudabilis sacrarum castimonia virginum iuxta mei facultatem ingeniali celebraretur.[25]

It is evident from this passage that Hrotswitha's intention was to provide an edifying version of Terence's immoral comedies.[26] This assertion is in keeping with the traditional understanding that Terence's plays were recited or read during the Middle Ages, at times with the accompaniment of mute miming.[27] Vinay observes that

> non è difficile . . . constatare come, da Isidoro in poi, si sia convinti, nel medioevo, che le commedie di Terenzio e di Plauto furono scritte per essere recitate con accompagnamento di gesti e di moti corporei in un luogo idoneo chiamato teatro, alla presenza di un pubblico di spettatori.[28]

Hrotswitha's knowledge of Terence and the dramatic possibilities inherent in her plays have caused certain scholars [29] to consider her as the germinal point of the revival, in the tenth century, of the Latin theater. The imitation of Terence and the possibility that her plays could be performed do not, however, warrant regarding Hrotswitha as a legitimate playwright.[30] To be considered such, one must be conscious of writing for the theater and have an objective understanding of its essential prerequisites: mise en scène, action, dialogue, and impersonation.

The poetic theme of Hrotswitha's pious legends is ill suited to the development of human passions and the creation of a dramatic situation,[31] for the *dramatis personae*, the virgins and martyrs, saints and sinners, emperors and executioners, are stereotyped and rigid. Her characterization of the martyrs and sinners, in particular, is so dominated by religious considerations that they lack tragic motivation and human sensibility. With martyrdom being not a catastrophe but a victory, the characterization and the sudden conversions are devoid of internal self-appraisal and conviction. The characters behave, generally, as allegorical personages, for the tragic situation is marked by the intervention of God, who as a *Deus ex machina* irregularly facilitates the development of action. Whatever the literary worth of Hrotswitha's tales, and whether or not they were ever acted out, the prevalent opinion today is that her writings had no influence on the subsequent development of drama [32] and cannot serve as ties between the classical theater and that of the Middle Ages.

RELIGIOUS VS. SECULAR THEATER

According to some recent investigations, the link can be found in the mime. In the wake of Reich, Nicoll, Reinhardt, and Borcherdt,[33] Hunningher, in particular, has strongly posited the persistence of a secular histrionic tradition in the Middle Ages. Resurrecting Winterfeld's [34] arguments, he asserted that the religious drama came into being through the dramatic tradition represented by the mimes who were employed by the clergy in the presentation of tropes and actually performed them. This was "how drama sprang from the tropes—or rather, how the tropes developed into drama." [35] Hunningher did not seem to realize that "if tropes were written as a sort of drama, the church did produce drama, and the question of who acted it on a given occasion is irrelevant." [36] Hunningher believes that the necessity to pull the masses away from the satanic entertainment they enjoyed "led the clergy to cooperate with the mimes and to develop theatrical attractions for the congregation." [37] But surely the Church did not need to employ the mimes for theatrical purposes, for beginning in the sixth century it possessed in the medieval monastery not only a house of a religious order, but also an establishment that functioned as a school, a university, a library, a publishing house, a center of culture.[38] As Helen Waddell has shown the monks were highly proficient in impish rhyme, classical learning, and religious fervor. Hunningher's hypothesis clearly disregards evidence indicating that the liturgical drama was acted by the clergy: priests and monks. For the representation of the Easter *Quem quaeritis*, for instance, it is specifically mentioned in the tenth-century *Regularis Concordia* that

> tres [fratres] succedant, omnes quidem cappis induti, turribula cum incensu manibus gestantes ac pedetemptim ad similitudinem querentium quid, ueniant ante locum Sepulchri. Aguntur enim hoc ad imitationem Angeli sedentis in monumento, atque Mulierum cum aromatibus uenientium ut ungerent corpus Jhesus.[39]

Furthermore, Cohen has shown how two eleventh-century reliefs, one from southern France and the other from Modena, Italy, offering a representation of the Holy Women at the sepulchre, can be properly interpreted by reference to the text of the liturgical drama. That the actors are priests taking the part of the Holy Women can be surmised by their pointed beards, the liturgical "amict," and the incense-burners of priests. The presence of the *Unguentarius*, too, indicates this vision could have come only from the liturgical drama.[40]

To reinforce his argument emphasizing the contribution of the mimes, Hunningher remarks that from the twelfth to the fourteenth century secular and religious dramatic productions were almost equal in quantity, although the artistic level of secular drama was much higher than that of the religious drama, for no Church play could compare with the well-constructed thirteenth-century *Jeu de la feuillée*. In addition, if the Church provided the stimulus to the development of drama, it appears to him highly "singular that before the beginning of the thirteenth century, there is no mention whatever of a dramatized Passion;" [41] a remarkable lacuna this, according to him, in view of the vast popularity achieved by Christ's Passion in later mystery plays.

In reply to the latter proposition it can be pointed out that we do have a dramatized Latin Passion of the twelfth century,[42] which is comparable in many ways to the *Jeu de la feuillée*. This fact is reason enough to question the alleged superiority of the secular drama. It is worth noting that scholars have pointed out the connection between the *Jeu de la feuillée* and the Church.[43]

As to the influence of the mimes, Hunningher bases their dramatic importance primarily on the strength of Isidore's *Etymologiae*, which describes the mimes and their activities,[44] and on his personal interpretation of a richly illuminated tenth-century troper from the abbey of St. Martial at Limoges, now in Paris (Bibl. Nat., lat. 1118), which shows "various mimes in their performances—acting, dancing, accompanying themselves on musical instruments." [45] That the portraits represent mimes is not definite but is merely the author's own allegation; an analysis of the miniatures strongly suggests to Ogilvy and myself that the persons represented may be the mimes of King David.[46] Hunningher's hypothesis is hardly tenable also since the Limoges manuscript cannot be dated earlier than the year A.D. 1000 (990) because of the appearance in it (f. 38ᵛ) of the names of Hugh Capet and Pope John XVI.[47] Professor Gamer, in a recent cogent study, has decisively solved the problem by demonstrating that Hunningher's conjecture is based on a wrong assumption about the date of the Paris manuscript. Gamer dates it about A.D. 1000–1050 and shows that the mimes or dancers represented in the miniatures are really in keeping with the best sacred tradition; she further identifies the first one of these figures as that of King David himself.[48] But even if the painted figures of the Limoges manuscript are worldly mimes, they are of no consequence in the inception of the religious play, nor can they be used as evidence, because by A.D. 1000 the *Visitatio Sepulchri* was an already well established form. It appears highly improbable, too, that during the tenth century—an age characterized by monastic reforms such as those emerging from Lorraine and Cluny, when education remained throughout ecclesiastical and mainly monastic [49]—the Church would employ the services of secular mimes to commemorate and represent the greatest and most sacred Christian mystery: Jesus' Passion and Resurrection.

As to Isidore's descriptions of the mimes, it would be misleading to use his evidence as a *post hoc ergo propter hoc* argument, for he is describing past practices, and when he speaks of the *mimi* he means mimicry, not play acting. Modern scholarship, too, has given evidence that "the information on representation by comedians and tragedians, *histriones* and *mimi*, transmitted by Isidore of Seville in the *Etymologiae* (XVIII, 42–51) was bare and limited, at second hand, chiefly from late sources of the empire when formal drama was already dead; errors in understanding the ancient drama accumulated in later learned tradition." [50] A common mistake by modern scholars has been their unwillingness to distinguish between traditional dramatic modes and contemporary theatrical conditions.[51]

It is now generally agreed that the performance of the mimes differed considerably from the modern theatrical production. Already during the Empire the old *histrio* (actor) had been supplanted by the *pantomimus*, and by the fifth and sixth centuries they came to be associated with the *mimus*, whose repertory consisted of a facile and clever imitation of human customs and lewd scenes in which panderers, prostitutes, and adulterers were portrayed.[52] Such, too, appears to be the medieval application of these terms, as indicated in Papias': "Mimus . . . idest ioculator et proprie rerum humanarum imitator sicut olim erant in recitatione comediarum quia, quod verbo recitator dicebat, mimi motu corporis exprimebant" [53] and Isidore's "Histriones sunt qui muliebri indumento gestus impudicarum feminarum exprimebant, hi autem saltando etiam historias et res gestas exprimebant." [54] Concerned in his work with transmitted knowledge and its sources, Isidore is here referring to past practices as evidenced by the tense used. To be sure, he must have known contemporary *mimi* and *histriones* who gave imitation of "human things" or stories. But one ought to distinguish, as Allardyce Nicoll does, between acting in the old classic tradition of mimic impersonation with its "imitation" of life and ancient or for that matter modern dramatic performance utilizing actors, dialogue, and action.

A more complete delineation of the mimes' inferior modes of performance is found in the tenth century in one of the *Sermones* of Attone bishop of Vercelli:

> Non laetentur in theatris, ut scenici; non in epithalamiis et cantilenis, ut mimi; non in saltationibus et circo, ut histriones vel idolorum cultores, quos, heu. quidam Christiani adhuc in multis imitantur. Quid enim miserabilius senibus, quid turpius juvenibus, quid perniciosius adolescentulis, quam strupa virginum et libidines meretricum turpi gestu et blanda voce cantare, ut spectatores suos talibus insidiis ad suas provocent corruptiones? [55]

The survival of mimes of this kind cannot be questioned, particularly in view of the frequent anathemas pronounced against them by the Church. Since we lack, however, all records of dramatic performance between the fifth and the ninth centuries, we need not assume as Winterfeld, Nicoll, and Hunningher do, that the *mimi* and *histriones* served to keep alive the traditions of the ancient Roman theater until the appearance of the religious drama of the Middle Ages,[56] nor that they were the *causa causans* of this theater. They simply attested the survival of some kind of histrionic instinct,[57] possessing within definite limitations what Fergusson calls "histrionic sensibility." [58]

As to the existence of a potential dramatic milieu established on recollection of the works of Plautus and Terence, it is significant that little is recorded of the three Latin dramatic authors who survived in the Middle Ages.[59] Of Plautus' twenty plays, only eight seem to have been generally known. Most often though, he is mentioned for the *flores* of his *eloquentia*,[60] and after the eleventh century as the alleged author of the *Querulus*. Seneca, too, and his ten tragedies are hardly referred to before the thirteenth century.[61] Terence appears to be the best known and the most widely mentioned and imitated in the many *florilegia* but only as an *auctor*, a master of style and clarity.[62] It was indeed Terence's *dulcedo sermonis* and *elegantia*, grace of idiom and refinement, which induced Hrotswitha to imitate him. There is, however, no dramatic concept connected with these authors in the Middle Ages, for "gli autori classici del teatro antico sopravvivono . . . soltanto nella cultura del Medio Evo; vengono letti nelle scuole, non rappresentati sulle scene." [63]

With the absence of the notion of dramatic representation Plautus and Terence were treated as *Lesedramen* [64] and read just as Virgil, Horace, Ovid, and Juvenal were.

Thus comedy came to be considered a kind of poetic narrative (Dante writes: "est comoedia genus quodam poeticae narrationis") that distinguishes itself from the others by the use of familiar, comical themes, a low style and the employment of ordinary personages. Placidus, for instance, wrote that: "Comoedia [est] quae res privatorum et humilium personarum comprehendit, non tam alto ut tragoedia stilo, sed mediocri et dulci," [65] and Isidore observed: "Tragoedi sunt qui antiqua gesta atque facinora sceleratorum regum luctuoso carmine, spectante populo, concinebant." [66] As late as the end of the fourteenth century medieval definitions of *tragoedia* and *comoedia* lack clear dramatic connotations. Maistre Nicole Oresme, the compiler of the first French translation (1370) of Aristotle's *Nicomachean Ethics*, and the first to use the word "tragédie" in French, states that tragedies "sont ditiéz, comme rommanz qui parlent et traictent de aucuns granz faiz notables." In evident reference to contemporary French mystery plays, he defines comedies as "aucuns gieux, comme sont ceulz ou .i. homme represente Saint Pol, l'autre Judas, l'autre un hermite, et dit chascun son personage et en ont aucuns roulles et rimes. Et aucunes fois en tels giex l'en dit de laides paroles, ordes injurieuses et deshonestes." [67] On the basis of such definitions, the words *tragoedia* and *comoedia* came to indicate particular kinds of style and were applied to narrative and lyrical forms of literature. The Virgil of the *Aeneid*, the Ovid of the *Elegies*, and Lucan and Statius were considered tragic authors, while Horace, Juvenal, Plautus, and Terence, the Virgil of the *Bucolics*, and Dante in his *Commedia* were regarded as comic ones.

Servius' comment on Virgil's third Eclogue appears to have initiated this misconception: "Apud poetas tres characteres sunt dicendi: unus in quo tantum poeta loquitur . . . Alius dramaticus in quo nusquam poeta loquitur, ut est in comoediis et tragoediis. Tertius mixtus. . . ." [68] He observes that all three styles of writings are represented in the *Bucolics* and that the first and third eclogues belong in the second class, the "dramatic." The fourth-century writer Diomedes, in the wake of Servius, more definitely ranks certain eclogues with tragedies and comedies (*Art. Gram.*, Lib. III. ed. H. Keil, *Gram. lat.*, I, 482): "dramaticon est vel activum in quo personae agunt solae sine ullius poetae interlocutione, ut se habent tragicae et comicae fabulae; quo genere scripta est prima bucolicon et ea cuius initium est 'quo te, Moeri, pedes?'" (Ecl. IX). Isidore of Seville (*Etymologiae*, VIII, 7) virtually follows Servius. Bede, in his *De Arte Metrica*, follows in the path of Diomedes, refers to the *Eclogues* of Virgil in his examples of drama and calls the *Song of Songs* "our" kind of drama. In the ninth century, Hrabanus Maurus closely follows Servius and Diomedes and changes but a few words.[69] By the time of Papias the notion is more clearly defined: "Poetarum tres sunt genera: unum in quo poeta loquitur, quod enarratium dicitur; aliud didramaticon [*sic*] in quo poeta nunquam loquitur, ut in comoediis; tertium in quo poetae et mixtae personae." [70]

Another cause of confusion appears to have been the prevalent misconception of the ancient methods of staging plays. From the fifth-century account of Calliopius to the tenth-century Terentian *Persona Delusoris*,[71] Terence's plays are described as having been recited by one man, with pantomimists acting out the scenes. The notion that the poet or *recitator* read the words while the pantomime performed the scenes with gestures seems to have originated from Livy's (VII, 2) and Valerius Maximus' (II, 4,4) descriptions of the introduction, in Rome, of dramatic art by Livius Andronicus, who appears to have required the service of a boy to sing the lyrics to preserve his voice while he mimed the scenes.[72] This peculiar manner of staging, the imperfect recollection of Empire mimes apparent in the definitions found in medieval dictionaries, the impressions gathered from the descriptions left by the early Church fathers,[73] have all contributed to widespread and enduring misconceptions.

COMOEDIA ELEGIACA

In the history of dramatic art particular importance has also been attributed to the "Comoedia elegiaca," a literary genre that developed during the twelfth century, particularly in France, and has been thought to have influenced the incipient medieval theater. By no means dramatic, these compositions in Latin are versified tales, written in distichs and treating comic or familiar subjects. Drawing for their themes mostly on Terence and for form on Ovid,[74] they are scholastic exercises without any plausible relationship with scenic representation.[75] They are called *comoediae,* for

> le commedie del sec. XII sono dette ora commedie, ora elegie, a causa del distico che vi è usato abitualmente, per effetto proprio delle idee che circolavano a quel tempo sui tre tipi di stile, evolgendo narrazioni che potevano essere benissimo novelle o romanzetti, laddove sono classificate per commedie a causa degli argomenti e dello stile, oltre che del metro.[76]

Most famous among these comedies are the twelfth-century *Geta,* known also as the *Amphitryo,* and the *Aulularia* of Vitalis Blesensis, which "are not plays but narrative." [77] A variation on the theme of Plautus' *Amphitryo, Geta*'s sustained interest hinges on the sophistry of the servant Geta who represents a parody of the metaphysical disquisitions typical of the age and of the uncouth dullness of Birria. Unrelated to Plautus' play and deriving from an anonymous fourth-century *Querulus,* Vitalis' *Aulularia* is another narrative comedy. In the prologue he identifies himself as the author of the *Amphitryo* as well and pretends to excel Plautus:

> Haec mea vel Plauti comedia nomen ab olla
> Traxit, sed Plauti quae fuit illa mea est.
> Curtavi Plautum, Plautum haec iactura beavit;
> Ut placeat Plautus scripta Vitalis emunt.
> Amphitryon nuper, nunc Aulularia tandem
> Senserunt senio pressa Vitalis opem.[78]

The work depicts some devious servants trying to deprive a credulous young man of his rightful inheritance. Among the elegiac comedies of the twelfth century, honorable mention is to be made of the *Alda* of William of Blois, the anonymous *Pamphilus* and the *Milo* of Matthew of Vendôme. One play, the *Babio,* by reason of its continuous and vivacious dialogue, has been thought to have been destined for some kind of dramatic representation. A composition made up of 486 verses in elegiac distichs, the *Babio* has variously been attributed to Vitalis of Blois and Petrus Babion. Henry Laye and Filippo Ermini have indicated that it was written for the theater; [79] Faral, while suggesting the possibility of its being destined to a mimed recitation, wrote nevertheless that it had all the characteristics of a fabliau.[80] Gustave Cohen described it as "extrêmement scénique," [81] while Franceschini is of the opinion that it was intended exclusively for reading, not performance.[82]

Scholars of the history of drama have long debated whether the *comoediae* of the twelfth century belong to general literature or to drama and, if the latter, about the nature of their theatrical performances, if any. Petit de Julleville refers to them as "écrits plus ou moins dramatiques . . . rédigés en latin . . . par des lettrés . . . qui se gardaient de les produire dans une représentation publique." [83] Cloetta considers them to have been destined for a half-dramatic recitation with distribution of parts; [84] and Creizenach maintains they were not represented, but read.[85] J. P. Jacobsen, on the other hand, accepts their recitation as a fact and asserts that "on est allé jusqu'à les représenter devant un public." [86] Manitius abstains from formulating a hypothesis based on inadequate evidence: "Weder die Dramen des Terenz noch ihre stofflichen Weiterbildungen, die elegischen und hexametrischen Komödien des Mittelalters scheinen aufgeführt worden zu sein, obwohl hierüber das letzte Wort noch nicht gesprochen ist." [87] Gustave Cohen, under whose direction a corpus of these *comoediae* was first collected, argues that though the existence of an actual representation of these comedies can hardly be ascertained, there exist "au contraire des arguments sérieux en faveur de cette possibilité." [88] Harald Hagendhal dismisses Cohen's suggestion by commenting that the dialogue of the greater number of the comedies is interrupted by long narratives and that anyhow "au moyen âge, on donnait au mot 'comédie' un sens tout différent de celui qu'il avait dans l'antiquité." [89] Cohen's reticence about making a firmer pronouncement on the subject may stem from the fact that, having set out to bring together *comoediae* that could be considered homogeneous from the quadruple standpoint of language, genre, time, and place of origin, it became apparent to him in the end that their only common characteristic is the employment of the elegiac distich.

With the disappearance of the classical dramatic tradition, and of concepts of tragedies and comedies, the men of the Middle Ages began to fashion a kind of theatrical *mimesis* that relied for expression on long dialogues, declaimed or read, and on pantomimic representation. These elements, however, do not constitute dramatic representation, nor do they imply the perpetuation of the classical dramatic tradition.[90]

It appears, then, that these *comoediae* are a product of the learned milieu of the schools[91] of the Middle Ages where they were composed and later adapted for public recitation or sporadic representation by the scholastic body.[92] They are essentially non-dramatic, and the fact that none of them is earlier than the twelfth century definitely substantiates the widely entertained belief that they were of no consequence in the formation or evolution of the liturgical drama.

Posterity's possession of some knowledge about the ancient theater and its *modus operandi* in representation has been at times posited on the strength of isolated information regarding the existence of theater in Rome since 55 B.C.,[93] and in Gaul from the second[94] to the fifth centuries.[95] Any knowledge posterity may have acquired from these accumulated references was certainly devoid of significance, for by the year A.D. 568 the Roman theater had been completely effaced and its dramatic function entirely blurred by the prominence of the mime, farce, and pantomime. Indeed, as early as 400 St. Augustine could write that "per omnes pene civitates cadunt theatra . . . cadunt et fora vel moenia, in quibus demonia colebantur."[96] The disintegration of the theaters was particularly swift in Rome, for the dramatic art never really took firm hold there, being impeded in its progress by the conservative Republican elements, which in their cult of traditional *romana simplicitas* disapproved of anything Greek and looked upon the theater as a corrupting creation.

Recent scholarship on the subject of medieval drama and theater, while acknowledging a limited understanding of the ancient drama during the Middle Ages, has nevertheless predicated the definite presence in the twelfth and thirteenth centuries of a substantial secular dramatic activity on the assumed position that theater buildings were then in existence. Recently Loomis [97] and Cohen argued the existence of theater buildings in the twelfth and thirteenth centuries on the basis of texts containing the words *theatrum* and *scena*. Their assumption was challenged by Bigongiari [98] who adduced evidence to show that the term *theatrum* meant at that time "scaffolding" or "platform." Medieval French [99] uses such terms as *lieux, estages,* and *chauffaulx* for the *mise-en-scène*, while in general in Europe one finds terms as *loca, loci, sedes, domus, mensa, stacio, loco deputato*. Mary H. Marshall, who made an exhaustive inventory of theatrical terminology from the sixth century to the late Middle Ages, found that "throughout the middle ages any place, usually but not necessarily out of doors, where public and secular entertainments were given—often public square or marketplace—might be called theatre" [100] and concludes that for the twelfth and thirteenth centuries "there seems . . . no evidence . . . for anything conceived as specific and regularly used theatre buildings of that period." [101] In view of these conditions, and considering the lateness of the period, it seems unlikely that a secular theater influenced the beginnings of medieval religious drama.

This brief survey we have made of the various attempts to link the theater of the Middle Ages to that of Rome should suffice to indicate the paucity of factual evidence and the tenuous nature of the arguments adduced. A much stronger case can be made for the generally accepted position that the true origin of the medieval drama is to be found in the Church. We shall examine rapidly the dramatic aspects of the liturgy, the origins and nature of the trope, and in the process show that the frequently expressed view that this new form of the theater originated in France needs to be reexamined in the light of recently discovered Italian parallels.

The true origin of modern drama must be found in the development of the medieval theater, which is a creation of the Church.[102] Action, impersonation, and dialogue, the *sine qua non* of drama, appear in the Roman liturgy, which provided during the liturgical year all kinds of antiphonal responses between a cantor and the Chorus, or between two alternating Choruses. The liturgy made provisions for "symbolic action, gesture, and there were also present the elements of impersonation, inherent in vestements and in the allocation or assignment of parts or roles in the service." [103] Karl Young, while stressing impersonation as the essential ingredient of drama, recognizes that "the Roman liturgy is abundantly dramatic" and that the Mass, along with the Canonical Office, "may have contributed suggestions as to the possibility of inventing drama, and may indirectly have encouraged it." [104] It is true, however, that Churchmen never considered the liturgy as theater, and the ceremonies, although potentially theatrical, cannot be said to constitute drama in the traditional sense of the word.

The intense dramatic feeling noted in the liturgy of the ninth and tenth centuries, the period when religious drama is supposed to have originated, is already present in the rituals of the early Christian Church.[105] Among the most ancient works describing the ritual of its *officia* is the *Aetheriae peregrinatio ad loca sancta*, first discovered and published by Gamurrini in 1887,[106] attributed to St. Sylvia of Aquitaine, sister of Rufinus, and now reputed to have been written at Constantinople by a Galician nun named Etheria, between 381 and 395.[107] The second is a *Lectionarius Armenianus* probably composed during the years 464–468; [108] the third, the *Kanonarion* of the Church of Jerusalem dated not earlier than 634–638.[109] The fourth is the *Typicon* (ordo) of the Church of Jerusalem, preserved in a manuscript of the twelfth century but written between the ninth and tenth centuries.[110] These are of considerable interest as sources of information in the study of liturgical offices, but by far the most important is the *Peregrinatio*, for it treats at length the rites of Holy Week of the Church of Jerusalem, the disposition of the canonical hours, the role of the clergy in the various ceremonies, and it contains a most vivid description of the processions to the holy places associated with Christ's Passion.[111] The *Peregrinatio*, transcribed in Cassino in the eleventh century by Petrus Diaconus at the order of the abbot Desiderius (1057–1086), who later became Pope Victor III,[112] has been unduly neglected by medievalists. Recent studies, particularly those of Bastiaensen and Pétré,[113] have shed much light on it, and its influence on the Montecassino liturgy has already been ascertained.[114] It is noteworthy that the earliest Latin Passion play appears at Montecassino in the twelfth century.

THE TROPES

The germinal point of religious drama is not, however, to be found in the liturgy but in the trope.[115] The trope is usually defined as a verbal amplification of a passage in the authorized liturgy—an introduction, interpolation, addition, or conclusion or a combination of these. Originally *tropos* was a musical term [116] for a short cadence or melisma added to a syllabic melody. Later it referred to a purely textual addition to a chant or a new composition combining a new text with a new melody. The custom arose during the eighth and ninth century of frequently troping the *Introitus*, the *Kyrie* and the *Gloria*. Freely troped, too, was the *Ite, missa est* of the Mass by the intercalation, with the Latin text, of appropriate phrases as a kind of expansion and commentary upon the liturgical text:

> *Ite* nunc in pace, spiritus sanctus super vos sit, iam *missa est.*
> *Deo* semper laudes agite, in corde gloriam et *gratias.*

The most important trope for the history of modern drama, however, was the *Quem quaeritis*, which was sung antiphonally before the Introit of the Easter morning Mass. In its most primitive form it is to be found in a manuscript of the tenth century from St. Gall; the oldest extant example, but less primitive in form, was composed between 923 and 924 at the monastery of St. Martial of Limoges:

> Trophi in Pasce
> Psallite regi magno, deuicto mortis imperio: Quem queritis in sepulchro, o Christicolae?
> Responsio:
> Ihesum Nazarenum crucifixum, o celicole.

19

Responsio:
>Non est hic, surrexit sicut ipse dixit, ite,
>nunciate quia surrexit. Alleluia, resurrexit
>dominus, hodie resurrexit leo fortis, Christus,
>filius Dei; Deo gratias, dicite eia!

This trope, as long as it lingered in its position before the Introit as an embellishment to the Mass, did not attain substantial dramatic significance. Its dramatic worth came to life during the tenth century when the *Quem quaeritis* was transferred to the conclusion of the Matins just before the final *Te Deum*.

Scholars have questioned the validity of this assertion, first postulated by Young,[117] on several grounds. To Hunningher, the transfer does not appear to constitute a particularly decisive argument for the dramatic quality of the tropes, for one would be hard pressed to understand "that it was space, merely space and growth, which changed the celebrant into an actor and delivered theater from religion." [118] Jude Woerdeman suggests that the most plausible reason for the transfer of the trope is not to be found in the general dramatic and literary tendencies proposed by Young but rather in "the substitution of the Roman Easter office, which had no . . . Gospel reading at Matins, for the monastic Easter office, at which the Gospel reading was performed with considerable ceremony." [119] The soundness of Young's explanation is also debated by Liegey but for different reasons. While acknowledging the importance of the transfer of the trope to the Matins, he questions nonetheless the "appropriateness of the location if, for its performance, a didactic motive is claimed." [120] If, reasons Liegey, the purpose of liturgical drama was didactic, the clergy could hardly have expected the untutored faithful to comprehend a play written and chanted in Latin or to attend the third responsory, the Invitatory, and the Gospel at the most unlikely hour of two in the morning. He believes the clergy had only itself in mind, particularly since it seems unlikely that the people were allowed in the Abbey churches.[121] In this respect he points out that in the *Regularis Concordia*, upon their discovery of the empty Sepulchre, the three Marys hold up the sudary or *linteum* to the Clergy and not to the faithful, which would have been desirable had there been a question of instructing them. He concludes by asserting that the purpose of the liturgical drama was not didactic, and that it was born of the Faith.[122] Nevertheless, to contend that the religious drama was not created with the manifest intention of edifying and instructing the masses is to disregard completely the stated purpose of the plays and contemporary commentary on them.[123] This evidence is hardly contestable, and Hardin Craig reflects present-day research on the subject when he writes that "the medieval religious drama existed primarily to give religious instruction, establish faith, and encourage piety. It did not exist as a free enterprise as did the Elizabethan drama, the French classical drama, or the drama of the modern world." [124]

The possibility that some of the faithful may not have understood all the Latin of the traditional ceremonies does not constitute a strong argument against a didactic intent since, for centuries, the entire body of Catholic liturgy has been given in Latin and it was only in 1967 that the Church, in the wake of the salutary impetus provided by the encyclical *Mediator Dei*, permitted a part of the Mass to be given in the vernacular. As will be shown later on, however, vernacular passages do appear in some of the earliest religious plays, including the twelfth-century Montecassino Latin Passion.

Furthermore the faithful were indeed allowed in the Abbey churches and in monastic houses, especially on the occasion of the most important liturgical festivities.[125] Dedicated by tradition to learning and charity, "monks and friars permeated the religious life of the Middle Ages and blended their functions with those of the secular clergy. They also lived in contact with ordinary people." [126] The miniatured *rouleux* and the *Exultets* from Southern Italy dating from the tenth, eleventh, and twelfth centuries show how, during the Easter season, after the singing of the *Lumen Christi* at the benediction of the Easter Candle, particularly in the monasteries of Montecassino and Capua, a deacon would display from the pulpit to both the Clergy and the faithful minatures representing scenes from the Passion of Christ while reading the Latin rubrics.[127] Not only did the monks live in the midst of the people but "monastic preachers taught the people and were the custodians of their culture." [128] Monastic centers occupied themselves with lay instruction, too, for "dès le début du IXᵉ siècle apparaît l'usage d'envoyer aux écoles monastiques ou presbytérales non seulement les clercs ou de futurs clercs, mais des élèves laïcs, apparentés aux clercs ou fils de chrétiens de la région et, ce qui est remarquable, quelle que soit leur naissance ou leur rang." [129]

Let us return again to the problem of the transfer of the *Quem quaeritis* trope to the Matins. It is agreed that this new position enhanced its dramatic potential, but no one has been able to explain convincingly why the change occurred. Nor can it be proved, as Young believed, that before this happened the trope was not performed or any attempt at impersonation considered or introduced. The pre-Matins trope certainly contained dramatic elements, as did the sermons of the time. G. R. Owst has shown that in pulpits "the sacred episodes had been declaimed with a freedom and dramatic intensity unknown to mere liturgical recitation," [130] and Keppler has stated that the dramatic range of medieval homilies is of some consequence in the understanding of medieval drama since it precedes the drama. [131] Thus the possibility remains that some form of impersonation may have preceded the trope in question. Decisively dramatic elements are also present in established and older Church ceremonies, such as the *Adoratio Crucis, Depositio Crucis* and the *Elevatio Crucis* with the accompanying movement to the various *sedes,* the symbolic representation of liturgical facts, and the participation of the people. Although not represented, these ceremonies lent themselves to possible impersonation, and it would be inaccurate to deny their importance in affecting and perhaps inspiring the essential beginnings of the religious drama. [132]

There is also the question of the priority of the French in the invention of the medieval religious play. By tradition, the composition of the earliest tropes is attributed to Tutilo, a monk of the Benedictine abbey of St. Gall, [133] and France is reputed to be the land in which its earliest form appeared. Cohen claimed that "la mission de l'inventeur appartient à la France," [134] and many scholars agree. The evidence for this conclusion is based entirely on two documents, both of the tenth century: the *Regularis Concordia* of St. Ethelwold of Winchester and the *Quem quaeritis* version from Saint-Martial of Limoges.[135] Composed between 965 and 975, the *Regularis Concordia* contains rules drawn up as guidance for the English monks and describes religious ceremonies for the edification of the masses. In it are found the earliest stage directions for the performance of an Easter play: the *Quem quaeritis:*

Dum tertia recitatur lectio, quatuor fratres induant se, quorum unus alba indutus ac si ad aliud agendum ingrediatur atque latenter Sepulchri locum adeat, ibique manu tenens palmam, quietus sedeat. Dumque tertium percelebratur responsorium, residui tres succedant, omnes quidem cappis induti, turribula cum incensu manibus gestantes ac pedetemptim ad similitudinem querentium quid, ueniant ante locum Sepulchri. Aguntur enim hec ad imitationem Angeli sedentis in monumento, atque Mulierum cum aromatibus uenientium, ut ungerent corpus Ihesu. Cum ergo ille residens tres uelut erraneos, ac aliquid querentes, uiderit sibi adproximare, incipiat mediocri uoce dulcisone cantare:

Quem queritis [in sepulchro, o Christicolae]?

Quo decantato fine tenus, respondeant hi tres uno ore:

Ihesum Nazarenum [crucifixum, o coelicola].

Quibus ille:

Non est hic, surrexit sicut predixerat; ite nuntiate quia surrexit a mortuis.

Cuius iussionis uoce uertant se illi tres ad chorum dicentes:

Alleluia, resurrexit Dominus, [hodie resurrexit leo fortis, Christus, filius Dei.]

Dicto hoc, rursus ille residens uelut reuocans illos dicat antiphonam:

Venite et uidete locum [ubi positus erat Dominus, alleluia]. Hec uero dicens surgat, et erigat uelum, ostendatque eis locum Cruce nudatum, sed tantum linteamina posita, quibus Crux inuoluta erat. Quo uiso, deponant turribula, que gestauerant in eodem Sepulchro, sumantque linteum et extendant contra clerum, ac ueluti ostendentes, quod surrexit Dominus et iam non sit illo inuolutus, hanc canant antiphonam:

Surrexit Dominus de sepulchro, [qui pro nobis pependit in ligno, alleluia].

Superponantque linteum altari. Finita antiphona, prior con-
gaudens pro triumpho regis nostri, quod deuicta morte surrexit,
incipiat hymnum *Te Deum laudamus.* Quo incepto, una pulsan-
tur omnia signa.[136]

In the prologue of the *Regularis Concordia* the author in-
forms us that he drew upon monastic practices in effect at
Fleury and Ghent. Some scholars inferred from this that the customs came from the Continent and that Fleury in particular and
France in general must be regarded as the fountainhead of the
liturgical drama. Young has pointed out, however, that there is
no proof the usages were brought in from the Continent.

The second evidence advanced by the French school is the
tenth-century Saint-Martial Easter trope,[137] which, considered
until recent times the oldest extant, seemed to confer on France
unquestioned priority in the evolution of the religious drama.
Yet others have attributed preeminence to the Swiss monastery
of St. Gall, for it contains the manuscript (n. 484) of the simplest version of the *Quem quaeritis* trope. To be sure, the monastery of St. Gall and that of St. Martial hold esteemed positions in
the study of the trope, but "one need not assume that troping
was invented at either place or the other." [138] Modern scholarship on the subject is slowly undermining this belief by re-
evaluating the origin of the tropes in view of recent evidence.
Jacques Chailley, for instance, believes that only few of the St.
Martial tropers originate from that monastery,[139] and Heinrich
Husmann offers evidence to show that the two earliest St. Gall
tropers are not a product of that monastery.[140] More recently,
on the strength of new evidence, a French scholar has written
that

> au lieu de faire à Tutilon l'honneur d'avoir inventé le trope
> *Quem quaeritis* et par là, le drame liturgique, il nous paraît plus
> vraisemblable que celui-ci se soit développé, étape par étape, à
> partir du culte que l'on vouait au Sauveur en Neustrasie et
> Austrasie, depuis la fin du VIIIe siècle; dés le milieu du même
> siècle, en tout cas à partir de 870, la Résurrection a pu être
> commémorée. . . . Il existe donc un décalage d'un demi-siècle
> au moins entre la date d'origine généralement assignée au drame

liturgique et le témoignage de certains documents liturgiques et iconographiques.[141]

Tropes flourished in England, Italy, and Germany, as well as in France and Switzerland, and one need not assume that a practice typical of one monastic center became such for all medieval Europe. One should not overlook the ties between St. Gall and Italy. Lehman noted that the Swiss monastery had connections with Bobbio since the days of Columba.[142] Two texts are known to have been imported directly from Italy: *M.S. Sangallensis 912* (containing parts of the grammar by Donatus of the tenth century and a fourth-century fragment of a manuscript of Terence, the oldest in existence) [143] and the *Codex St. Gallensis 908*, the king of palimpsests. It is a known fact that the richest source of books for the Benedictine monastery of Fleury was Italy.[144] The *Officium Sepulchri* of Cividale [145] as well as that from Parma are virtual duplications of the ceremonies described by St. Ethelwold, although of a later period. Liuzzi has even postulated a primitive form (archetipo) of the liturgical drama which, composed in Italy, soon spread to France and was there faithfully reproduced by the English Benedictines for their *Regularis Concordia*,[146] many of whose sources are of Cassinese origin or connection.[147] The Italian *Quem quaeritis* texts—one from Abruzzi dates back to the tenth century [148]—are closer to the Easter representation illustrated in the *Regularis Concordia* than are those of France.[149]

Italy's contribution to the rise of liturgical drama has never been fully recognized. In 1892 Gaston Paris, reviewing D'Ancona's *Origini del teatro italiano*, could assert without fear of contradiction that "toute l'évolution du drame religieux telle qu'elle s'est produite en France du IXe au XVe siècle est étrangère à l'Italie." [150] Paris's attitude is reflected in the works of later scholars who, like Sepet, Creizenach, Cohen, Young, Craig, and Frank,[151] have perpetuated the thesis of French invention on the basis of the evidence offered by the *Regularis Concordia* and the tropes of St. Martial of Limoges.

In view of the important new evidence that has recently come to light, it is time to reexamine the thesis that liturgical drama evolved from an expansion and histrionic elaboration of the St. Gall Easter trope from Switzerland. The text reads as follows:

> Quem quaeritis in sepulchro, christicolae?
> Jesum Nazarenum crucifixum, o caelicolae.
> Non est hic surrexit sicut praedixerat.
> Its nunziate quia surrexit de sepulchro.[152]

This trope differs only slightly from the text in the *Liber Responsalis* of Gregory the Great, which had been in existence for several centuries:

> Scio quod Jesum quaeritis crucifixum: surrexit . . .
> Jesum quem quaeritis non est hic sed surrexit . . .
> Cito euntes dicite discipulis quia surrexit Dominus. . . .[153]

The essential features of the St. Gall version are the added words: *christicolae, o caelicolae, sicut praedixerat, nunziate,* which imply dramatic action and impersonation. If this text was the actual starting point of religious drama, we would expect the key words to reappear constantly. In fact, however, they do not appear in many of the texts originating in Italy, Germany, and France itself. The various *Officia sepulchri* from Rouen, Narbonne, Klosterneuberg, Tours, Sens, Einsiedeln, Gotha, Wurzburg, Rheinau, Châlons, and Halberstadt do not adhere to the St. Gall trope; neither do those from Brescia, Parma, Sutri, Aquileia, or Cividale.[154] They offer new additions and original expressions that show independence from the St. Gall Easter type.

The identifying expressions are lacking, for example, from the following eleventh-century trope from Montecassino, which reveals a primitive attempt at dramatization:

> Dominica Sancta Pascha. Finita tercia vadat Unus Sacerdos ante altare alba veste indutus et versus ad Chorum dicat alta voce:
>
> Quem queritis
>
> Et Duo Alii Clerici stantes in medio Chori Respondeant:
>
> Jesum Nazarenum.
>
> Et Sacerdos:
>
> Non est hic. Surrexit.
>
> Illi vero conversi ad Chorum dicant:
>
> Alleluia. Ressurexit Dominus.[155]

Many tropes in Italy, France, and Germany have *tremulae mulieres* and *in hoc tumulo* instead of *christicolae* and *de sepulchro*. Grace Frank believes that the former are reworkings of the latter.[156] It seems peculiar to me, though, that such should be the case as the substitution would not have affected in any fashion the dramatic quality of the trope; both sets of expression have the same histrionic value. All logical deductions appear to designate the Montecassino Easter trope as one of the earliest and simplest types. As Dom Inguanez reasons:

> E più logico pensare che le frasi: *in sepulchro christicolae— crucifixum o caelicolae—Surrexit sicut praedixerat; ite, nunziate quia surrexit de sepulchro,* del testo di S. Gallo siano delle aggiunte al testo primitivo, e non il contrario, che esse cioè siano state soppresse da esso posteriormente. Questa ipotesi trova una conferma nel fatto che nella serie dei numerosi testi del *Quem queritis,* possiamo rilevare che esso, da un secolo all'altro, è venuto man mano ampliandosi ma non accorciandosi, dando origine, insieme con altri elementi, a quel vero dramma che è *l'Officium sepulchri.*[157]

Miss De Vito's hypothesis that the drama did not originate from the trope [158] is hardly tenable in view of the overwhelming evidence offered by the texts—over four hundred—and the attached rubrics. Nor does it seem logical, in view of present-day scholarship on the subject, to maintain the theory of Pascal, who, on the strength of Stumpfl's [159] anthropological, archaeological, and literary research into the rituals and customs of primitive religion, thought the Easter play represented the grafting of pagan rituals, particularly the theme of death and rebirth, on Christian ones.[160] Equally untenable is a recent theory advanced by O. B. Hardison, Jr., who contends that the Easter play derives from a ninth-century Resurrection ceremony celebrated as part of the Vigil Mass after midnight on Easter Sunday.[161] It appears to me, therefore, that a more plausible answer to the problem has to be found in a plurigenetic origin in that both the St. Gall and the other extant tropes represent primitive, parallel, but separate versions that owe their remarkable similarity to the extensive communication existing between different monasteries and churches, and their clergy, and primarily to their having a common origin in the Roman liturgy and Bible.

Notes to Chapter II

1 Paolo Toschi, *Le origini del teatro italiano* (Torino: Edizioni Scientifiche Einaudi, 1955); Ezio Franceschini, *Teatro latino medievale* (Milano: Nuova Accademia Editrice, 1960); Vincenzo de Bartholomaeis, *Origini della poesia drammatica italiana* (Torino: Società Editrice Internazionale, 1952).

2 Hans Knudsen, *Deutsche TheaterGeschichte* (Stuttgart: Alfred Kröner Verlag, 1959); Rudolf Vey, *Christliches Theater in Mittelalter und Neuzeit* (Zürich: Christiana-Verlag, 1960); Heinz Kindermann, *TheaterGeschichte Europas I. Antike und Mittelalter* (Salzburg: Otto Müller Verlag, 1957); Eduard Hartl, "Das Drama des Mittelalters" in Wolfgang Stammler *Deutsche Philologie Im Aufriss*, II (Berlin: Erich Schmidt Verlag, 1954), 903–47; Richard Froning, *Das Drama des Mittelalters* (Darmstadt, 1964).

3 Jeanne Hamelin, *Le théâtre chrétien* (Paris, 1957); Robert Pignarre, *Histoire du théâtre* (Paris, 1957); Léon Moussinac, *Le théâtre des origines à nos jours* (Paris, 1957); Gustave Cohen, *La grande clarté du Moyen Age* (Paris, 1954); Gustave Cohen, *Etudes d'histoire du théâtre en France au Moyen Age et à la Renaissance* (Paris, 1956); Jean Frappier and A. M. Gossart, *Le théâtre religieux au Moyen Age* (Paris, n.d.).

4 Harold C. Gardiner, *Mysteries' End* (New Haven, 1946); Grace Frank, *The Medieval French Drama* (Oxford, 1954; reprinted 1960); Hardin Craig, *English Religious Drama* (Oxford, 1955); Richard B. Donovan, *The Liturgical Drama in Medieval Spain* (Toronto, 1958); Robert Speaight, *The Christian Theatre* (New York, 1960); O. B. Hardison, Jr., *Christian Rite and Christian Drama in the Middle Ages* (Baltimore, 1965).

5 Karl Young, *The Drama of the Medieval Church* 2 vols. (Oxford, 1933).

6 C. Magnin, *Les origines du théâtre moderne* (Paris, 1838); E. Du Méril, *Les origines latines du théâtre moderne* (Leipzig, 1897); Hermann Reich, *Der Mimus* (Berlin, 1903); E. K. Chambers, *The Mediaeval Stage* 2 vols. (Oxford, 1961); also his *English Literature at the Close of the Middle Ages* (Oxford, 1961).

7 Silvio D'Amico, *Storia del teatro drammatico* 2 vols. (Milano, 1953).

8 Benjamin Hunningher, *The Origin of the Theater* (New York, 1961).

9 W. Bridges-Adams, *The Irresistible Theater* Vol. I (London, 1957).

10 D'Amico, *op. cit.*, p. 220.

11 *Ibid.*, p. 230.

12 Knudsen, *op. cit.*, p. 11.

13 Sister Mary Marguerite Butler, *Hrotswitha: the Theatricality of Her Plays* (New York, 1960), p. 184.

14 Edwin H. Zeydel, "Were Hrotswitha's Dramas Performed During Her Lifetime?" *Speculum* 20 (1945), p. 443.

15 Chambers, *Mediaeval Stage,* II, 207; Craig, *op. cit.,* pp. 24–25; Chambers, *English Literature,* p. 2.

16 Young, I, 2–6; Grace Frank, "Introduction to a Study of the Mediaeval French Drama" in *Essays and Studies in Honor of Carleton Brown* (New York, 1940), pp. 71–78; Charles Homer Haskins, *The Renaissance of the Twelfth Century* (New York, 1961), p. 171.

17 Zeydel, *loc. cit.,* pp. 444–48.

18 Max Manitius, *Geschichte der lateinischen Literatur des Mittelalters* 3 vols. (München: Beck'sche Verlagsbuchhandlung, 1911–1931, in Handbuch der klass. Altertumswissenschaft, IX, vol. II), 524.

19 Jacques de Ricaumont, "Le théâtre de Hrotsvitha" *La Table Ronde,* 166 (November, 1961), p. 54.

20 Rosemary Sprague, "Hrotswitha—Tenth-Century Margaret Webster" *The Theatre Annual* 13 (1955), 30; Charles W. Jones, *The Saint Nicholas Liturgy and its Literary Relationship* (Berkeley, 1963), pp. 99–102.

21 Filippo Ermini, "Hrotsvita" in *Medio evo latino* (Modena, 1938), 163–81, p. 178.

22 Young, I, 2; Frank, "Introduction", pp. 62–64; Franceschini, *op. cit.,* p. 22.

23 W. Cloetta, *Beiträge zur Literaturgeschichte des Mittelalters und der Renaissance* (Halle, 1960), 2–54; De Bartholomaeis, *Origini,* 26–28; R. S. Loomis, with comment by G. Cohen, "Were There Theatres in the Twelfth and Thirteenth Centuries?" *Speculum,* 20 (1945), 92–8; R. S. Loomis, "Some Evidence for Secular Theatres in the Twelfth and Thirteenth Centuries," *Theatre Annual,* (1945), pp. 33–43. Cf. the reply to these by D. Bigongiari, "Were There Theaters in the Twelfth and Thirteenth Centuries?" *Romanic Review* 37 (1946), 201–24. A learned contribution to the subject is Mary H. Marshall's "Theatre in the Middle Ages: Evidence from Dictionaries and Glosses," *Symposium* 6 (1950), 1–39, 366–89.

24 Manitius, *Geschichte,* III, 1041; M. O'C. Walshe, *Medieval German Literature* (Cambridge, 1962), p. 31; George R. Coffman, "A New Approach To Medieval Latin Drama" *Modern Philology* 22 (1924–25), p. 263.

25 Karl Strecker, *Hrotsvithae Opera* (Leipzig, 1906), p. 113.

26 This is also the opinion of knowledgeable scholars on the subject. Ezio Franceschini, "Per una revisione del teatro latino di Rosvita," *Rivista Italiana del Dramma,* 1 (1938), p. 308; Hugo Kuhn, "Hrotsviths von Gandersheim Dichterisches Programm" in *Dichtung und Welt in Mittelalter* (Stuttgart, 1959), 91–104; p. 100; Pignarre, *op. cit.,* 42; Eva Mason-Vest, *Prolog, Epilog und Zwischenrede im deutschen Schauspiel des Mittelalters* (Basel, 1949), p. 44.

27 Franceschini, *Teatro,* 15; Knudsen, *op. cit.,* 11; Marianne Kesting, *Das Epische Theater* (Stuttgart, 1959), p. 25; F. Gabotto, *Appunti sulla*

fortuna di alcuni autori romani nel Medio-Evo (Verona, 1891), p. 13; Frank, *Introduction*, 67; M. Manitius, "Beiträge zur Geschichte röm. Dichter im Mittelalter," *Philologus*, (1893), p. 546; H. Dziatzko, "Zu Terentius in Mittelalter," *Jahrbücher für klass. Philologie*, (1894), 465–77; G. Pacetto, *La fortuna di Terenzio nel medio evo e nel rinascimento* (Catania, 1918); Ezio Franceschini, "Il teatro post-carolingio" in *I Problemi comuni dell'Europa post-carolingia*, II (Spoleto, 1955), 295–312, p. 296.

28 Gustavo Vinay, "La commedia latina del Secolo XII" *Studi Medievali* 2 (1954), 209–71, p. 230.

29 Ermini, *op. cit.*, p. 178; Ettore Paratore, *Storia del teatro latino* (Milano, 1957), p. 189.

30 Marcella Rigobon, *Il teatro e la latinità di Hrotsvitha* (Padova, 1932), p. 5.

31 Philip S. Allen, "The Mediaeval Mimus. II" *Modern Philology* 8 (1910–11), 41–43.

32 W. T. H. Jackson, *The Literature of the Middle Ages* (New York, 1960), p. 305; Haskins, *op. cit.*, pp. 171–2; Fernando Ghilardi, *Storia del teatro* 2 vols. (Milano, 1961), pp. 111–12. In the most recent book on Hrotswitha, *Hrotswitha of Gandersheim* (New York, 1965), Anne Lyon Haight writes, p. 19: "It is not known if the plays were ever produced during the lifetime of Hrotswitha, but she must have written them with that purpose in mind."

33 Reich, *op. cit.*, Allardyce Nicoll, *Masks, Mimes and Miracles* (New York, 1931), p. 146; Heinz Reinhardt, "Uber den Ursprung des Dramas," *Die Pforte* 3 (1951–52), 339; Hans Heinrich Borcherdt, "Geschichte des Deutschen Theaters," in Wolfgang Stammler's *Deutsche Philologie Im Aufriss* III (Berlin, 1957), cols. 418–20.

34 Paul von Winterfeld, "Der Mimus in Mittelalter" *Herrig's Archiv*, CXIV, 48–75, 293–324; Winterfeld's belief that the medieval *mimus* derives straight from the Roman has been opposed by Philip Schuyler Allen in " 'Mimus' in the Tenth Century" in his *Medieval Latin Lyrics* (Chicago, 1931), pp. 148–83.

35 Hunningher, *op. cit.*, p. 76.

36 J. D. A. Ogilvy, "*Mimi, Scurrae, Histriones:* Entertainers of the Early Middle Ages," *Speculum* 38 (October, 1963), 603–19, p. 617.

37 Hunningher, *op. cit.*, p. 77; also John Speirs, *Medieval English Poetry* (London, 1957), pp. 307–11.

38 Allen, *Medieval Latin*, p. 154.

39 Dom Thomas Symonds, ed., *Regularis Concordia* (New York, 1953), pp. 49–50.

40 Gustave Cohen, "The Influence of the Mysteries on Art in the Middle Ages," *Gazette des Beaux-Arts*, 24 (1943), pp. 329–30.

41 Hunningher, *op. cit.*, p. 77.

42 Sandro Sticca, "The Priority of the Montecassino Passion Play," *Latomus* 20 (1961), 381–91, 568–74, 827–39.

43 M. Sepet, "Les origines de la comédie au Moyen Age" in his *Origines catholiques du théâtre moderne* (Paris, 1901), p. 402.

44 Hunningher, *op. cit.*, p. 67.

45 *Ibid.*, p. 73.

46 Ogilvy, *loc. cit.*, p. 616.

47 Jean Porcher, *French Miniatures from Illuminated Manuscripts* (London, 1960), p. 28.

48 Helena M. Gamer, "Mimes, Musicians, and the Origin of the Mediaeval Religious Play," *Deutsche Beiträge zur Geistigen Überlieferung*, 5 (1965), 9–28, 10, 17, 18, *passim*.

49 F. J. E. Raby, *Christian Latin Poetry* (Oxford, 1927), p. 203; also Luitpold Wallach, "Education and Culture in the Tenth Century," *Medievalia et Humanistica*, 9 (1955), 18–22, p. 18.

50 Mary H. Marshall, "Boethius' Definition of *Persona* and Mediaeval Understanding of the Roman Theater," *Speculum*, 25 (October, 1950), 471–82, p. 471.

51 Bigongiari, *loc. cit.*, pp. 202–06.

52 Philip Schuyler Allen, *The Romanesque Lyric* (Chapel Hill, 1928), p. 265; Franceschini, *Teatro*, 17; Paratore, *op. cit.*, 21–3. The mimes' scurrility was known to Roman poets (Mart. iii. 86, *non sunt haec mimis improbiora;* Ovid. *Trist.* 2. 497, *mimos obscena iocantes*); Craig, *op. cit.*, p. 24.

53 Vinay, *loc. cit.*, p. 230.

54 W. M. Lindsay, ed., *Isidori Etymologiae* 2 vols. (Oxonii, 1911), II, Bks. XVIII, XLIX.

55 Migne, *P.L.*, CXXXIV, col. 844.

56 See also Wolfgang Stammler, "Zum Fortleben des antiken Theaters im Mittelalter" in his *Kleine Schriften zur Literaturgeschichte des Mittelalters* (Berlin, 1953), 26–8; Bridges-Adams, *op. cit.*, p. 8.

57 De Bartholomaeis, *op. cit.*, p. 27; Frank, *Medieval French*, 3–5.

58 Francis Fergusson, *The Idea of a Theater* (Garden City, 1953), 251–55.

59 Cloetta, *op. cit.*, p. 14; Frank, *Medieval French*, 5–6.

60 F. Gabotto, *Appunti sulla fortuna di alcuni autori romani del medio-evo* (Verona, 1891), p. 13 and foll.; Max Manitius, "Beiträge zur Geschichte der Ovidius und ander. röm. Schrifstell. im Mittelalter." *Philologus*, Suppl. 7, (1899), p. 758.

61 Cloetta, *op. cit.*, p. 14; Giorgio Brugnoli, "La tradizione manoscritta di Seneca tragico alla luce delle testimonianze medio-evali," in *Atti della Accademia nazionale dei Lincei*, Anno CCCLIV (Roma, 1957), *Memorie, Classe di Scienze Morali, Storiche e Filologiche*, s. VIII, vol. VIII, fasc. 3, 201–85; also G. Brugnoli, "Le tragedie di Seneca nei Florilegi medio-

evali," *Studi Medievali*, ser. 3, 1 (1960), 138–52, p. 138; Ezio Franceschini, "Glosse e commenti medievali a Seneca tragico" in his *Studi e note di filologia latina medievale*. (Milano, 1938), 1–105, pp. 1–19.

62 H. Dziatzko, "Zu Terentius in Mittelalter," *Jahrbücher für klass. Philologie*, (1894), 465–77; also Pacetto, *La Fortuna*, *op. cit.*; James Stuart Beddie, "The Ancient Classics in the Mediaeval Libraries," *Speculum*, 5 (1930), 3–20, p. 8.

63 Franceschini, *Teatro.*, p. 15.

64 Kesting, *op. cit.*, p. 25.

65 Cloetta, *op. cit.*, pp. 21, 16–54 on the subject; also under the term *comoedia* in J. W. Pirie and W. M. Lindsay *Glossaria Latina Iussu Academia Britannicae Edita*, 5 vols. (Paris, 1926–31).

66 Isidore, *Etymologiae.*, XVIII, 45 in Lindsay's edition.

67 Albert Douglas Menut, ed., *Maistre Nicole Oresme. Le livre de éthiques d'Aristote* (New York, 1940), p. 137. Oresme also states, p. 247, that comedies "sont ditiéz ou chancons de choses deshonestes que les desactrempés escoutent volentiers."

68 Cloetta, *op. cit.*, p. 19; Thilo and Hagen eds., *Servii Gram. in Virg. Bucolica Com.* (1887), III, p. 29.

69 Migne, *P.L.*, CXI, 666: "Dramaticum vel activum, in quo personae solae agunt, sine ullius interlocutione, ut se habent tragicae et comicae artes, quo genere scriptum est prima Bucolicon, et ea cuius initium est: 'Quod, te, Moeri, pedes.' "

70 Cloetta, *op. cit.*, p. 24.

71 For fifth and tenth-century manuscripts of Terence see Karl E. Weston, "The Illustrated Terence Manuscripts," *Harvard Studies in Classical Philology*, 14 (1903), 37–54; John Calvin Watson, "The Relation of the Scene-headings to the Miniatures in Manuscripts of Terence," *Harvard Studies in Classical Philology*, 14 (1903), 55–172; C.E. Geppert, "Zur Geschichte der Terentianischen Texteskritik," *Neue Jahrbücher für Philologie und Pädogogik*, Supplementband 18 (1852), 28–87; R. Sabbadini, "Biografi e commentatori di Terenzio," *Studi Italiani di Filologia Classica*, 5 (1897), 289–327; Edward Kennert Rand, "Early Mediaeval Commentaries on Terence," *Classical Philology*, 4 (1909), 359–89; also J. D. Craig, "Jovialis and the Callopian Text of Terence," (London, 1927), St. Andrew Publications, XXII.

72 Creizenach, *op. cit.*, I, 5.

73 Marshall, "Theatre in the Middle Ages," p. 17.

74 Haskins, *op. cit.*, p. 171; F. J. E. Raby, *Secular Latin Poetry in the Middle Ages* 2 vols. (Oxford, 1934), II, 54; also Young, I, 7.

75 Franceschini, *Teatro*, pp. 14–15; Raby, *Secular Latin*, II, 55.

76 Dante Bianchi, "Per la commedia latina del sec. XII" *Aevum*, no. 2, 29 (1955), 171–78, p. 178; J. W. H. Atkins, *English Literary Criticism: The Medieval Phase* (New York, 1943), p. 32.

77 Donald Clive Stuart, *The Development of Dramatic Art* (New York, 1960), p. 179.

78 Raby, *Secular Latin*, II, 59.

79 Henry Laye, in G. Cohen's *La comédie latine en France au XIIe siècle* (Paris, 1931), 2 vols. II, 16–17; Filippo Ermini, "Il Babio, commedia latina del secolo XII," in *Medio evo latino* pp. 241–50.

80 Edmond Faral, "Le fabliau latin au Moyen Age," *Romania*, 50, (1924), 321–85, pp. 375–79.

81 Gustave Cohen, "La comédie latine en France du XIIe siècle" in his *Etudes d'histoire du théâtre*, pp. 71–106, p. 79.

82 Franceschini, *Teatro latino*, 93.

83 Petit de Julleville, *Les comédiens en France au Moyen Age* (Paris, 1885), p. 15.

84 Cloetta, *op. cit.*, pp. 127–38.

85 Creizenach, *Geschichte*, I, 32–35.

86 J. P. Jacobsen, "La comédie en France au Moyen Age," *Revue de Philologie Française et de Littérature* 23 (1909), 1–22, 81–106, 161–96, p. 82.

87 Manitius, *Geschichte der lateinischen*, III, 1041.

88 Cohen, *Etudes d'histoire*, p. 79.

89 Harald Hagendhal, "La comédie latine au XIIe siècle et ses modèles antiques," in ΔΡΑΓΜΑ Martino P. Nilsson dedicatum (Lund, 1939), 222–55, p. 231.

90 Margarete Bieber, *The History of the Greek and Roman Theater* (Princeton, 1961), p. 254.

91 Bianchi, *loc. cit.*, p. 172; D'Amico, *op. cit.*, p. 220.

92 Ermini, *Il Babio*, p. 241.

93 Marshall, "Theater," IV, no. 1, p. 5; Chambers, I, 2.

94 Albert Grenier, "La Gaule Romaine" in T. Frank, *An Economic Survey of Ancient Rome*, III (1937), 381–644, p. 540.

95 Samuel Dill, *Roman Society in the Last Century of the Western Empire* (London and New York, 1898), p. 117.

96 St. Augustine, *De Consensu Evangelistarum.*, I, 33 in Migne's P.L., XXXIV, 1,068; also M. P. Nilson, "Zur Geschichte des Bühnenspiels in der römischen Kaiserzeit," *Acta Universitatis Lundensis* XL, no. 3 (1904) printed 1906, 11–14. A. Muller, "Das Buhnenwesen in der Zeit von Constantin d. Gr. bis Justinian," *Neue Jahrbücher für das klassische Altertum; Geschichte und deutsche Literatur*, 23 (1909), 36–55.

97 Loomis and Cohen, "Were There Theatres," pp. 92–98.

98 Bigongiari, "Were There Theatres," p. 222.

99 Gustave Cohen, "Un terme de scénologie médiévale: 'lieu' ou 'mansion'" *Mélanges de philologie et d'histoire littéraire offerts à Edmond Huguet* (Paris, n.d.), p. 58.

100 Marshall, *Theater*, 32.

101 *Ibid.*

102 Young, I; Frank, *Medieval French*, 18–43; Franceschini, *Teatro*, 9–21.

103 Craig, *English Drama*, p. 20.

104 Young, I, 79–85; Otto Georg von Simon, too, agrees that liturgy is not drama and that the Mass did not and could not furnish the initial movement in the creation of the medieval religious drama. "Das abendländische Vermächtnis der Liturgie," *Deutsche Beiträge zur geistigen Überlieferung*, 1 (1947), 7–9.

105 Hardison, *Christian Rite*, Chapter 3: "The Lenton Agon," pp. 80–138.

106 Johannes Franciscus Gamurrini, *S. Hilarii Tractatus de Mysteriis et Hymni et S. Silviae Aquitanae Peregrinatio ad Loca Sancta* (Romae, 1887). The entire text with philological comments by Edward A. Bechtel has been published in *The University of Chicago Studies in Philology*, 4 (1902).

107 J. B. Thibaut, *Ordre des offices de la Semaine Sainte à Jérusalem du IVᵉ au Xᵉ siècle* (Paris, 1926), p. 8; Hélène Pétré, *Ethérie. Journal de voyage* (Paris, 1948), p. 15.

108 Thibaut, *op. cit.*, p. 9.

109 *Ibid.*, p. 10.

110 *Ibid.*

111 As Thibaut observes, "ces offices commémoratifs, accomplis sur les Lieux Saints qui furent le théâtre de la douloureuse Passion de Notre-Seigneur, Jésus-Christ, s'étendirent bientôt à toutes les Eglises de la chrétienté, y compris celle de Rome." (*Ibid.*, p. 127). Pope Damasus appears to have introduced this *Ordo* in the Roman liturgy: "Id est primus beatus Damasus papa adjuvante sancto Hieronimo presbytero vel ordinem ecclesiasticum descriptum de Hierosolyma permissu sancti ipsius Damasi transmittentem instituit et ordinavit." In Martin Gerbert's *Monumenta Veteris Linguae Alemanicae* (Saint-Blasien, 1790), p. 185.

112 D. Mauro Inguanez, "Montecassino e l'Oriente nel Medio-Evo" in *Atti del IV Congresso Nazionale di Studi Romani*, I, (Roma, 1938), 377–84, p. 380; Harry J. Leon, "A Medieval Nun's Diary" in *The Classical Journal*, 59 (1963), 121–7, p. 121. Gamurrini, *op. cit.*, p. IX, writes about the *Peregrinatio*: "Sane quidem Petrus Diaconus, qui saeculo duodecimo ineunte post Leonem Marsicanum vel Ostiensem bibliothecarius valde laboriosus in illo floruit coenobio, quum librum vel Itenerarium—De locis sanctis—confecisset, eamdem Peregrinationem in manus versavit, multa ad verbum prosecutus excepit, atque in sua inserenda curavit." Petrus Diaconus is more widely known as the compiler of Montecassino's *De viris illustribus* and for having continued to 1138 the famous *Chronica Casinensis* of Leo of Ostia, who, as the first chronicler, recorded the events of the monastery covering the years 1098 to 1107. For an edition of the *Chronica Casinensis* see W. Wattenbach ed., *Leonis Marsicani et*

Petri Diaconi Chronica Monasterii Casinensis, in *Monumenta Germaniae Historia,* Fol. seria *Scriptorum,* VII (Hanover, 1846), 551–844.

113 A. A. R. Bastiaensen, *Observations sur le vocabulaire liturgique dans l'Itinéraire d'Égérie* (Utrecht, 1962); Pétré, *op. cit.*

114 Teodoro Leutermann, *Ordo Casinensis Hebdomadae Maioris Saec. XII* in *Miscellanea Cassinese,* 20 (Montecassino, 1941), pp. 16–19.

115 Young, I, 178–97; Craig, *English Drama,* 30–47; Frank, *French Drama,* 19–30; Knudsen, *op. cit.,* 1–9; Vey, *op. cit.,* 12–24; Franceschini, *Teatro,* 22–28; Hans Heinrich Borcherdt, "Geschichte des deutschen Theaters" in Wolfgang Stammler's *Deutsche Philologie Im Aufriss,* III (Berlin, 1957), 421–3; Gustave Reese, *Music in the Middle Ages* (New York, 1940), pp. 185–6; Cohen, *Le Théâtre,* I, 1–14; H. F. Müller, "Pre-History of the Mediaeval Drama," *Zeitschrift für romanische Philologie,* 44 (1924), 544–75, p. 573.

116 Jacques Handschin, "Trope, Sequence, and Conductus," in *Early Medieval Music up to 1300,* ed., A. Hughes (New Oxford History of Music, II; Oxford, 1954), 128–74; Willi Apel, *Gregorian Chant* (Bloomington, 1958), 429–42; W. L. Smoldon, "The Easter Sepulchre Music-Drama" *Music and Letters,* 27 (1946) 1–17, on page 3, writes that the Easter Dramas "were indeed music-dramas, the earliest European examples." Ferdinando Liuzzi on p. 105 of his "L'espressione musicale nel dramma liturgico" in *Studi Medievali,* n.s. 2 (1929), observes that "la musica è . . . nel teatro medievale, l'elemento propriamente, squisitamente estetico. Ne è anzi in un certo senso il solo: certo il più puro." J. Schwietering was the first to derive the drama of the medieval Church from the spirit of the music in the liturgy in his "Uber den liturgischen Ursprung des mittelalterlichen geistlichen Spiels," in *Zeitschrift für deutschen Altertum und deutsche Literatur* 42 (1925), 1–20. Martin Gerbert, *De Cantu et Musica Sacra* (Monast. S. Blasii, 1774), Lib. I, p. 340 states that trope "in re liturgica est versiculus quidam aut etiam plures Ante vel Post alios ecclesiasticos cantus appositi."

117 Young, I. 231.

118 Hunningher, *op. cit.,* p. 59.

119 Jude Woerdeman, "The Source of the Easter Play," *Orate Fratres,* 20 (1945–46), 262–72, p. 263.

120 Gabriel M. Liegey, "Faith and the Origin of Liturgical Art," *Thought,* 22 (1947), 126–38, p. 137.

121 *Ibid.,* pp. 137–8. The music may well have been the principal source of enjoyment for some of the audience, as competent scholars have recently suggested.

122 *Ibid.;* also Speirs, *Medieval English Poetry,* p. 311.

123 Timothy Fry, "The Alleged Influence of Pagan Ritual on the Formation of the Mystery Plays," *American Benedictine Review,* 9 (1958–59), 187–201, p. 196; J. De Ghellinck, *L'essor de la littérature latine au XIIe siècle* 2 vols. (Paris, 1946), II, 261; Barbara Craig, "Didactic Ele-

ments in Medieval French Drama" *Esprit Créateur*, 2 (1962), 142–8, pp. 142 and 148.

124 Craig, *English Drama*, p. 15.

125 Etymologically the Greek word λειτουργια really means people's work, (λήιτον ἔργον) in the sense of a service performed in the interest of the community.

126 Craig, *English Drama*, 14.

127 Leutermann, *op. cit.*, 80–82; also Jean Alazard, *L'art italien des origines à la fin du XIVe siècle* (Paris, 1949), p. 104; Paolo D'Ancona, *La miniature italienne du Xe au XVIe siècle* (Paris, 1925), p. 6; Emile Bertaux, *L'art dans l'Italie méridionale* I (Paris, 1904), p. 237; B. G. Nitto de Rossi e Nitti di Vito, Francesco, *Codice diplomatico barese* 2 vols. (Bari, 1897–1899), I. pp. 204–15.

128 Friederich Heer, *The Medieval World* (New York, 1963), p. 61.

129 Dom Jean Leclercq, "L'humanisme bénédictin du VIIIe au XIIe siècle," *Studia Anselmiana*, 20 (1948), 1–20, p. 3.

130 G. R. Owst, "Sermon and Drama," in his *Literature and Pulpit in Medieval England* (New York, 1961), 471–547, pp. 473–4.

131 P. Keppler, "Zur Passionspredigt des Mittelalters," *Historisches Jahrbuch*, 3 (1882), 285–315; 4 (1883), 161–88; 4, p. 182.

132 Solange Corbin, for instance, does not take into account the all-pervading mimetic action of the Latin liturgy when she refuses to acknowledge the presence in the *Depositio* of the most rudimentary dramatic elements. *La déposition Liturgique du Christ au Vendredi Saint* (Paris, 1960), pp. 245–7.

133 Joseph Szövérffy, "L'hymnologie médiévale: recherches et méthode," *Cahiers de Civilisation Médiévale. X^e–XIIe siècles*, IVe Année, n. 4 (October–November, 1961), 389–422, p. 397; H. Leclercq, "Tutilo, Notker, Ratpert," *Dictionnaire d'Archéologie Chrétienne*, 15 (1950), 2,848–84, and "trope," *Ibid.*, 2,799–2,802; Young, I, 205; Manitius, *Geschichte*, III, 220; also Borcherdt, *Geschichte*, 423, writes: "Notker Balbulus galt als der Schöpfer der Sequenzen, Tutilo als Schöpfer des Ostertropus"; Knudsen, *Deutsche Theater*, 4, "in St. Gallen war des älteren Notker Zeitgenosse Tutilo . . . als Verfasser und Komponist von Tropen bekannt"; these statements find their strength in the famous *De Casibus monasterii Sancti Galli* where Ekkehard attributes the earliest tropes to Tutilo.

134 Cohen, *Théâtre en France.*, I, 12.

135 Edith Wright, in *The Dissemination of the Liturgical Drama in France* (Bryn Mawr, 1936), p. 31, writes: "St. Martial seems to have been the true creator of the liturgical drama in France and perhaps in Europe." Frank, *Medieval French*, p. 66, observes: "It seems probable . . . that both the Easter and Christmas plays arose in France . . . and thence they spread over the Continent."

136 London, *Brit. Mus.*, MS *Cotton Tiberius A*. III, fol 21–21^v; in Young, I, 249; in Symons, *Regularis Concordia, op. cit.*, pp. 49–50.

137 Paris, *Bibl. Nat., MS lat. 1240, Trop. Sancti Martialis Lemovicensis saec. X*, fol. 30ᵛ.

138 Paul Evans, "Some Reflections on the Origin of the Trope," *Journal of the American Musicological Society*, 14 (1961), 119–30, p. 119.

139 Jacques Chailley, "Les anciens tropaires et séquentiaires de l'Ecole de Saint-Martial de Limoges (Xᵉ–XIᵉS.)" *Etudes Grégoriennes*, 2 (1957), 163–88, pp. 163–4; also Smoldon, "The Easter Sepulchre," p. 4.

140 Heinrich Husmann, "Die älteste erreichbare Gestalt des St. Galler Tropariums," *Archiv für Musikwissenschaft*, 13 (1956), 25–41, p. 25; R. Pascal, "On the Origins of the Liturgical Drama of the Middle Ages," *Modern Language Review*, 36 (1941), 369–87, p. 377; Joseph Klapper suggested Jerusalem as the place of origin of the Easter trope in "Der Ursprung der lateinischen Osterfeiern," *Zeitschrift für deutsche Philologie*, 50 (1923), 46 foll.

141 Carol Heitz, *Recherches sur les rapports entre architecture et liturgie à l'époque carolingienne* (Paris, 1963), pp. 220–1.

142 Paul Lehman, "The Benedictine Order and the Renaissance of the Literature of Ancient Rome in the Middle Ages," in his *Erforschung des Mittelalters* (Stuttgart, 1950), III, 172–83, p. 178.

143 *Ibid.*

144 *Ibid.*, p. 177.

145 De Bartholomaeis, *Origini*, 465; Maria Sofia de Vito, *L'origine del dramma liturgico* (Milano-Genova-Roma, 1938), pp. 33–43; Paolo Toschi, "L'origine romana del dramma liturgico" *Rivista Italiana del Dramma*, II (November, 1938), 257–68.

146 Liuzzi, *L'espressione musicale*, pp. 82–3.

147 Symonds, *Regularis Concordia*, p. xlviii.

148 *Bibl. Vatic., MS lat. 4770, Miss. Benedictinum Sancti Petri in Aprutio saec. X-XI*; see also Young, I, 207–8.

149 As in the *Regularis Concordia*, the *Officium Sepulchri* of Cividale too takes place Easter day, at Matins, "*finito tertio Responsorio.*" Here the three Marys carry the turible and incense just as the *tres fratres* do in the *Regularis*. The dialogue too is similar and at the end of the ceremony, as in the *Regularis*, the three Marys enter the sepulchre and show Christ's linteum to the Clergy. Both the *Regularis* and Cividale plays end with the singing of the Antiphon: *Surrexit Dominus de sepulchro qui pro nobis pependit in ligno* and of the *Te Deum*.

150 Gaston Paris, "Origines du théâtre italien" *Journal des Savants*, (1892), 670–85, p. 672.

151 Grace Frank, although aware of the existence of the Montecassino Latin Passion, for in *RR* 30 (1939) she reviewed De Vito's book, still states in her *Medieval French Drama* (1954, 1960), p. 29: "Only two liturgical Passion plays survive, both in the *Carmina Burana*."

152 Young, I, 201.

153 Migne, P.L., LXXVIII, col. 769.

154 De Vito, *op. cit.*, pp. 31–38.

155 De Bartholomaeis, *Origini*, pp. 31–38.

156 Frank, *RR*, (1939), pp. 69–71.

157 D. Mauro Inguanez, "Il 'Quem quaeritis' pasquale nei codici Cassinesi," *Studi Medievali* 14 (1941), 142–49, p. 148.

158 De Vito, *op. cit.*, p. 38.

159 Robert Stumpfl, *Kultspiele der Germanen als Ursprung des mittelalterlichen Dramas* (Berlin, 1936).

160 Pascal, *loc. cit.*, pp. 386–7.

161 Hardison, *op. cit.*, chap. V.

II. The Origin of the Latin Passion Play

AS WE HAVE SEEN, the tropes—the kernel of the liturgical drama—first appeared in the eighth century, continued to be produced in the ninth, and flourished in the tenth century. Some were in dialogue, such as the famous Easter trope *Quem quaeritis in sepulchro*, which was antiphonally sung.

In the tenth century this Easter trope was supplied with rubrics that show dramatic impersonation and action. In its simplest and perhaps earliest form the *Quem quaeritis* trope comes down to us in a tenth-century manuscript of the monastery of St. Gall in Switzerland.[1] It was an addition to the liturgical service of the Mass of Easter. When the single dialogue is assigned to Marys and angels, with rubrics for action, the trope becomes a play, the *Visitatio Sepulchri*.[2] Young discusses more than 400 texts of these Easter versions of the *Visitatio Sepulchri*,[3] which became actual drama.

Imitative of the *Quem quaeritis* of Easter, nativity tropes began to appear in the eleventh century.[4] These also were given dramatic form, as rubrics show. It is generally accepted that the Easter and Christmas tropes were the original germ of later Latin Easter and Christmas liturgical plays.

The origin of the Latin Passion play, however, is more doubtful since very few Latin ones exist, and also because the full development of vernacular Passion plays belongs to the late Middle Ages. The distinguished scholar Karl Young writes in *The Drama of the Medieval Church* that "in comparison with the multitude of medieval Latin Church plays treating events relating to the Resurrection, the number of dramatic representations of the Crucifixion is astonishingly small."[5] Christ's Passion was rarely dramatized within the Church. The Crucifixion and the events that led up to it are non-existent in the liturgical drama, for it focuses on the Resurrection and its characteristic emotion is joy. The reason for the scarcity and late appearance of these Latin dramas may be found, as Young observes, in the fact that the Mass itself offered to the medieval worshiper in visible and audible form an actual repetition of Christ's Passion.[6] The eucharistic mystery on the altar is primarily a *memoria passionis*, and "particularly after the ninth century the whole Mass was explained as a comprehensive representation of the Passion of Jesus."[7] Indeed, as far back as the tenth century, Amalarius of Metz, in the preface to his *De ecclesiasticis officiis*, wrote:

> Sacramenta debent habere similitudinem aliquam earum rerum quarum sacramenta sunt. Quapropter, similis sit sacerdos Christo, sicut panis et liquor similia sunt corpori Christi. Sic est immolatio sacerdotis in altari quodammodo ut Christi immolatio in cruce.[8]

The Mass was, in fact, conceived as an authentic drama by medieval commentators on its symbolism. Interesting and peculiar, for instance, is what Honorius d'Autun writes around the year 1100:

> Sciendum quod hi qui tragoedias in theatris recitabant, actus pugnantium gestibus populo repraesentabant. Sic tragicus noster pugnam Christi populo Christiano in theatro Ecclesiae gestibus

suis repraesentat, eique victoriam redemptionis suae inculcat. Itaque, cum presbyter "Orate" dicit, Christum pro nobis in agonia positum exprimit, cum apostolos orare monuit.[9]

It would seem, then, that for Honorius d'Autun the church is already the theater, the priest the tragic actor, the Mass a rememorative drama. Du Méril[10] and E. K. Chambers[11] have expressed the same idea about the ritual of the Mass. It seems to have been, in part, one of the factors responsible for the late appearance of the Passion plays, for originally the people appear to have been satisfied with contemplative liturgy, which possessed in itself some elements of dramaturgy.[12] The crucifix, a familiar and impressive reminder to the faithful of the meaning of the Passion, needed no realistic and immediate elaboration in liturgy or literature. The symbolical importance of the Cross, moreover, can be perceived in the liturgical observances of Holy Week called *Adoratio Crucis*, *Depositio Crucis*, and *Elevatio Crucis*. Performed at Jerusalem as early as the fourth century and known to the Roman liturgy as early as the eighth, the *Adoratio* took place on Good Friday with both the clergy and the congregation adoring and later kissing the Cross. The *Depositio* and the *Elevatio*, symbolizing the Burial and Resurrection, took place respectively on Good Friday and Easter morning before Matins. These latter ceremonies seem to have been attached to the *Adoratio* as a kind of progression.

Although lacking genuine dramatic elements, these ceremonies exhibit unmistakably vivid attempts at some sort of representation commemorating some of the events of Christ's Passion. They cannot be considered, however, as the religious source from which a drama of the Passion stemmed.[13] Nor can the formation of it be found, as Young at first firmly and later cautiously suggested, in the singing of the *Passio* during Holy Week.[14] Although the singing of the *Passio* with the distribution of the principal parts was primarily instituted to dramatize the Gospel narrative,[15] this ceremony cannot be considered true drama nor can it have had any influence on the origin of the Latin Passion play. As to the theory that the *planctus* must be looked upon as the germinal point of the Latin Passion, I will observe at this time that the *planctus* is an essentially non-dramatic, simple lyric expression and will reserve discussion of it until the fifth chapter.

The literary genesis of the Latin Passion play must be found in a shift in emphasis that took place both in art and in literature. The realization of the first Latin Passion was made possible by general artistic and cultural changes which, starting in early Christian art, liturgy, and literature, reached their climax in the eleventh and twelfth centuries. These new manifestations brought about a growing interest in and concentration on Christocentric piety, which found its greatest expression in an increased dwelling on the subject of the Passion. In art the shift is manifested by a more humanistic treatment of Christ and in literature, by a consideration of the scenes of the Passion as dramatic human episodes. In both, the change is from a contemplative to a more vivid visual experience.

It would be impossible, I think, and unprofitable to present all available evidence of the liturgical, artistic, and literary activity that from the earliest centuries of the Christian era centered on the Passion. From the tenth century on, however, Christ's Passion acquired a continuous and ever-increasing popularity as one of the favorite sacred mysteries, until, within the general framework of Christian worship, by chance and coincidence, new forces were produced in Southern Italy that allowed a more eloquent and humane visualization and description of Christ's anguish in his Passion. Thus was laid the foundation of a religious *Zeitgeist* that permitted the creation, early in the twelfth century, of the first Latin Passion play in the monastery of Montecassino.

The new forces at work were the mystical concentration on Christ's human suffering as articulated primarily by St. Anselm and St. Bernard; the Romanesque revival of the eleventh century, which introduced a fresh interest in humanism; and the Byzantine school of miniature and painting in Southern Italy.

In *The Making of the Middle Ages* R. W. Southern recognizes the value of these new attitudes by remarking that "the theme of tenderness and compassion for the sufferings and helplessness of the Savior of the world was one which had a new birth in the monasteries of the eleventh century."[16] Some scholars find the heralds of this Christocentric piety early in that century in monastic figures such as St. William of Volpiano (d. 1031), St. Richard of Verdun (d. 1046), and especially Volpiano's nephew and favorite disciple John of Fécamp (d. 1078).

It was left to St. Anselm (1033–1109), however, to supply the theological and theoretical justification for Christ's sufferings through a new interpretation of the necessity of the Redemption. In the *Cur Deus Homo,* a Christological treatise reminiscent of those of the second to fifth centuries, St. Anselm emphasizes the true significance of the humanity of Christ by stressing that the redemptive act took place on a human level.

The devotion to Christ's Passion that stirred in the souls of pious monks early in the eleventh century and was fostered in the same generation by the delicate sensibility of St. Anselm finds its greatest expression in the concentrated pathos devoted to it by St. Bernard (1091–1153). An unremitting love for Jesus crucified was the focal point of St. Bernard's life and the guide for his interior feelings and emotions: "haec mea sublimior interim philosophia, scire Jesum, et hunc crucifixum."[17] St. Bernard's treatment of Christ's suffering founded a new strain of spirituality for his writings "dès le XIIe siècle, orientèrent les coeurs vers les mystères de la vie terrestre, en particulier vers ceux de sa naissance et de sa passion."[18]

There can be no doubt that the mystical contemplation on the doctrine of the Incarnation must have contributed to the desire to represent the Passion dramatically. The Christocentric mysticism of St. Anselm and St. Bernard soon acquired a religious universality by being incorporated into the common body of Christian opinion. By virtue of their examples and personal reputations—St. Anselm as the Primate of England and the so-called Father of Scholasticism and St. Bernard as the renowned *doctor mellifluus,* the founder of the Cistercians, the preacher of the Second Crusade, and both through the efforts of their various pupils and monastic orders that fostered the perpetuity of their teachings—medieval spirituality came to know Christ with a more delicate intimacy and dwelt primarily on his Passion.

This general shift towards a realistic handling of the Passion is not peculiar to literature but can also be traced and observed in the visual arts. We had occasion to point out earlier how the Romanesque revival of the eleventh century, with its preference for emotional rather than intellectual apprehension of dogma, had produced a fresh interest in humanism. One of the first results in religious terms was a new trend in the iconography of Christ on the Cross.[19] From the fifth century to the beginning of the eleventh the prevalent type of the Crucified, in Europe, is the *Christus triumphans*, the Pantocrator, Lord and Master of the Universe. This type shows Christ alive on the Cross, with his eyes open, the body erect and without signs of pains to indicate the triumphant and divine qualities of Christ. The attempt is always to transcend the real, to negate the value of the transient, to deny the natural and earthly in its evocation of permanent values.

Although such early iconographical monuments as the Rabula crucifixion of 586 exhibit a desire toward a more dramatic and humanizing representation of Christ on the Cross, and although the substitution of the figure of Christ for that of the Lamb in crucifixion scenes was decreed by the council *in Trullo* of Constantinople in the year 692 for the avowed purpose of emphasizing the humanity of the theological mystery, the figure of the Crucified remained devoid of realistic details and followed even throughout the Carolingian artistic revival the compositional laws of early hieratic iconography.

From the eleventh century on a second type becomes increasingly common: expressing suffering and human nature, Christ is now represented dead on the Cross, eyes closed, head lowered, the body slightly bent in a rhythmic curve, and blood and water issuing from his wounded side.[20] Art too appears to be exploiting and conveying the deep emotion that Christ's sacrifice had aroused at that time. The dramatic potentialities suggested by this new iconography of the Crucified in the formulation of a Latin Passion in Southern Italy will become readily apparent when one considers that although sporadic representations of Christ dead on the Cross appear in Europe as early as the eighth century, this type was unfamiliar in Italy as late as the first half of the eleventh century,[21] and was introduced there in the same century by way of Byzantine influence.

This influence was made possible, in part, by the close relations existing for centuries between Montecassino and Byzantium and by the fact that geographically, politically, and racially the south of Italy has been comparatively isolated from the rest of the peninsula. The most conspicuous time of Byzantine influence, however, begins in the eleventh century, when the Beneventan noble Desiderius, who later became Pope Victor III, was elected abbot (1058–1086) of Montecassino. One of Desiderius' first acts was to set about the reconstruction of the entire monastery, and especially the basilica of St. Benedict. To this end, he not only ordered and imported works of art from Constantinople but summoned Greek craftsmen skilled in mosaic, in metal works, and in the illumination of manuscripts.

The most characteristic activity that developed at Cassino under the stimulating influence of Byzantine artists is the art of illumination. Under Desiderius Montecassino became one of the chief centers for the production of South Italian manuscripts, particularly the *Exultet Rolls*,[22] which in the liturgy of the Roman Church were used in the ceremony of the Blessing of the Paschal Candle on Easter Eve. Inscribed on a long strip of parchment or vellum, the text of the *Exultet Roll* was annotated with musical neumes and illustrated with illuminated pictures. The peculiar feature of the roll is that the pictures are in reverse to the text. As the deacon chanted and unrolled the scroll, the illustrations of the unrolled portion he had just read, would fall over the back of the ambo before him, thus displaying them right side up in front of the congregation.

The distinctive value of these rolls lies in their liturgical use, for "lo scopo principale di questi rotoli era di ottenere in tutta la cerimonia una più completa comprensione e partecipazione da parte del popolo."[23] The dramatic aspects of the *Exultet Rolls* cannot be questioned since the people, as spectators, were given a vivid representation in tableaux, in a kind of cinematic sequence, of some of the most memorable events in Christ's life from his birth and ministry to his Passion and Resurrection.

The influence of Byzantine iconography is perceptible everywhere in Southern Italy, particularly in the frescoes which, from the eleventh to the thirteenth centuries, appeared on the walls of its churches. Of particular interest are the Byzantine frescoes appearing on the walls of the south Italian church of St. Angelo in Formis, which was presented to Desiderius in 1072 by Richard, Prince of Capua. Here the sequences of New Testament paintings that decorate the central nave reproduce the events leading to the Passion of Christ with scrupulous fidelity. The paintings show unusual attention to the dramatic and the pathetic as can be gathered from the violent scene of Judas' betrayal and the sorrow and tears on the face of the Virgin and the Holy Women at the Crucifixion. The historical significance of the entire cycle of frescoes of St. Angelo in Formis in understanding medieval spirituality at Montecassino cannot be emphasized enough.

The decoration on the walls of St. Angelo in Formis, many of which bear underneath appropriate Latin phrases, must be seen in strict analogy with Desiderius' method of decorations used in the basilica of Montecassino. The method of decorating the text under consideration with suitable pictures is conspicuous at this time in all the artistic productions associated with the Montecassino renaissance of the eleventh and twelfth centuries, whether it be the illumination of the *Exultet Rolls* and other manuscripts, the beautification of church walls, or later on the illumination with Passion scenes of the very text on which the first Latin Passion was written.

Although Passion cycles were known to the Southern Italian monastic communities since the seventh century,[24] none of them can be compared in faithfulness to the gospel account and in fullness of details to the great Gospel and Passion cycles of the eleventh century introduced into Southern Italy through Byzantine influence. It is for these reasons that Paul Weber, in 1894, with critical and literary foresight could describe the frescoes of St. Angelo in Formis as "die erste gemalte Darstellung eines mittelalterlichen Passionspiel" [25] and point out its importance for the history of the religious drama by remarking: "das ist eine

46

Erscheinung, mit der die Forschung über das geistliche Schauspiel von nun an zu rechnen haben dürfte." [26]

The purpose of this last discussion has not been to overemphasize the importance of the Passion frescoes of St. Angelo in Formis but rather to indicate that, through Byzantine influence at Montecassino and within its religious domain, artistic forces were at work, which, coupled with mystical and literary trends and attitudes towards a deeper interest in Christ's suffering and Passion and with the general artistic revival inaugurated by abbot Desiderius in all the arts, produced a milieu in which the first Latin Passion could originate early in the twelfth century. When one considers that whether in art, literature, or mystical ideas, monastic residents of Montecassino held the same Christocentric attitude, it would not be surprising if a competent monk should have decided to express those very attitudes in a dramatic form. The Montecassino Latin Passion play bears witness to the fact that indeed he did.

Notes to Chapter III

1 Young, I, 201–05.

2 Julius Schwietering, "Ueber den liturgischen Ursprung des mittel-alterlichen geistlichen Spiels," *Zeitschrift für deutsches Altertum* 62 (1925), 1–20; also Henning Brinkmann, "Zum Ursprung des liturgischen Spiels," *Xenia Bonnensia* (Bonn, 1929), pp. 106–43; Young, I, 231–8.

3 Young, I, 239–40.

4 *Ibid.*, II, 1–196; Craig, *English Religious Drama*, p. 49.

5 Young, I, 492.

6 *Ibid.;* Erwin Wolff, "Die terminologie des Mittelalterlichen Dramas in Bedeutungsgeschichtlicher Sicht," *Anglia*, 78, no. 1 (1960), 1–27, pp. 7–8.

7 Joseph A. Jungmann, *The Mass of the Roman Rite: its Origin and Development* 2 vols. (New York, Boston, 1950), I, p. 177. Henri Ghéon, in *The Art of the Theatre* (New York, 1961), 21, states: "The Mass, the central act of worship, is essentially a drama: for the faithful it is the drama of dramas, the real drama in which the Son of God in person participates each morning."

8 Migne, *P.L.*, CV, 989.

9 *Ibid.*, CLXXII, 570.

10 E. Du Méril, *Les origines latines du théâtre moderne* (Paris, 1897), p. 41.

11 Chambers, *The Mediaeval Stage*, II, 75.

12 Luigi Tonelli, *Il Teatro italiano* (Monza, 1924), p. 11; also De Vito, *L'origine*, pp. 163–4. As late as the twelfth century, Alanus de Insulis comments on the rememorative, liturgical and symbolical meaning of the Mass: "O quantum misse misterium, ubi Christi passio representatur, ubi crux Christi figuratur, ubi sacerdos ad interpellandum mittitur, ubi panis in corpus Christi mutatur, ubi Christus Deo Patri offertur, ubi angelus ad consecrandum delegatur . . ." (Marie-Thérèse d'Alverny, ed., *Alain de Lille. Textes Inédits* (Paris, 1965), *Sermo de Cruce Domini*, p. 280.

13 Werner, Wilfred. *Studien zu den Passions und Osterspielen des deutschen Mittelalters in ihrem Ubergang vom Latein zur Volkssprache* (Berlin, 1963), p. 19.

14 Karl Young, "Observations on the Origin of the Medieval Passion Play" *PMLA*, 25 (1910), 309–54; also his *Drama of the Medieval Church*, I, 539.

15 Paolo Ferretti, "Il canto della Passione nella Settimana Santa," *Rivista Liturgica*, 5 (1918), 69–75, p. 70; Vincenzo Coosemans, "Il canto del *Passio*," *Rivista Liturgica*, 6 (1919), 49–55, pp. 54–5; G. Römer, "Die Liturgie des Karfreitags" *Zeitschrift für Katolische Theologie*, 77 (1955), 39–93, p. 64.

16 R. W. Southern, *The Making of the Middle Ages* (New Haven, 1959), p. 232; Dom Jean Leclercq, *L'amour des lettres et le désir de Dieu* (Paris, 1957), p. 240. P. Amedée de Zedelgem, O.F.M. writes that

48

"à partir du XIᵉ siècle, la dévotion à la passion du Christ entre dans une nouvelle phase, à savoir une dévotion tendre envers la passion de Notre-Seigneur, qui se manifeste dans une compassion profonde pour Jésus souffrant et dans une véritable participation à ses souffrances et à ses douleurs." ("Aperçu historique sur la Dévotion au Chemin de la Croix," *Collectanea Franciscana*, 18–19 (1948–49), 45–142, p. 53.

17 Migne, P. L., CLXXXIII, St. Bernard, *Sermones in Cantica*, Sermo XLIII, 4, col. 995. St. Bernard appears to be echoing St. Paul's: "Non enim iudicavi me scire aliquid inter vos, nisi Iesum Christum, et hunc crucifixum." (*Ad Corinthios*, 1:2–3)

18 P. Pourrat, *La spiritualité chrétienne* 2 vols. (Paris, 1947–51), II, 481; Felix Vernet, *La spiritualité médiévale* (Paris, 1929), p. 18.

19 Gabriel Millet, *L'iconographie de l'évangile* (Paris, 1916), p. 398; Paul Thoby, *Le crucifix des origines au concile de Trente* (Nantes, 1959), p. 79; L. H. Grondijs, *L'iconographie byzantine du Crucifié mort sur la Croix* (Utrecht, 1947), p. 4; Bernard Teyssèdre, *Le sacramentaire de Gellone* (Paris, 1959), p. 110.

20 J. R. Martin, "The Dead Christ on the Cross in Byzantine Art," in *Late Classical and Mediaeval Studies in Honor of Albert Mathias Friend, Jr.* (Princeton, 1955), 189–96, p. 189; Victor Leroquais, *Les sacramentaires et les missels manuscrits des bibliothèques publiques de France* 3 vols. (Paris, 1924), I, p. XXXV; M. Didron, *Iconographie chrétienne* (Paris, 1843), p. 235; Grondijs, *op.cit.*, p. 25.

21 Martin, *loc.cit.*, p. 192.

22 Emile Bertaux, *L'art dans l'Italie méridionale* (Paris, 1904), pp. 201–12; Dom Agostino Maria Latil, *Le miniature nei rotoli dell'Exultet* (Montecassino, 1899); Paolo D'Ancona, *La miniature italienne du Xᵉ au XVIᵉ siècle* (Paris, 1925), p. 4; David Diringer, *The Illuminated Book. Its History and Production* (London, 1958), p. 295.

23 Leuterman, *Ordo Casinensis Hebdomadae Maioris*, in *Miscellanea Cassinese*, 20 (1941), p. 82.

24 P. F. Russo, "Attività artistico-culturale del monachismo calabro-greco anteriormente all'epoca normanna" in *Atti dello VIII Congresso di Studi Bizantini* Vol. I (Roma, 1953), pp. 463–75.

25 Paul Weber, *Geistliches Schauspiel und Kirchliche Kunst* (Stuttgart, 1894), p. 52.

26 *Ibid.*

III. The Tradition of the Passion Play

T HIS LATIN PASSION was found at the monastery of Montecassino by D. M. Inguanez,[1] who first published it in 1936 in the *Miscellanea Cassinese*. The Montecassino text is not complete: it records the events of the Passion from Judas' bargain to the Crucifixion and the *Planctus* of the Virgin Mary.

The primary importance of the text is that it is a century older than any other western Passion play yet known; paleographical evidence places it, in fact, in the twelfth century. Secondly, it allows us to augment an already known fragment, the *Officium Quarti Militis*, a fourteenth-century document of Sulmona, Italy, by providing the part of a fourth soldier.

In a bibliographical survey C. S. Gutkind refers to the Montecassino Passion as "not only the earliest Passion play which has come down to us from Italy, but perhaps even the earliest for the whole Western Church." [2] F. Neri expressed the same view when he wrote that our twelfth-century play is the earliest Passion known, "for the two monastic texts, which had been thought the earliest until now, and which come from the monastery of Benediktbeueren (it too a Benedictine center), are preserved in MSS. of the 13th century." [3] These observations are alone sufficient to demonstrate the value of our document for the history of the Passion play in the Middle Ages.

Before the discovery of the twelfth-century Latin Passion play at Montecassino,[4] the oldest known Passion plays were of the thirteenth century or later, other extant Latin ones being the two thirteenth-century plays from the Benediktbeueren collection[5] and a fourteenth-century fragment known as the *Officium Quarti Militis*.[6] This fragment was so named because "the passage preserved is a player's part, providing only the role of a subordinate character, the 'fourth soldier,' along with certain cues." [7] The Montecassino text is the same Passion from which the *Officium Quarti Militis* of Sulmona derives and permits us to add to it.[8]

Although the extant texts are few, information has come down to us about the extensive representations of the Passions from the thirteenth century: perhaps at Siena around 1200,[9] certainly at Padua in 1243 and 1244,[10] and then at Cividale in Friuli in 1298 and 1302.[11]

Concerning a representation of the Passion at Siena about the year 1200, Chambers wrote that it is the "first recorded Passion in Italy," [12] and Kretzmann also shared this opinion.[13] About the same play D'Ancona wrote that, according to a certain Uberto Benvoglienti, similar plays were performed at Siena around 1200, but that one should not put too much trust in this reference because it is full of generalities.[14]

Adolf Ebert thought that the oldest reference to the religious drama in Italy dates from the year 1244 and refers to the Padua Passion.[15] Creizenach, too, regarded the *Repraesentatio Passionis et Resurrectionis Christi* of Padua as the oldest reference to early religious drama in Italy.[16]

The representation of comprehensive Passion plays at Cividale in 1298 and 1303 is documented by the following passage:

Anno Domini mcclxxxxviii. die vii.
exeunte Majo, videlicet in die Pentecostes,
et in aliis sequentibus duobus diebus,
facta fuit repraesentatio Ludi Christi;
videlicet Passionis, Resurrectionis,
Ascensionis, adventus Spiritus Sancti, et
adventus Christi ad Judicium in Curia
Domini Patriarchae . . . honorifice, et
laudabiliter per Clerum Civitatensem, ...
Anno Domini mccciii, facta fuit per Clerum,
sive per Capitulum Civitatense Repraesentatio: . . . .
de Passione et Resurrectione, Ascensione et
adventu Spiritus Sancti.[17]

Until the Montecassino Passion was found, one could safely observe with Young [18] and Hunningher, among others, "that before the beginning of the thirteenth century, there is no mention whatever of a dramatized Passion." [19] One of the curious phenomena of literary history has been the tenacity with which modern scholarship on the medieval drama has fostered the erroneous belief that the two thirteenth-century Benediktbeueren Latin Passion plays are the earliest extant.[20] In the most recent study on the subject, completely unaware of the existence of the Montecassino Passion, Wilfred Werner states: "Die einzige umfassenden und verhältnismässig vollständig überlieferten lateinischen Passionsspiele sind das kleine und das grosse Benediktbeurer Spiel." [21]

Of the early extant Latin Passion plays in the *Carmina Burana* manuscript of Benediktbeuern, one, the *Ludus breviter de Passione* comes from the end of the thirteenth century.[22] Wilhelm Meyer believed that this play, since it is entirely composed of prose Latin passages from the Evangelists, probably draws on some Harmony of the Gospels, rather than on a longer Passion play.[23] Young feels that although it is comprehensive, this play is devoid of literary originality.[24] The other Benediktbeuern play in the *Carmina Burana*, the *Ludus de Passione*, gives a far more elaborate dramatization of the Passion than is to be found in the first. Creizenach calls this latter text "the oldest till now known, in which the Passion, this main subject of the dramatic arts of the Middle Ages, was produced." [25]

From the beginning of the thirteenth century we witness in Germany a flourishing of German and Latin-German Passion plays such as the Muri *Passion* of the thirteenth century,[26] which is the oldest German religious play, the Vienna *Passion* play of the beginning of the fourteenth century,[27] and the St. Gall *Passion*, also of the fourteenth century,[28] which is "the most complete and typical of early German plays." [29]

The earliest manuscripts of Passion plays in French date in general from the fourteenth century, though one may be as early as the thirteenth. These are the Sion fragment published by Bédier in *Romania*,[30] the so-called *Passion d'Autun*,[31] the Provençal *Passion* contained in the Didot manuscript,[32] and *La passion du Palatinus*.[33] *La passion Sion*, which consists of a fragment of only eighty-seven lines, has been dated by Gaston Paris as of the last years of the thirteenth century.[34] *La passion d'Autun*, dated by Frank at the end of the thirteenth century or maybe at the beginning of the fourteenth,[35] is written mostly in octosyllabic couplets. The Provençal *Passion* of the Didot manuscript, dated 1345, is written, as almost all the mysteries were, in the vernacular and exhibits no relation to any French model. This manuscript is important for the abundance of its rubrics, especially on those pages devoted to the Passion.[36] *La passion du Palatinus*, dated by Frank [37] as from the fourteenth century was discovered recently in the Vatican library. Written in verses of eight syllables, it served, Frank believes, for reading rather than for performance.[38] Together with the Sion fragment it is "the earliest French Passion that we possess." [39]

Spanish Passion plays are still shrouded in complete mystery. One of the reasons has been the traditional lack of interest shown by scholars of the medieval drama in undertaking a careful and systematic research in Spanish libraries. Creizenach, for instance, could write that in Spain very few monuments of medieval drama have been preserved.[40] Crawford, too, asserted that the "material is almost lacking for a study of the liturgical drama in Spain." [41] That a liturgical drama did exist in Spain was made apparent, however, by a twelfth-century trope of Ripoll,[42] two Easter tropes from Silos showing the earliest European form,[43] and a thirteenth-century regulation governing plays that was found in Castile in one of the *Partidas* of Alphonse X, the Wise. In this *Partida* it is specified that

> reprecentación hay que pueden los cléricos fazer; así como de la Nascencia de Nuestro Señor Jesu Christo, en que muestra como el ángel vino a los pastores e cómo les dixo como era Jesu Christo nacido. E otrosí de Aparición, cómo los tres Reges Magos lo vinieron a adorar. E de su Resurrectión, que muestra que fué crucificado e resucitó al tercer día.[44]

It was left to Richard B. Donovan to fill this lacuna by gathering valuable information about the medieval drama of Spain.[45] In his study he does not offer any example, Latin or vernacular, of Spanish Passion plays.

England's religious drama does not offer us any complete Passion plays until we reach the English mystery cycles in the fourteenth century, which survive chiefly in later manuscripts. Passion plays, as distinguished from comprehensive religious cycles, did exist in England in the later fourteenth century, especially in London. Hardin Craig in *English Religious Drama* writes that

> The medieval religious drama in England has been too narrowly conceived of because chance has given us four great *Corpus Christi* plays with a good deal of information about them and has left us little about the great contemporary rival of the *Corpus Christi* play, namely, the Passion play of London and southern England. What for lack of information can hardly be imaginatively restored is the situation in London and the south of England, where the Passion play prevailed. In London in 1378 minor clergy of St. Paul's were presenting the 'History of the Old Testament' at Christmas. In 1384 a mystery play at Skinners Well lasted five days, and in 1409 we learn of a play there by certain *clerici Londoniae* that apparently lasted for five days and told 'How God created Heaven and Earth out of nothing, and how he created Adam and so on to the Day of Judgment'. It may be inferred that the Passion plays of southern England were played on stationary stages and that in London perhaps the performers were minor clergy. The 1409 play at Skinners Well seems to have been of full scope. What relation, if any, it had to guilds and trading companies we do not know, although we know that London had its *Corpus Christi* procession and that guilds regularly went in it in a specified order of precedence. The London plays must have attained the height of medieval magnificence. We may conjecture with reasonable assurance

that the Passion plays of southern England were in form somewhat like those of France and Germany.[46]

Craig's speculations about the English Passion plays are founded
upon relatively little evidence. Indeed, although the English
mystery cycles have preserved for us complete Passion plays, the
origin of the Passion plays in England still remains a moot question. It is unknown also when the Passion plays first appeared in
England, although it has been shown, for instance, that of the
four extant English mystery cycles, only Chester did not make
extensive use of the *Northern Passion,* a poem written in
England at the close of the thirteenth century,[47] largely based
on the French poem called *La Passion des Jongleurs,* which also
influenced some of the French plays.

Since the *Northern Passion* is dated at the close of the thirteenth century, the first English plays may have been produced
soon after. In fact such material as the Bible, narratives of the
Passion, and religious treatises were ready for "an author of
about the year 1300, setting his hand to compose a narrative of
the Passion." [48]

It is evident from the above survey that the discovery of the
Montecassino Latin Passion, earlier than any of those thus far
noted, is extremely important from both an historical and a literary point of view.

The four Montecassino sheets, in which the play appears, are
of Beneventan or Longobardic-Cassinese handwriting,[49] a type
that was used at Montecassino, where monastic scribes "were
masters of the elaborate and difficult Beneventan script." [50] It is
permissible, therefore, to conjecture that the text was written at
Montecassino.

In dating a manuscript we must remember a rule given to us
by Mabillon: "non ex sola scriptura neque ex uno solo character-
ismo, sed ex omnibus simul de vetustis chartis pronuntiandum." [51]
Mabillon's criteria of manuscript analysis are also practiced
by the distinguished paleographer E. A. Lowe. In the *Beneventan Script* Lowe observes that, in dating any manuscript, the
general impression should be the paleographer's first guide. The
next step is to confirm or correct that impression by an examination of details.[52]

According to D. M. Inguanez, the first impression created by these Cassinese sheets in Beneventan handwriting is that they are not later than the twelfth century.[53] To this may be added the fact that other manuscripts of similar handwriting, such as the Codd. Cassin. nn. 165, 166, 167, have been assigned by Lowe to the twelfth century also.[54] The paleography of our Montecassino text definitely suggests a twelfth-century date to Lowe and E. Carusi.[55] A short stay at Montecassino has enabled the present writer to examine the manuscript and to confirm the twelfth-century dating.

After a close examination of the text itself, both orthographically and stylistically, Inguanez dates it more precisely as of the first years of the second half of the twelfth century.[56] It would even be possible paleographically to date it still earlier in the twelfth century, for Lowe writes that "the script of Montecassino is often half a century in advance of the writing produced in other centres."[57]

In my view, metrical evidence also suggests the second if not the first half of the twelfth century. The Passion of Montecassino is written in the type of Latin Sequence verse called *versus tripartitus caudatus*, the invention of which is attributed to Adam of Saint Victor (1110–1192).[58] Indeed, as Raby observed,

> the history of the Sequence in the twelfth century centres around the name of Adam of St. Victor, to whom tradition assigns the glory of having brought to perfection this most characteristic achievement of medieval poetry.[59]

Composed as early as the eighth and ninth centuries,[60] the Sequence grew out of a series of musical notes called *sequelae* or *jubili*, sung upon the final *a* of the Alleluia at the end of the Gradual.[61] In the ninth century words or phrases were provided in order to remember these melodies or musical sequences.[62] The resulting production came to be known as the *Sequentia cum prosa* or *prosa ad sequentiam*. The invention of the Sequence is usually associated with Notker Balbulus (ca. 840–912), a monk of St. Gall,[63] although some question it.[64] After a transitional stage during the eleventh century, in which accentual meter, assonance, and rudimentary rhyme were replaced by regular accentual meter, the Sequence reached the highest perfection with Adam and his school in the twelfth century.[65] His type of Sequence, in particular, "became a prime favourite with other Sequence-writers, and remained so as long as Sequences continued to be written." [66]

This favorite strophe of Adam of St. Victor is the six-line stanza of accentual trochaic dimeters, of which lines 3 and 6 are catalectic in stanzas 1,2,3,4,9,10, and acatalectic in 5,6,7,8. The rhyme is usually *aabccb*. Ferdinand Wolf, in *Uber die Lais, Sequenzen und Leiche*, writes that the verses *tripartiti caudati* were made up of

> two directly rhymed lines (pair of rhymes) and a final line (mostly shorter) by means of which rhyme, all, several, or at least two half-strophes (originally long-lines) were tied together; these half-strophes or long lines were called *versus tripartiti caudati* in the terminology of the medieval teaching of verses or rhymes, from the tripartition of the long lines and that rhyme of the final line (cauda).[67]

Wolf puts the *versus tripartitus caudatus* under the direct influence of that type of religious poetry called Sequence,[68] whose history in the twelfth century is tied, as we have seen, to the name of Adam of St. Victor. The following are some of the characteristics of the Sequence in its full metrical development:

1. The rhythm is regular and is based wholly on the word-accent, with occasional transpositions of stress, especially in the short line which ends a strophe.

2. The caesura is regular, and should occur at the end of a word.

3. The rime is regular, and at least two-syllabled.

4. The Sequence measure par excellence is the trochaic line of eight syllables, repeated one or more times, and followed by a trochaic line of seven syllables.[69]

L'Abbé E. Misset in *Les Proses d'Adam de Saint-Victor*, after having stated that Adam's verse rests on the triple basis of accent, syllabism, and rhyme, writes that

> les mots ne doivent y être considérés que comme une suite de syllabes accentuées et de syllabes non accentuées. S'ils sont

monosyllabiques, ils prennent ou ne prennent pas l'accent, *ad libitum*. S'ils ont deux syllabes, ils sont toujours accentués sur la pénultième. S'ils comptent plus de deux syllabes, ils reçoivent l'accent sur la-pénultième, quand elle est longue, et sur l'antépénultième, quand la pénultième est brève. Dans ce cas, de deux en deux syllabes, avant et après l'accent principal, ces mots reçoivent en outre un accent secondaire.[70]

These are Adam's simple metrical rules. If we take for comparison one strophe from one of Adam of St. Victor's hymns and one from the Montecassino Passion, we shall see how well the above rules apply. Before proceeding into the comparison it seems opportune to observe that the Montecassino dramatist appears to have chosen Adam's favorite Sequence type with the intent of emulating by means of the dramatic form that exposition of the Scriptural truth so eminently practiced by Adam in his Sequences. To provide a striking parallel in the comparison, we shall take the last stanza of Adam's hymn *De Trinitate* and one from the Passion of Montecassino.

Adam's *De Trinitate*	Montecassino Passion
Nós in fíde glóriémur	[I]ésus dóli séminátor
Nós in úna módulémur	Nóstre géntis súpplantátor
Fídei constántiá:	tétro fráudis nóminé.
Trínae sít laus Únitáti	Múltos nóstrum íam sedúxit
Sít et símplae trínitáti	In errórem quós perdúxit
cóaetérna glóriá.[71]	fráudulénto nóminé.[72]

It is obvious from the above that these two stanzas are metrically identical, both in meter and accent. Both are made up of verses that "expand into a six-line stanza by doubling the first stave in a riming couplet twice and using the second stave between the two couplets and the riming end." [73] Such is also the scheme of the Montecassino Passion, in general. The redaction of this Passion in the Victorine poetical sequence allows us to observe that although "sequences, such as those by Adam of St. Victor, did not find their way into the drama" [74] nevertheless the Victorine sequence meter was used for dramatic purposes; the meter, moreover, provides evidence to refute the theory that the earliest Passion plays were written in Latin prose.[75]

We have demonstrated, therefore, that the stanza used nor-

mally by Adam of St. Victor in his Sequences and the stanzas
of our Passion are metrically the same, and that the Sequence
verse created by Adam flourished in the twelfth century and
was available to the Montecassino author. The monks of that
monastery distinguished themselves during the eleventh century
in the composition of hymns (abbot Guaiferus, Peter Damian,
Alphanus, Alberic of Montecassino being the most prominent) [76] and of the *artes dictaminis* (prose and verse) and *cursus
rhythmorum*,[77] which dominate the rhetoric of the twelfth century. Thus we have additional evidence that our Passion was
produced during the first half of that century, its *terminus ad
quem* being around 1150.

Since the Montecassino Passion is written entirely in the hymnodic sequence form, there remains another line of research
which seems to offer interesting suggestions. The poetic production of the twelfth century appears to have given preeminence
particularly to three genres: the hymns, the tropes and the sequences.[78] The evidence offered by the medieval Latin drama
indicates that of these three poetic forms, especially in the
twelfth century, the sequence assumes an extraordinary popularity and the widest diffusion.

An examination of the medieval drama seems indeed to indicate that it evolved poetically and musically from rudimentary
towards more complex rhythmic forms, particularly through the
constant utilization of the hymnodic sequential technique.[79] Sequences such as *Victimae paschali laudes, Fideles animae*, and
Planctus ante nescia, appear in Latin dramas, which exhibit a
certain degree of dramatic sophistication both in themselves and
through the presence of these lyrical additions.

Sequences were notably employed to celebrate canonical
feasts and seasons such as Advent, Nativity, the Passion, Easter,
Ascension, Pentecost, Trinity, Annunciation, Visitation, Purifi-
cation, Assumption and many others. But it is particularly in the
twelfth century that one observes a growing relationship between Latin hymnody and the arts, the more obvious being the
one between the sequence and the liturgical drama.

The most popular and typical of the rhythmic and rimed sequences of the twelfth century is precisely the trochaic stanza of

two eight syllable couplets,[80] with a third trochaic line of seven syllables as employed by the Montecassino author. As sequences were becoming quite prominent in liturgical dramatic representations, it is not surprising that our unknown dramatist should have chosen for the redaction of his drama the most widely used sequence form of his time.

A much more important reason for the use of the sequence form in the Montecassino Passion can be found in the fact that, whereas the Latin hymn was traditionally tied in with daily secular worship and later with canonical monastic hours, the sequence was associated with the celebration of the divine sacrifice,[81] which is also the main theme of the Montecassino Passion.

The above observations, then, paleographical, metrical, and liturgical, establish conclusive evidence that the Passion of Montecassino was written in the twelfth century. This date throws new light upon the epoch in which the drama of the Passion was first created and allows us to abandon the older idea that the Passion drama was introduced later into southern Italy through French influence with the famous *Ludus Paschalis* of Tours,[82] which shares a few lines with the Sulmona fragment. In fact, as Toschi observes,

> until the Passion of Montecassino was discovered the *officium Quarti Militis* of Sulmona was placed in direct dependence upon a text of Tours: now it has been observed that a good part of the verses of which it is composed, finds an exact reproduction with as many verses of the *Cassinese Passion:* and it is easier to think of a relationship between Montecassino and Sulmona (the Benedictines of the famous convent expanded their activity in many centers of Abruzzi) than between Sulmona and Tours.[83]

Moreover, relations were entertained between St. Peter Celestine —the founder, near Sulmona, in 1285, of the Badia of S. Spirito del Morrone through which the French influence was reputed to have come to Italy [84]—and Montecassino.[85] In addition, we know that the Celestines were followers of the rule of St. Benedict.[86] Of course, we do not know if the Passion discovered at Montecassino was composed by a monk from the monastery— although paleographical, liturgical, and literary reasons as we have seen make it reasonably certain—or in one of the Benedictine monasteries under Montecassino's influence. It is certain, however, that the Passion of Montecassino ends with three lines of a *Planctus* of Mary, which is in the Italian centro-meridional vulgar tongue. The careful rubrics for actors and the existence of this vernacular *Planctus* here give definite suggestions that the play was performed in Italy, at Montecassino or within its immediate religious domain. This is substantiated by the fact that three verses of this *Planctus* offer a striking resemblance to four lines of a far longer Italian *Planctus* found in the region of Marche, which are preserved in a good text of about seventy quatrains of double quinary monorhymes.[87]

Montecassino *Planctus*	Marchigiano *Planctus*
. . . te portai nillu meu ventre	Io nove misi en ventre te portai . . .
Quando te beio [mo]ro presente	
Nillu teu regnu agi me a mmente.[88]	Con ce cte vejo cosine morire. . . .
	Con ce Kte vejo lu core se parte . . .
	Et se morrai, sera ennu miu Rignu.[89]

We may add to this that Francesco Ugolini has published a collection of vernacular *planctus* ranging from the thirteenth to fifteenth centuries, some of which show marked similarities both to the Montecassino Passion *Planctus* and to each other.[90] Judging by the density relative to geographical origin, these *planctus* appear to have their epicenter in the region of Abruzzi.[91] In view of the fact that Montecassino had kept close ties with Abruzzi through its dependent monastic houses there,[92] Ugolini suggests that perhaps this flourishing of vernacular *planctus* ought to be viewed in terms of this relationship. From the above evidence we may safely conjecture that, while the Montecassino Passion was written at that monastery, the vernacular *planctus* may have been added there or within one of its dependent monastic houses with a view to local performance before the congregation. Scholars have already established that the transition from Latin to vernacular religious drama occurred beginning with the twelfth century, and in Italy, the Montecassino *Planc-*

tus marks "certamente l'inizio d'una evoluzione dal dramma latino a quello volgare." [93] This evolution was partly aided and partly prevented by the development of the *Lauda*.

The Montecassino text offers us twelve scenes, which may be summarized as follows:

I. vv. 1–33.

The play starts by introducing Judas bargaining with Caiaphas for the life of Christ, after which Judas guides the soldiers to the place where Jesus was to be found.

II. vv. 34–51.

The second scene includes Judas' kissing of Jesus on the cheek, the soldiers' declaration of the purpose for their coming, and Jesus' noble entreaty to the soldiers to take Him but spare those with Him.

III. vv. 52–69.

Peter cuts off the ear of Malchus and is rebuked by Jesus.

IV. vv. 70–102.

Scene four presents Jesus being accused by the soldiers before Caiaphas and his inquiries to know if Jesus thought Himself to be the Son of God, and his subsequent rage upon hearing Christ's affirmative answer. After this, Jesus is struck and spat upon.

V. vv. 103–126.

Scene five begins with the presentation of the false witnesses who do not give any testimony, but are only alluded to in the rubrics. Peter is then accused of being a follower of Christ by a housemaid, and he denies the charge. After Peter's third denial the rooster crows. Deeply moved, Peter then goes to where the disciples are in hiding and tells them that he has denied Jesus.

VI. vv. 127–138.

Scene six shows Christ briefly before Pilate, then gives Peter's lament and, finally, Judas' repentance and suicide by hanging.

VII. vv. 139–171.

Scene seven again places Jesus before Pilate. Jesus is accused by the soldiers who ask that Jesus die for referring to Himself as king. To Pilate's query of whether or not He is the king of the Jews, Christ answers affirmatively, while the soldiers demand that He be crucified.

VIII. vv. 172–228.

The next scene includes the flagellation of Jesus but concerns itself primarily with Pilate, his wife, and her maid. The scene begins by presenting Pilate's wife, very much perturbed by a sleepless night caused by visions stirred up by the devil. The nature of these visions is not revealed. While under the anxiety caused by these visions, Procula sends her maid to her husband Pilate entreating him not to harm that just man (Christ), for she has been disturbed during the night by strange visions. Pilate sends back the maid with the assurance that he will not spill innocent blood. On her return the maid joyfully announces to Procula her husband's decision, and invites her to be merry. Procula praises the name of God for such a happy report and bids her maid attend to her weaving.

IX. vv. 229–273.

Scene nine again presents Jesus before Pilate, who entreats Jesus to say something against the soldiers' accusations, since Pilate has the power to kill Him or set Him free. Jesus answers Pilate by telling him that whatever power he may have has been given to him from above. At this point Pilate abruptly addresses the priests and the soldiers, asking them whether they want Barabbas or Jesus freed. The soldiers and the priests demand that

Christ be crucified, for he who proclaims himself king contradicts Augustus. Pilate, as if trying to overlook what the priests had said, asks them what he is to do with Jesus. They protest against Jesus, demanding that He be crucified. At this point Pilate washes his hands before the crowd, disclaiming any responsibility for Jesus' blood. The priests then claim that responsibility by asking that Christ's blood fall on them and their heirs. Scene nine ends with Pilate's bidding the priests to take Jesus to be crucified.

X. vv. 274–288.

Jesus is led to another place where the priests and the soldiers dress Him in a red tunic, put a reed in His hands, and spit on His face. They then place a crown of thorns on His head and kneeling before Him say: "Hail, king of the Jews."

XI. vv. 298–317.

Scene eleven presents Christ being taken to Calvary, His fragmentary prayer for His crucifiers, and the crucifixion. The priests and Caiaphas taunt Jesus crucified, asking Him to try and free Himself, He who had promised to destroy the temple and rebuild it in three days. Caiaphas' address is followed by the incident of the two thieves and Christ's subsequent promise of eternal happiness in paradise from that same day to one of them.

XII. vv. 318–320.

The last three verses, in vernacular Italian, contain a brief lament of the Virgin, which translated read in the following manner:

> I bore you for nine months in my womb,
> When I see you I presently will die,
> In your kingdom, remember me.

Since the text in the *Miscellanea Cassinese* is relatively inaccessible I here reprint Inguanez' 1939 edition with the permission of the abbot of Montecassino.

[I. vv. 1–33. Judas' bargain]

Iudas dicat:

> Vos salvete sacerdotes
> quos adornant morum dotes
> et virtutum gloria.

Cayphas respondeat Iude et dicat:

> [F]rater Iuda tu salveris
> 5   iam revela si quid queris
> nostra peten[s l]imina.

et Iudas respondeat Cayphe:

> [I]esus doli seminator
> nostre gentis supplantator
> tetro fraudis nomine.
> 10   Multos nostrum iam seduxit
> in errorem quos perduxit
> fraudulento nomine.
> Cui si vita perdurabit
> totus populus errabit
> 15   suis blandis monitis.
> Tradam vobis ipsum vere
> si vos vultis respondere
> digne meis meritis.

Ad hec Cayphas respondeat et dicat ei:

> [S]i [q]uod dicis perpetrabis
> 20   sic a nobis impetrabis
> quicquid expetieris.
> Si tu comples quod optamus
> nos triginta tibi damus
> numbos iusti ponderis.

Ad hec Cayphas det denarios Iude et Iudas dicat eis:

> 25   [E]rgo factum maturetis
> et clientes mihi detis
> probos atque strenuos.

et Cayphas precipiat loricatis ut eant cum Iuda et dicat:

> Istos optimos clientes
> arma plurima ferentes
> 30   ducas tibi socios.

66

[II. vv. 34–51. Judas betrayal]

Post hec exeat Iudas cum loricatis et consilium cum eis st[atuen]s
[eat ad locu]m ubi orat Iesus e[t di]cat:

>Vos hoc signum habeatis,
>illum caute teneatis
>cui iam tradam osculum.

Post hec Iudas eat ad illum locum ubi Iesus orat sicut super
scriptum est. et Iudas dicat alta voce inclinans se ei et osculans
eum Iesum et dicat:

>Ave rabi veritatis etc.
>[A]ve rabbi veritatis
35   in quo nullus falsitatis
>adinvenit scrupulum.

et Iesus respondeat Iude et dicat ei:

>[O] amice quid venisti?
>mecum fu[rtim tu] existi
>ut latronem perdere.
40   Cur me tunc non tenebatis
>cum docentem videbatis
>in templo consistere?
>Venientes cum lanternis
>armis fustibus lucernis
45   dicite quem queritis.

Ad hec loricati respondeant alta voce et dicant:

>[I]esum [vi]rum [nazarenum]
>virum multa fraude plenum
>et orrendis meritis.

Ad hec respondeat Iesus arm[atis et] dicat eis:

>Si me queritis sineatis
50   hos abire quos spectatis
>adque mecum cernitis.

[III. vv. 52–69. Peter and Malchus]

His dic[tis] loricati capiant Iesum et ligent eum et discipuli
fugiant, et Petrus incid[at] auriculam Malcho dicens:

>[S]et [cur] nequam re[t]exosa
>cur verborum venenosa
>tu sagittas spicula?

67

55 Tu magis [trum] vis tenere,
iam te faciam carere
penitus auricula.

Ad hec dominus Iesus dicat Petro:

[E]rras Petre nunc aperte,
in vaginam tu converte
60 quem vibrasti gladium.
Namque gladio qui ferit
gladiatus tandem perit,
illud non est dubium.
Quod si pat[rem] rogitarem
65 plus duodecim spectarem
angelorum agmina.
Sic impletur ver[a] scripta
prophetarum vera dicta
nec non testimonia.

[IV. vv. 70–102. Jesus before Caiaphas]

Post hec ducant loricati Iesum ligatum ad sacerdotes. quem dum
ducunt dicant alta voce:

70 [E]cce Iesum teneamus
quem ligatum p[erduc]amus
Cayphe in atrium.
Ubi populi maiores
scribe nec non seniores
75 faciunt concilium.

Post hec dum Iesus stat ligatus coram sacerdotibus surgant duo
ex loricatis et clament contra eum dicentes:

Vos audite

[V]o[s a]ud[ite circ]umsta[nt]es
namque sumus confirmantes
verax testimonium.

[Templum] dei d[est]r[uc]turus
80 [h]ic predixit et facturum
se fore post triduum.

Ad hec Iesus nichil respondeat set Cayphas clamet contra eum
et dicat:

[N]il respondes ad obiect[a]?
non sunt ista verba tecta,
non est hoc mendacium.

68

85   Per [d]eum te coniuramus
   tibi [et int]e[rro]gamus
   si sis dei filius.

Ad hec dominus Iesus respondeat Cayphe et dicat:

   [Quem vi]d[etis a]udien[tem]
   vos cernetis venientem
90   ethereis nubibus.
   Et videbitis sedentem
   [de]i filium potentem
   ad virtutis dexteram.

Ad hec Cayphas clamet contra Iesum alta voce. et scindat vestimenta sua et surgat de solio et excu[t]eat se et dicat:

   [B]lasphemavit, cur tacemus?
95   quid i[am te]stibis egemus?
   ecce scindo tunicam.

Ad hec loricati respondeant contra Iesum alta voce et percutiant
eum et expuant in faciem eius et dicant:

   [R]eus mortis puniatur
   collum colaphis cedatur
   quid est hoc quod protulit?

100   Prophetiza nobis Christe
   dicas nobis quis est iste
   qui te modo perculit.

[V. vv. 103–126. Peter's denial]

Dum hec suprascripta fiunt. silicet dum falsi test[es accus]ant
Iesum coram Caypha, ancilla clamet contra Petrum et dicat:

   Tu cum Iesu galileo
   eras [inqua]m tu cum eo
105   [vi]di sine dubio.

Et Petrus [responde]at ancille et dicat:

   Certe nescio quid dicas
   cur sic verb[a] falsa plicas
   tetro sub mendacio?

et iterum ancilla veniat ad Petrum et dicat ei:

   Nonne tu cum nazareno
110   eras in[quam cor]de pleno,
   quid nobis cooperis?

69

et Pet[rus iterum ne]get et dicat:

> Deum teste michi posc[o]
> quia hominem non nosco
> nescio quid loqueris.

Iterum veniat ancilla et clamet contra Petrum et dicat:

115
> Licet tibi sit molestum
> te loquela manifestum
> facit adque cognitum.

Et Petrus tertio neget et iuret et dicat:

> Iuro verbo veritatis
> quod non novi quid dicatis,
120
> . . . . falsissimum.

Ad hec gallus cantet et Iesus respiciat Petrum. ad hec . . .
coram Caypha. et Petrus lamentetur et eat ad discipulos qui
stant in absco[ndito et dicat]:

> Heu quam graviter peccavi.
> Iesum tertio negavi
> et nunc [ga]llus cecinit.
> Ecce fleo nunc amare,
125
> quem promiseram amare
> mea lingua renuit.

[VI. vv. 127–138. Judas' repentance]

Inter hec tollatur Iesus a presentia Cayphe et ducant eum ligatum
ante Pilatum dicentes:

> Iesum strictum religatum etc.
> Religemus ad columpnam etc.

Item dum Petrus lamentatur Iudas reportet denarios et proiciat
in mensa coram Caypha clamans et dicens:

> Ecce numbos reportavi,
> heu quam graviter peccavi
> tradens iustum sanguinem.

Ad hec Caypha respondeat Iude:

130
> Quid ad nos? hoc tu videbis,
> iam nec aliud habebis
> iam tenemus hominem.

et Annas recipiat denarios Iud[e] et dicat:

[Co]r[b]ona non sit locatum
agr[o] figuli set datum
135   sanguinis [est pre]tium.
[In hoc ca]mpo peregrini
sue vite ducti fini
suscipiant tumulum.

[VII. vv. 139–171. Jesus before Pilate]

et Iudas exit et suspendit se. Interim loricati ducant Iesum
ligatum coram Pilato dicentes:

   Iesum strictum religatum
140   perducamus ad Pilatum
   iudeorum presidem.
   Religemus ad columpnam
   demergentem in erumpnam
   Iesum mortis obsidem.

Post hec milites tenentes Iesum ligatum flexis genibus dicant
coram Pilato:

145   [Preses] inclite salvete,
   semper prosperis gaudete,
   preses benignissime.

et Pilatus respondeat militibus et dicat:

   Fratres bene veniatis,
   quid est istud quod portatis?
150   dicite citissime.

et milites dicant:

   [Ec]ce vobis seductorem
   gentis nostre perversorem
   sacerdotes dirigunt.
   Ut in ligno suspendatur
155   adque clavis configatur
   postulant et cupiunt.
   Nam se dixit regem [esse]
   ipsum mori est necesse
   contradicens cesari.

Ad hec Pilatus dicat domino Iesu:

160   [Ve]r[e] rex es iudeorum?
   infinite voces quorum
   te accusant graviter.

71

Et Iesus respondeat Pilato et dicat:

> [Tu] dixisti quod non nego
> iudeorum rex sum ego
> 165   loqueris veraciter.

Ad hec sacerdotes et milites clament contra Iesum et dicant:

> [C]rucifige preses bone
> mori debet ratione
>   qui sic peccat graviter.

et Pilatus dicat domini Iesu:

> Iam non audis que dicuntur,
> 170   quot adversus te loquuntur
>   isti testimonia?

[VIII. vv. 172–228. Dialogue of Pilate's wife's maid with Pilate and Pilate's wife]

Ad hec nichil Iesus respondeat set tollatur a presentia Pilati. dum uxor eius dormit et ligatur ad columpnam et flagelletur. et tamdiu stet Iesus ligatus quo usque ancilla redierit a Pilato.

[D]um hec superscripta fuerit scilicet dum Iesus stat ligatus ad columpnam uxor Pilati dormiat. et diabolus appareat ei dum dormit in sompnis. Uxor Pilati dicat ad ancillam:

> [T]olle moras et festinas,
> meo viro dic inclinas
>   ne ledat innocuum.
> 175   Ne molestet illum iustum
> et mira[c]ulis venustum,
>   prophetam magnificum.
> Pro quo multum fatigata
> et diversis sum turbata
> 180   sompnii laboribus.
> Hac in nocte non quievi
> sicut condam consuevi
>   mota visionibus.

Ad hec ancilla eat ad Pilatum et salutet eum et dicat:

> Preses inclite Pilate
> 185   morum fulges honestate
>   aures huc accomoda.

Et Pilatus respondeat ancille et dicat:

> Aures tibi commodabo
> vide modo si spectabo
> provenire commoda.

et ancilla respondeat Pilato et dicat ei:

190
> [A]d te mittit speciosa
> prudens adque gratiosa
> uxor tua Procula.
> Quod dum sompno potiretur
> contigit ut pateretur
195
> gravia pericula.
> Dum quieti se dedisset
> nec quietem invenisset
> videns terribilia.
> Multas vidit visiones
200
> nec non apparitiones
> et orrenda sompnia.
> Unde supplica[t] devota
> quod tu complens sua vota
> hoc sibi des premium.
205
> Non offendas istum iustum
> et virtutibus robustum,
> non offendas hominem.

et Pilatus respondeat ancill[e] et dicat ei:

> Vade nunctia uxori
> quod non ipsum cogam mori
210
> nec effundam sanguinem.

Post hec ancilla revertatur ad uxorem Pilati et dicat ei:

> [C]ur sic stipida moraris
> vultu pallens contristaris
> et demisse loqueris?
> Iucundare vehementer
215
> cum sit factum condec[e]nt[er]
> quod michi preceper[is].
> Vester subdidit maritus
> quod non sponte set invitus
> talem regit [cu]ri[am].
220
> Vultu retulit sereno
> quod nequaquam nazareno
> inferet iniuriam.

73

Ad hec [uxor] Pilati levet manus suas ad celum et dicat:

> [N]omen domini laudetur
> quia non inficietur
> 225   pres[es iust]o sangu[ine].

et uxor Pilati precipiat ancille et dicat ei:

> [V]ade sede cum ancillis
> operare iam cum illis
>   pleno filans stamine.

[IX. vv. 229–273. Jesus before Pilate and condemnation of Jesus]

[A]d hec uxor Pilati et ancilla tunc recedant. [Tunc] solv[atur Iesu]s a c[o]lumn[a] et reinducatur coram Pilato cui Pilatus dicat:

> [V]alde miror te tacentem
> 230   et nequaquam respondentem
>   ad verba tam gravia.
> Michi non vis respondere
> quem sic vides presidere
>   qui te vinctum teneo?
> 235   [N]escis quia dimictendi
> teque ipsum occidendi
>   potestatem habeo?

Iesus respondeat Pilato et dicat ei:

> Non habere potestatem
> neque ullam facultatem
> 240   in me ipso penitus
> Nisi desuper collata
> tibi esset adque data
>   hec potestas celitus.

Post hec surgat Pilatus et dicat sacerdotibus et militibus alta voce:

> Quem dimicti vobis vultis
> 245   Barabam an Iesum multis
>   condempnatum testibus?

et milites respondeant contra Iesum et dicant:

> [I]esus hic crucifigatur
> Barabas set dimictatur
>   populis petentibus.

74

Ad hec sacerdotes dicant:

250   [S]i servatur hic iniquus
    non es cesaris amicus,
      preses esto prescius.
    Esse regem se qui dicit
    hic Augusto contradicit
255   quod egit hic pessimus.

Ad hec Pilatus respondeat sacerdotibus:

    [D]e Iesu quid sum facturus
    quid de illo tractaturus?
      pandite consilium.

et sacerdotes extendant manus contra Iesum et dicant alta voce:

    [C]rucifige, crucifige,
260   penis variis afflige,
      preses hunc nequissimum.

Ad hec Pilatus surgat et lavet manus suas coram omnibus dicens:

    [N]on me tangat s[angu]is hu[ius]
    [Sum immu]nis morte cuius,
      et ablutis manibus.

Ad hec sacerdotes respondeant alta voce et dicant:

265   Sanguis hic in nos fundatur
    nobis crimen non parcatur
      nec nostris heredibus.

Post hec Pilatus tradat Iesum ligatum per funem sacerdotibus quibus dicat:

    E[cce I]esum flagellatum
    vobis trado condempnatum
270   ite cruci[figi]te.
    Barabb[an] vobis dimissus
    set Iesus sit crucifissus,
      sicut vultis facite.

[X. vv. 274-219. Jesus in the Praetorium]

Post hec sacerdotes et milites capiant Iesum et ducant eum ad alium locum et exuant vestimenta sua et dicant:

    Vestimentis sit exutus
275   iste Iesus et indutus
      clamide coccinea.

75

Genu flexo [salute]mus
ipsum adque corone[mus]
de corona spinea.

280   Illudamus sibi multum
[conspu]amus eius vultum
dextre dantes calamum.

Hic ponant calamum in manu Iesu et expuant in faciem et
dicant:

Iesum grave puniamus,
capud ictibus plectamus
285   sic et occipitium.

Hic induant eum purpuram et ponant coronam spineam super
caput eius cum arundine et flexis genibus loricati dicant:

Ave nunc rex iudeorum
ave decus [angelorum?]
[dex]tra tenens calamum.

et statim [clament] dicentes:

set no . . . dif[feramus]
290   [et Jesum] crucifigamus
ad mont[em] cal[varium].

[XI. vv. 292–317. Jesus is brought to Calvary. Crucifixion]
Post hec loricati exuant Iesum [clamide et in]duant eum
vestimenta sua [et ducant ad] locum ubi debet crucif[igi] . . .
. . . . in collo eius et fingant . . . . . . crux. Dominus Iesus
flectat g[enua et levet manus] suas ad celum orans pro crucifixo-
ribus Iudeis dicit al[ta voce]:

Omn . . . .   Sta. . . . . .
pien . . . .
. . . .
. . . .
dul   no . . . . . .
. . . .   dei . . li . .

Post hec surgat Iesus [de te]rra et milites exu[ant] . . .
. . . . . . [po]nant eum in cruce et duo latrones . . . .
[cru]ce. Milites dividant vestimenta Christi et [dicant]:

[V]estes sorte sortiatur
Ut in par . . . .
. . . .

tes . . . as et Cayphas stantes ante crucem moveant capita.

[Vah qui templum destrueba]s
295 et destructum construebas
        ipsum die tertio.
      Se deponat [crucifixum]
      . . . . [s]alvet semetipsum
        crucis de supplicio.

. . . respondeat. His dictis sacerdotes redeant ad loca sua et
. . . . stans a longe . . . . . . et scindat vestimenta
sua . . . . s et loquantur contra Iesum. Unus
duorum latronum [cruci]fi[xorum] clamet contra Iesum et
dicat:

300   [Tu dixi]sti esse christum
        [fa]c te salvum me et istum
          mergens de supplicio.

et alius [latro dicat]:

        [Quid dixi]sti miser latro?
        iam nos digni sumus atro
305   torqueri iudicio.
        Nonne [times?] verum deum?
        non cognoscis esse reum
          eadem sententia?
        Nos dampnati recto [iure?]
310   [h]i[c] quid fecit ut tam dure
          subiret exitia?

et subsequenter dicat latro ad Iesum:

        [Domine] memento mei
        [du]m veneris in regnum dei
          in quo regnas iugiter.

Et Iesus respondeat ei et dicat:

315   Amen dico tibi latro
        mecum hodie in sacro
          paradiso veniens.

[XII. vv. 318-20. The Virgin's lament]

. . . mater . . . stans cum I[oann]e et aliis mulieribus ante
crucem . . . versus . . . quasi ostendens ei v[entre]m in quo
christum portavit. Unde dolens beatad, vir[go qui]a loquen[do
la]troni et matri sue flenti nunquam loquitur cum ingenti

77

cla[more i]psa bea[ta] vir[g]o vocat filium crucifixum et coram
lo[ricatis] . . . .
. . . . . mag . . . . .
. . . . te portai nillu meu ventre
Quando te beio [mo]ro presente
Nillu teu regnu agi me a mmente.

One notable feature of this drama is that the disposition of the
text clearly demonstrates certain scenes were to be illustrated by
pen designs or miniatures, which unfortunately were not exe-
cuted. But the text transcribed near the space left free and the
rubrics let us know the subject which the designs or miniatures
were to represent:

I. p. 1: Judas' betrayal.

II. p. 2: The false witnesses.

III. p. 3: Peter's denial.

IV. p. 3: Judas' repentance.

V. p. 4: Jesus before Pilate.

VI. p. 5: Interview between Pilate and his wife's servant.

VII. p. 6: Jesus before Pilate.

VIII. p. 6: Pilate washes his hands.

IX. p. 7: Jesus in the *praetorium* mocked by the soldiers.

X. p. 7: Jesus crowned with thorns.

XI. p. 7: Jesus praying for his crucifiers.

XII. p. 8: Crucifixion.

Even with the twelve scenes in the play, we still lack a few
scenes which we should expect, such as: the initial speech of the
soldiers with Pilate, part of the scene of Judas' betrayal, Jesus
before Herod, the scene of Simon of Cyrene, some episodes in
the Crucifixion, of the grave watch and the final scene of the annunciation of the Resurrection.

Notes to Chapter IIII

1 D. M. Inguanez, "Un dramma della Passione del secolo XII," in *Miscellanea Cassinese*, 12 (1936), 7–38; reprinted, with the addition of a Sulmona fragment, in *Miscellanea Cassinese*, 17 (1939), 7–50. Hereafter all quotations from Inguanez are from the 1936 text. Any references to the second edition, which has been available to me through inter-library loan, will be identified as such. For reviews of the play see C. S. Gutkind, "Italian Literature to the Renaissance," in *Year's Work in Modern Language Studies*, 8 (1938), 13–20, p. 14; F. Neri, "D. M. Inguanez: Un dramma della Passione del secolo XII," *Giornale Storico della Letteratura Italiana*, 109 (1937), 129–30; Paolo Toschi, "D.M. Inguanez: Un dramma della Passione del secolo XII," *Archivum Romanicum*, 21 (1937), 397–400; M.P., "Drammatica liturgica," *Studi Romanzi*, 27–30 (1937–43), 147–8.

2 Gutkind, *loc.cit.*, p. 14.

3 Neri, *loc.cit.*, pp. 129–30.

4 Tonelli, *Il teatro italiano*, p. 11; De Vito, *L'origine del dramma*, pp. 163–4.

5 Young, I, 514–33; Chambers, *Mediaeval Stage*, II, 76; Du Méril, *Les origines latines*, pp. 126–47; Wilhelm Creizenach, *Geschichte des Neuren Dramas*, 5 vols. (Halle, 1893), I, 92.

6 For text see Young, I, 701–8.

7 *Ibid.*, p. 537.

8 Toschi, *Archivum*, pp. 397–400; Neri, *loc.cit.*, pp. 129–30.

9 Alessandro D'Ancona, *Origini del teatro italiano* 2 vols. (Torino, 1891), I, 90; Young, I, 697; Chambers, II, 75.

10 *Ibid.*, p. 87; Creizenach, I, 300.

11 D'Ancona, *op.cit.*, I, 87–91; Young, I, 506; Creizenach, I, 300; Chambers, II, 77–8.

12 Chambers, II, 75.

13 Paul Edward Kretzmann, "The Liturgical Element in the Earliest Forms of the Medieval Drama," *Studies in Language and Literature of the University of Minnesota*, I–IV (1916), 1–170, p. 90.

14 D'Ancona, *op.cit.*, I, 90; Young, I, 698.

15 Adolf Ebert, "Die ältesten italienischen Mysterien," *Jahrbuch für Romanische und Englische Literatur*, 5 (1864), 51–74; Hans Heinrich Borcherdt, *Das europäische Theater in Mittelalter und in der Renaissance* (Leipzig, 1935), p. 61; Heinz Kindermann, *Theatergeschichte, Europas I.*, p. 324.

16 Creizenach, I, 300.

17 D'Ancona, *op.cit.*, 91; Young, II, 50; Chambers, II, 77–8.

18 Young, I, 492.

19 Hunningher, p. 68.

20 Frank, *Medieval French Drama*, p. 29; Craig, *English Religious Drama*, pp. 42–3, 255; Hans Heinrich Borcherdt, "Geschichte des deut-

schen Theaters," in Wolfgang Stammler's *Deutsche Philologie Im Aufriss*, III (Berlin, 1957), 418–558, cols. 428–9; W. L. Smoldon, "Liturgical Drama," in Anselm Hughes' *Early Medieval Music to 1300* (New Oxford History of Music, II; London, 1954), p. 194; Hennig Brinkmann, "Das religiöse Drama im Mittelalter: Arten und Stufen," *Wirkendes Wort*, 9 (1959), p. 27; Jackson, *The Literature of the Middle Ages*, p. 287.

21 Werner, *Studien zu den Passions*, pp. 19–20.

22 Young, I, 54.

23 Wilhelm Meyer, *Fragmenta Burana* in *Festschrift zur Feier des Hundertfünfzigjahrigen Bestehens der Königlichen Gesellschaft der Wissenschaften zu Gottingen, Philologisch-Historische Klass*, (Berlin, 1901), p. 122.

24 Young, I, 516.

25 Creizenach, I, 95.

26 Karl Bartsch, "Das älteste deutsche Passionsspiel," *Germania*, 8 (1863), 273–97; Hunningher, 90; Craig, *op.cit.*, p. 103; Knudsen, *op.cit.*, 12–13.

27 Creizenach, I, 120; Hunningher, 90.

28 Craig, *op.cit.*, p. 105.

29 *Ibid.*

30 Joseph Bédier, "Fragment d'un ancien mystère," *Romania*, 24 (1895), 86–94.

31 Grace Frank, *La Passion d'Autun* (Paris, SATF, 1934).

32 William P. Shepard, *La passion provençale du manuscrit Didot* (Paris, SATF, 1928).

33 Grace Frank, *La passion du Palatinus* (Paris, CFMA, 1922).

34 Bédier, *loc.cit.*, p. 87.

35 Frank, *Autun*, p. 29.

36 Shepard, *op.cit.*, p. xii.

37 Frank, *Palatinus*, p. iv.

38 *Ibid.*, p. x. W. Noomen has clearly shown that many narrative passages in the *Passion d'Autun* and in the *Passion du Palatinus* were recited by a reader. ("Passages narratifs dans les drames médiévaux français: essai d'interpretation," *Revue Belge de Philologie et d'Histoire*, 36 (1958), 761–85, p. 772.

39 Frank, *Medieval French Drama*, p. 126.

40 Creizenach, I, 346.

41 J. P. Wickersham Crawford, *Spanish Drama before Lope de Vega* (Philadelphia, 1922), p. 9.

42 Young, I, 212.

43 Alexander A. Parker, "Notes on the Religious Drama in Medieval Spain and the Origin of the 'Auto Sacramental,' " *Modern Language Review*, 30 (1935), 170–82.

44 Angel Valbuena Prat, *Historia del teatro español* (Barcelona, 1956), p. 11.

45 Richard B. Donovan, *The Liturgical Drama in Medieval Spain* (Toronto, 1958).

46 Craig, *op. cit.*, pp. 152–3.

47 Francis A. Foster, *The Northern Passion* in Early English Text Society 2 vols. (London, 1913–16), II, p. 1.

48 *Ibid.*, II, 47.

49 Inguanez, pp. 12–13.

50 F. J. Raby, *Secular Latin Poetry*, 1, 375.

51 Jean Mabillon, (Dom) *De re diplomatica* (Luteciae Parisiorum, 1709), p. 241.

52 E. A. Lowe, *The Beneventan Script* (Oxford, 1914), p. 315.

53 Inguanez, p. 13.

54 Lowe, *op.cit.*, p. 345.

55 Inguanez, p. 13.

56 *Ibid.*, p. 14.

57 Lowe, p. 96.

58 Neri, p. 130; Creizenach, I, 315, noted its use in the Sulmona fragment; Jacques Handschin, "Trope, Sequence, and Conductus," *Early Medieval Music up to 1300*. ed., A. Hughes (New Oxford History of Music, II; Oxford, 1954), 128–74, p. 162; Szövérffy, *L'hymnologie médiévale*, p. 400; De Ghellinck, *L'Essor*, II, p. 296; L. Gautier, *Oeuvres poétiques d'Adam de S. Victor* 2 vols. (Paris, 1858), I, p. clviii; Digby S. Wrangham, *The Liturgical Poetry of Adam of St. Victor* 3 vols. (London, 1881), I, pp. xix–xxviii.

59 Raby, *Christian Poetry*, p. 348.

60 Bruno Stäblein, "Zur Frühgeschichte der Sequenz," *Archiv für Musikwissenschaft*, 28 (1961), 1–33, p. 1.

61 Raby, *Christian Poetry*, 210–11; Young, I, 182–4; Stablein, *loc.cit.*, 1–33.

62 Allen Cabanis, "Alleluia: a word and its Effect," *Studies in English*, 5 (1964), 67–74, pp. 67–9; Heinrich Husmann, "Sequenz und Prosa" *Annales Musicologiques*, II (1954), 61–91.

63 Heinrich Husmann, "Die St. Galler Sequenz-tradition bei Notker und Ekkehard," *Acta Musicologica*, 26–29 (1954–57), 6–18; Young, I, 183; Raby, *Christian Latin Poetry*, p. 211; W. von den Steinen, "Die Anfänge der Sequenze-dichtung," *Zeitschrift für schweizeren Kirchengeschichte*, 40 (1946), 190–212; 241–68; 41 (1947), 19–48; 122–62.

64 Egon Wellesz, "The Origin of Sequences and Tropes," in his *Eastern Elements in Western Chant* (Oxford, 1947), 153–74, pp. 158–9.

65 Zumthor, *Histoire littéraire*, p. 139.

66 F. Brittain, *The Medieval Latin and Romance Lyric to A.D. 1300* (Cambridge, 1951), p. 15.

67 Ferdinand Wolf, *Über die Lais, Sequenzen und Leiche* (Heidelberg, 1841), pp. 31–2.

68 *Ibid., passim*, pp. 30–2.

69 Raby, *Christian Poetry*, p. 348; John F. Benton, "Nicolas of Clairvaux and the Twelfth-Century Sequence, with special Reference to Adam of St. Victor," *Traditio*, 18 (1962), 149-79, p. 155.

70 E. Misset, *Les proses d'Adam de Saint-Victor* (Paris, 1900), p. 29.

71 *Ibid.*, p. 196.

72 Inguanez, p. 21.

73 Charles Sears Baldwin, *Medieval Rhetoric and Poetic* (New York, 1928), p. 201.

74 Rembert Weakland, "The Rhythmic Modes and Medieval Latin Drama," *Journal of the American Musicological Society*, 14 (1961), p. 136.

75 Eduard Hartl, *Das Drama des Mittelalters*, *loc.cit.*, p. 910; Marius Sepet, *Origines catholiques du théâtre moderne* (Paris, 1901), p. 59.

76 Szövérffy, *L'Hymnologie médiévale*, pp. 400-1.

77 D. M. Inguanez and M. H. Willard, *Alberici Casinensis Flores Rhetorici* in *Miscellanea Cassinese*, 14 (1938), 9-59; Charles H. Haskins, "Albericus Casinensis," in *Casinensia*, I (Montecassino, 1929), p. 118; Owen J. Blum, "Alberic of Monte Cassino and the Hymns and Rhythms attributed to Saint Peter Damian," *Traditio*, 12 (1956), *passim*, also pp. 124-7; De Ghellinck, *L'Essor*, II, 57-8.

78 De Ghellinck, *L'Essor*, II, 287.

79 Giuseppe Vecchi, "Innodia e dramma sacro," *Studi Mediolatini e Volgari*, I (1953), p. 237.

80 De Ghellinck, *L'Essor*, II, 296.

81 Ruth Ellis Messenger, *The Medieval Latin Hymns* (Washington, 1953), p. 45

82 For the text of the *Ludus Paschalis* see Young, I, 438-77.

83 Toschi, *Le Origini*, pp. 668-9; also Sandro Sticca, "A Note on Latin Passion Plays," *Italica*, 41, n. 4 (1964), 430-3.

84 Vincenzo de Bartholomaeis, *Le origini della poesia drammatica italiana* (Bologna, 1924), p. 172; Edith A. Wright, *The Dissemination of the Liturgical Drama in France* (Bryn Mawr, 1936), p. 180.

85 Inguanez, p. 17.

86 Ignazio Baldelli, "La lauda e i disciplinati," *Rassegna della Letteratura Italiana*, 64 (1960), p. 401; Arsenio Frugoni, *Celestiniana* (Roma, 1954), p. 129.

87 Toschi, *Le Origini*, p. 674.

88 Inguanez, (1939 ed.), p. 42.

89 Benvenuto A. Terracini, "Un dramma della Passione del secolo XII," *Archivio Glottologico Italiano*, 29 (1937), 92-4; for the entire text see Carlo Salvioni, "Il Pianto delle Marie in antico volgare Marchigiano" *Rendiconti della R. Accademia dei Lincei* (Classe di scienze morali, storiche, filologiche.), serie V, VIII (1900). Given their geographical vicinity, it is not difficult, according to Baldelli (p. 401) and Frugoni (p. 129) to imagine literary encounters between Abruzzi and Marche.

90 Francesco A. Ugolini, *Testi volgari abruzzesi del Duecento* (Torino, 1959), pp. 1–24.

91 *Ibid.*, p. 23.

92 Inguanez, p. 17; Enrico Carusi, "Il 'Memoratorium' dell'abate Bertario sui possessi Cassinesi nell'Abruzzo teatino, e uno sconosciuto vescovo di Chieti del 930," in *Casinensia* I (Montecassino, 1929), 97–9.

93 Fernando Ghilardi, "Le origini del teatro italiano e San Francesco," *L'italia Francescana*, 30 (1955), 341–51; 31 (1956), 81–87, 345; De Bartholomaeis, *Origini della poesia*, pp. 135–6.

IV. The Montecassino and Sulmona Passions

COMPARISON OF THE Montecassino Passion with the Sulmona fragment reveals a close kinship. The Montecassino text not only supplies a number of missing scenes—Judas' bargain with Caiaphas, a few episodes in the betrayal scene, Peter's denial, the repentance of Judas, and that of the maid of the wife of Pilate—but it provides in addition the full text for passages alluded to in the fragment merely by incipits. By combining the two texts we get an extensive Passion play of 543 lines, 317 coming from the earlier play, 226 from the fragment, with some 60 lines common to both.

The seven Sulmona incipits with the corresponding passages from the Montecassino text follow:

Sulmona Text:	Montecassino Text:

I. cum veniunt ad
Personam [Jesus],
et Persona dicit:
 	
O amice, quid.[1]
	Et Iesus respondeat Iude et
	dicat ei:
	
	[O] amice quid venisti?
	mecum fu[rtim tu] existi
	   ut latronem perdere.
	Cur me tunc non tenebatis
	cum docentem videbatis
	   in templo consistere?
	Venientes cum lanternis
	armis fustibus lucernis
	   dicite quem queritis.[2]

II. Et ex magno tremore cadant omnes in terra, et persona dicat: Si me queritis.[3]	Ad hec respondeat Iesu arm[atis et] dicat eis: Si me queritis sineatis hos abire quos spectatis adque mecum cernitis.[4]
III. Pilatus respondeat: Fratres bene.[5]	et Pilatus respondeat milittibus et dicat: Fratres bene veniatis, quid est istud quod portatis? dicite citissime.[6]
IV. Pilatus dicit: Quem dimitti.[7]	Post hec surgat Pilatus et dicat sacerdotibus et militibus alta voce: Quem dimicti vobis vultis Barabam an Iesum multis condempnatum testibus? [8]
V. Pilatus dicit: De Ihesu quid sum.[9]	Ad hec Pilatus respondeat sacerdotibus: [D]e Iesu quid sum facturus quid de illo tractaturus? pandite consilium.[10]
VI. Pilatus dicit: Non me tangat.[11]	Ad hec Pilatus surgat et lavet manus suas coram omnibus dicens: [N]on me tangat s[angu]is hu[ius] [Sum immu]nis morte cuius et ablutis manibus.[12]

85

Sulmona Text:	Montecassino Text:
VII. Primus Milex dicat:	Hic induant eum purpuram et ponant coronam spineam super caput eius cum arundine et flexis genibus loricati dicant:
Ave, rex tu Iudeorum.[13]	Ave nunc rex iudeorum ave decus [angelorum?] [dex]tra tenens calamum.[14]

Clearly the Cassinese text does complete in part the Sulmona fragment, and we may also infer that only Cassinese passages were not developed in the Sulmona text because they were not relevant to the role of the fourth soldier.

The combined texts of Montecassino and Sulmona give us, as already noted, a total of 543 verses, 317 in the Cassino, and 226 in the Sulmona fragment; [15] 60 verses are common to both texts, so that the earlier Passion from Montecassino offers us 257 new verses. But the verses in common to both texts do not follow the same order, and therefore I shall give them according to a table of comparison compiled by Inguanez:

Montecassino Text:	Sulmona Text:
vv. 46——8	vv. 31——3
70——5	34——9
97——102	40——5
139——141	49——51
142——4	46——48
145——7	52——4
151——6	55——60
166——68	97——9
247——9	95——6
250——5	109——14
259——61	103——5
265——7	106——8
274——6	118——20
277——82	121——6
289——91	127——9
294——6	139——41.[16]

According to Inguanez, the different disposition of the text and "several variations which are not due to the simple errors of a copyist, suggest that the two texts, the Cassinese and the Sulmonese derive from two different redactions of the drama." [17] This possibility is supported by the fact that while the Montecassino text has made use exclusively of the Victorine measure, *versus tripartitus caudatus*,[18] the Sulmona is polymetric. It contains predominantly the above verse form, and it has eight stanzas in hendecasyllabic lines and four in various other meters.

Before proceeding with the comparison, we note that the Cassinese author in reproducing the events of the Passion permits himself little textual license, but adheres closely to the Gospel narrative as supplied by the Evangelists, more particularly the Gospel narrative of St. Matthew. A few examples will be sufficient to demonstrate this particular trait. For instance, the scene in which Jesus reproaches Peter for cutting Malchus' ear is reported by the Montecassino author through a faithful rendition of Matthew's passage:

Matthew's Gospel	Montecassino Passion

Tunc ait illi Iesus: Converte gladium tuum in locum suum. omnes enim, qui acceperint gladium, gladio peribunt. An putas, quia non possum rogare patrem meum, et exhibebit mihi modo plusquam duodecim legiones angelorum? Quomodo ergo implebuntur Scripturae, quia sic oportet fieri? [19]	[E]rras Petre nunc aperte
	in vaginam tu converte
	    quem vibrasti gladium.
	Namque gladio qui ferit
	gladiatus tandem perit
	    illud non est dubium.
	Quod si pat[rem] rogitarem
	plus duodecim spectarem
	    angelorum agmina.
	Sic impletur ver[a] scripta
	prophetarum vera dicta
	    nec non testimonia.[20]

Later, when Jesus is brought before the priests and Caiaphas asks Him to tell whether or not He be the Son of God, Jesus' answer is strikingly similar to that in Matthew:

Matthew	Montecassino

amodo videbitis filium hominis sedentem a dextris virtutis Dei, et venientem in nubibus caeli.[21]	[Quem vi]d[etis a]udien[tem]
	vos cernitis venientem
	    ethereis nubibus.
	Et videbitis sedentem
	[de]i filium potentem
	    ad virtutis dexteram.[22]

Upon hearing Jesus's answer Caiaphas exclaims:

Matthew	Montecassino
Blasphemavit: quid adhuc egemus testibus.[23]	[B]lasphemavit, cur tacemus? quid i[am te]stibis egemus? ecce scindo tunicam.[24]

After this, the soldiers abuse Jesus by striking Him and spitting in His face, while asking:

Matthew	Montecassino
Prophetiza nobis Christe quis est qui te percussit? [25]	Prophetiza nobis Christe dicas nobis quis est iste qui te modo perculit.[26]

After having betrayed Jesus, Judas repents, and returning the *denarii* to Caiaphas, exclaims:

Matthew	Montecassino
Peccavi tradens iustum.[27]	. . . . heu quam graviter peccavi tradens iustum sanguinem.[28]

The similarities could be illustrated by many other passages in the Cassino Passion. They clearly show that our unknown author used Matthew as his primary source. However, he does not always follow Matthew closely. Indeed, when not motivated by mere didactic impulse, the narrative becomes more fluid and is rekindled here and there by pictorial touches; the shaping of the scenes, even in its fidelity to pre-established forms, is wisely disposed to amplify dramatically and render more perceptible the profound reality of the liturgical mystery. The entire composition reveals in the author noteworthy literary and dramatic qualities.

Judas' Bargain with Caiaphas

The Montecassino Passion starts on a realistic note: Judas' bargain with the high priests. Religiously and dramatically, it is an effective beginning for it marks the critical moment and the initial movement towards the realization of Christ's Passion. Concomitantly, it gives the audience an insight into Judas' true nature by pointing out his ungratefulness to Jesus and by contrasting the apostle's sanctimonious concern for the people's moral well-being with his overt venality:

> [I]esus doli seminator
> nostre gentis supplantator
> tetro fraudis nomine.
> Multos nostrum iam seduxit
> in errorem quos perduxit
> fraudulento nomine.
> Cui si vita perdurabit
> totus populus errabit
> suis blandis monitis.
> Tradam vobis ipsum vere
> si vos vultis respondere
> digne meis meritis.[29]

In describing Judas' betrayal the author has combined three scenes, namely: The Kiss of Judas, Jesus' Arrest, and The Encounter between Peter and Malchus. Again he appears to have followed Matthew's narrative:

> Qui autem tradidit eum, dedit illis signum, dicens: Quemcumque osculatus fuero, ipse est, tenete eum. Et confestim accedens ad Iesum, dixit: Ave Rabbi. Et osculatus est eum. Dixitque illi Iesus: Amice, ad quid venisti? Tunc accesserunt, et manus iniecerunt in Iesum, et tenuerunt eum. Et ecce unus ex his, qui erant cum Iesu, extendens manum, exemit gladium suum, et percutiens servum principis sacerdotum amputavit auriculam eius.[30]

Following the gospel account of St. Matthew (xxvi:48) and St. Mark (xix:44) the Montecassino author adopts Judas' agreed-on betrayal signal:

> Vos hoc signum habeatis,
> illum caute teneatis
> cui iam tradam osculum.[31]

Medieval exegetes have provided different solutions in justifying the necessity of the kiss as a means of identifying Jesus. Origen, for instance, justified it by indicating that Jesus could assume

89

different faces;[32] Anselm of Laon too, in the twelfth century, comments about the kiss:

> Habet adhuc de verecundia discipuli, qui non eum palam tradidit persecutoribus, sed per signum osculi. Et nota, quia signa quae viderat ab eo facta, non divinitus, sed magice facta putabat, et quem in monte transformatum audierat, timebat ne tali modo nunc de manibus eorum liberaretur, et ideo signum dedit.[33]

The greater number of commentators, however, found the reason in the close physical resemblance which James, one of Jesus' disciples, bore to his Master. Judas, then, would kiss Jesus as a sign of identification for the Jews:

> Judas dixit Judaeis: Duo consimiles sunt, scilicet Jacobus et Jesus; unde do vobis signum.[34]

Later tradition emphasizes exclusively this point:

> Frater quidem domini dicitur ex eo, quod simillimus sibi fuisse perhibetur, adeo ut plenique in eorum specie fallerentur. Unde cum Judaei ad capiendum Christum pergerent, ne forte Jacobum in persona Christi caperent, a Juda, qui Christum a Jacobo tanquam eorum familiaris optime discernebat, signum osculi acceperent.[35]

Of peculiar interest is the fact that, in the Montecassino Passion, in kissing Jesus, Judas bows towards Him: "inclinans se ei." As iconography suggests, tradition appears to have considered Judas to be shorter than Jesus. The Virgin Mary describes the scene thus to St. Bridget:

> Isto tempore patiebatur Filius meus, qui appropinquante Juda traditore suo inclinavit se ad eum, quia Judas brevis staturae erat. . . .[36]

Of the extant Latin Passion plays, the Montecassino is the only one to present the encounter between Peter and Malchus. Strangely enough, unusual interpretations have been given of the character of Malchus. Mone felt "dass die Person des Malchus aus dem Französischen genommen sei,"[37] and Émile Roy considered him "un personnage légendaire . . . qui devait jouir dans toute l'Europe chrétienne d'une popularité égale à celle de Botadieu ou du Juif errant."[38] There is, however, a scriptural basis for the existence of Malchus; in the Gospel of St.

John he is identified by name and mentioned as the servant of the high priest:

> Simon ergo . . . percussit Pontificis servum, et abscidit auriculam ejus dexteram. Erat autem nomen servo Malchus.[39]

In the Montecassino Passion, after His capture, it is to the home of Caiaphas, the high priest, that Jesus is first led, where He is accused by two soldiers of having expressed the desire of destroying the temple and rebuilding it in three days. Later, upon Caiaphas' direct questioning, He proclaims Himself to be the Son of God. Whereupon in horror at such a sacrilege Caiaphas cries out:

> [B]lasphemavit, cur tacemus?
> quid i[am te]stibis egemus?
> ecce scindo tunicam.[40]

Peter's Denial

Peter's threefold denial was predicted by Jesus at the Last Supper (Matthew, 26–34; Mark 14:30; Luke, 22:34; John, 13:38). According to the narrative of Matthew and Mark, after Jesus' arrest in the Garden of Gethsemane Peter had followed Him to the court of the high priest. There Peter is identified twice by two of the maid-servants and the third time by bystanders. According to Matthew, Luke, and John the cock crows once at the end of the third denial. Mark, however, reads: "priusquam gallus vocem bis dederit, ter me es negaturus." And the cock does crow twice, once after the first denial, and again after the third. Once more the author of our Passion follows Matthew's account.

Possibly to increase the dramatic action the Montecassino author has the same maid-servant accuse Peter three times before the high priest Caiaphas.[41] This tightly knit scene in its directness seems designed to heighten and emphasize for the audience, through the crowing of the cock, the silent but highly dramatic confrontation between Jesus and Peter: "Ad hec gallus cantet et Iesus respiciat Petrum." [42] Indeed the playwright of the Montecassino Passion was quick to see the dramatic possibilities inherent in Jesus' glance and conveniently took advantage of this detail which is given only by St. Luke: "Et conversus Dominus respexit Petrum."[43] The cathartic impact of Jesus' action reaches soon its climax in Peter's disconsolate regret:

> Heu quam graviter peccavi
> Iesum tertio negavi
>   et nunc [ga]llus cecinit.
> Ecce fleo nunc amare,
> quem promiseram amare
>   mea lingua renuit.[44]

Jesus' Trial

In the trial before Pilate the Montecassino dramatist follows the narrative of Matthew, who together with Mark and John records Jesus' appearing before Pilate only once, while Luke states that Jesus was subjected to two trials before the Roman governor, one occurring before, and the other after, Jesus' trial in the house of Herod.

The trial before Pilate in our play is significant because it appears that its author drew on available iconographical material for dramatic effects. Specifically, he seems to have utilized the Rossano Gospels' miniatures of the trial, which are a record of a monumental and canonical *Acta Pilati*, that is, "a representation of the trial that is faithful both to the Gospel account and to that state of Roman jurisprudence which obtained when the prototype was made."[45] Much more than with the juridical, I shall concern myself with the liturgical and literary side of these miniatures.

Written in silver uncials, the *Codex Purpureus Rossanensis*[46] (preserved in the Rossano Cathedral, in Calabria, Italy) has been assigned to the sixth century. In its present state it contains 188 sheets, about half of the original number. The style of the Rossano miniatures reflects the illumination of the first Byzantine Golden Age, and their liturgical character is established by the fact that the disposition of the miniatures devoted to the Passion and those leading to it presents a virtual correspondence to the liturgy of Holy Week in the Greek Church.[47] Our interest here is centered, however, upon the miniatures concerning Jesus' trial before Pilate.

The *Codex Purpureus Rossanensis*, [48] our earliest existing illustrated manuscript of the Gospels, like the Montecassino Passion, presents the trial in three acts. In the first, Jesus is brought before Pilate and is accused, and in the second, the choice between Jesus and Barabbas is presented. The third act of the trial, the Washing of Pilate's hands, has not been preserved among Rossano's miniatures, but as Muñoz suggested [49] it must have been part of the trial. The miniature disappeared when the *Codex* was rifled; fortunately, however, Loerke has located the miniature. [50]

The dependence of the Montecassino's Passion trial scene on the trial miniatures of the *Codex Purpureus Rossanensis* is evidenced not only by the fact that, like the *Codex*, it too follows Matthew's narrative, but also in that it combines in one scene, like the *Codex*, Jesus' appearance before Pilate, Judas' returning the money to Caiaphas, and Judas' hanging himself.

As it appears on fol. 8 of the *Rossano Codex*, the trial scene presents Pilate enthroned high in his tribunal. To his right, but lower, is Jesus, and to his left, at the same level, a group of bystanders. The upper left of the miniature reads: "καὶ δήσαντες αὐτὸν ἀπήγαγον καὶ παρέδωκαν Πιλάτῳ τῷ ἡγεμόνι." (Matthew. 27:2; "And when they had bound him, they led him away to Pilate the governor.") The bottom of the miniature shows at its right Judas throwing the pieces of money before Caiaphas and to its left Judas suspended from a tree. The inscription at the bottom of it is a not too careful rendition of Matthew: "ἰδὼν δὲ ἰούδας ὅτι κατεκρίθη μεταμεληθεὶς ἀπεστρέψεντα λ α[ργύρια] τοῖς ἀρχιερεῦσιν λέγων ἥμαρτον παραδοὺς αἷμα ἀθῷον οἱ δε[ξατο] τί πρὸς ἡμᾶς; καί ἀπελθὼν ἀπήγ[ξατο]." [51] (Matthew. 27:3–5; my italics show the words omitted in the inscription: "Tunc videns Iudas, *qui eum tradidit*, quod damnatus esset; poenitentia ductus, retulit triginta argenteos principibus sacerdotum, *et senioribus*, dicens: Peccavi, tradens sanguinem iustum. At illi dixerunt: quid ad nos? *tu videris. Et proiectis argenteis in templo, recessit:* et abiens laqueo se suspendit.")

It may be objected here that the fact that both the *Codex Ros-*

sanensis and the Montecassino Passion follow Matthew's account does not prove any dependence of the latter on the former. A careful comparison of the two texts will reveal, however, a partial dependence, in those areas where the Montecassino author, out of dramatic considerations, has deviated slightly from Matthew's text. Indeed, when Judas returns the thirty silver pieces, Matthew reads: "retulit triginta argenteos principibus sacerdotum." The high priests are not identified. The Montecassino Passion, however, reads: "Judas reportet denarios et proiciat in mensa coram Caypha." [52] The substitution in the play of *proiciat* (throws, let him throw) for *retulit* (brought back) and of *coram Caypha* for *principibus sacerdotum* could only have been suggested to the dramatist by this miniature, where indeed Judas is seen throwing the pieces of money before Caiaphas. As in the miniature, in the play too, Judas is made to hang himself immediately after returning the money.

In all probability the author of the Montecassino Passion had occasion to see the miniature either at Montecassino or in one of its monastic houses. Muñoz has remarked on the monastic origin of the *Codex* and on the fact that its liturgical character suggests it was employed for ecclesiastical use only. [53] Composed in Syria, the *Codex Rossanensis* probably reached Calabria towards the middle of the seventh century, brought there by the first oriental monastic expedition. [54] From Calabria the monks soon established themselves in Campania, [55] bringing with them their liturgical treasures and other monks who excelled in the arts of architecture, calligraphy, and miniature. They founded monasteries that became centers of Graeco-Oriental culture, which penetrated even into Germany and France. The first stop in their cultural penetration, particularly from a calligraphic point of view, was Montecassino. [56] The Calabrian monks maintained cordial relations with the Benedictine abbey through the following centuries and were even invited to visit it and celebrate there the office in their native tongue. [57] It is through these contacts that Oriental iconographical cycles were absorbed by the Benedictine school. Muñoz, for instance, stresses the similarity existing between the pictures of S. Angelo in Formis and the miniatures of the *Codex Rossanensis*. [58] He also points out the resemblance between the miniatures of the *Codex Rossanensis* and the twelve Passion miniatures of the sixth-century Cambridge Gospels of St. Augustine, which were composed in southern Italy.[59]

It is evident, then, that besides the Byzantine, of which we have spoken earlier, other iconographical cycles of the Passion were available at Montecassino to an author setting out to write a Passion play. Just as the artists working on the frescoes of S. Angelo in Formis drew on Byzantine cycles, the Montecassino Passion author also must have taken inspiration from both. In one specific case—to heighten the drama of the trial scene—he must have drawn on the Rossano trial miniature.

We shall see once again in the following apocryphal scene, the dream of Pilate's wife, how the author of the Montecassino play has departed from the literal text of the Gospel in order to introduce dramatic incident. A close analysis will afford insight into his psychological understanding of human motivation and his literary skill.

The Dream of Pilate's Wife

After the flagellation of Jesus, scene eight presents Pilate's wife, Procula, sleeping. The rubrics reveal that the devil appears to her in her sleep, after which Procula tells one of her maids:

> [T]olle moras et festinas
> meo viro dic inclinas
>   ne ledat innocuum.
> Ne molestet illum iustum
> et mira[c]ulis venustum,
>   prophetam magnificum.
> Pro quo multum fatigata
> et diversis sum turbata
>   sompnii laboribus.
> Hac in nocte non quievi
> sicut condam consuevi
>   mota visionibus.[60]

Upon awakening, Procula would normally have recalled first her sleepless night and then have ordered her maid to inform Pilate of her wishes. The author cleverly reverses this order to achieve a dramatic effect:

[T]olle moras et festinas,
meo viro dic inclinas
ne ledat innocuum.

The two bi-syllabic (Tolle moras) and the imperative suggest her excitement and preoccupation. Procula then explains the nature of the command:

Ne molestet illum iustum
et mira[c]ulis venustum
prophetam magnificum.

and finally the reason for it:

Pro quo multum fatigata
et diversis sum turbata
sompnii laboribus.

This sequence effectively focuses the reader's attention on the last stanza's lines, which represent the central idea of the whole passage. After all, Procula is not sending the maid to her husband because she is very much concerned over Jesus' welfare, but as she says, because:

Hac in nocte non quievi
sicut condam consuevi
mota visionibus.

The author's psychological insight is illustrated in another part of the scene. Before the maid has the opportunity of delivering the actual message, Pilate indicates that he will try his best to attend to the matter:

Aures tibi commodabo
vide modo si spectabo
provenire commoda.[61]

Upon hearing the message, without hesitation, Pilate assures the maid that he will abide by his wife's wishes:

Vade nunctia uxori
quod non ipsum cogam mori
nec effundam sanguinem.[62]

The motivation for Pilate's prompt acquiescence to his wife's request is found in the next stanzas. The maid returns to Procula with the happy news and says:

96

> [C]ur si stipida moraris
> vultu pallens contristaris
> et demisse loqueris?
> Iucundare vehementer
> cum sit factum condec[e]nt[er]
> quod michi preceper[is].[63]

Be merry. Rejoice. Everything went according to your plans.
Once again:

> Vester subdidit maritus
> quod non sponte set invitus
> talem regit [cu]ri[am].[64]

Psychologically, the *non sponte set invitus* depends on *vester
subdidit maritus* even though syntactically it governs *talem . . .
curiam*. The *vester subdidit maritus* implies both a psychological
as well as an administrative weakness in the character of Pilate.

It is regrettable that our author does not allow himself such
liberties more often. The reason could be, of course, that the
monastic rules forbade any literary interpolation in the sacred
text, although they allowed a free hand in those passages whose
origin was apocryphal.

In the redaction of this scene he relied on apocryphal and
patristic sources. At the beginning of the scene we read in the
rubrics: "Iesus . . . ligatur ad columpnam et flagelletur." [65]
Matthew and John are the only ones to record Jesus' flagellation
and they do not mention the column. A tradition about the column, however, soon arose and was incorporated into the liturgy.
In the *Missale Romanum*, a prayer for the Vespers Office reads:

> Deus, qui pro salute nostra in
> Assumptae carnis infirmitate ad
> columnam alligari et flagellis coedi
> voluisti. . . .[66]

Early and later medieval commentators provided new details
that elaborated upon the scriptural account. Peter Comestor, for
instance, writes: "adhuc columna cui alligatus fuit Jesus, vestigia
cruoris ostendit." [67] St. Anselm offers other details:

> Pilatus autem sperans crudelitati Judaeorum satisfacere, appre-
> hendit Jesum et flagellavit statua illigatum ita ut a planta pedis
> usque ad verticem non esset in eo sanitas. Haec statua ita spissa
> fuit quod circa duas spannas manus manum tangere non potuit.[68]

97

Before commenting on the source of the prophetic dream of Pilate's wife it may be pointed out that the name *Procula* has an apocryphal origin. It appears for the first time in the *Acta Pilati*.[69] As to the dream, the Montecassino author found this reference in Matthew (27:19) who alone relates that while Pilate sat in his tribunal his wife sent him a message not to harm that just man since because of Him she had suffered much in a dream.

Medieval exegetes commenting on Matthew's passage held two opposing views. One tradition believed that the dream had been sent by God to Pilate's wife both to save her and to have Jesus' innocence proclaimed. After quoting Matthew Origen adds:

> Et Jesus quidem per invidiam traditus erat, et ita per invidiam manifestam, ut etiam Pilatus eam non ignoraret. Volunt autem evangelistae non praeterire rem divinae providentiae laudem Dei continentem, qui voluit per visum convertere Pilati uxorem, ut, quantum ad se, vetaret virum suum ut ne audeat contra Jesum proferre sententiam.[70]

St. Ambrose,[71] St. Chrysostom [72] and St. Augustine,[73] all share the same belief.

According to a second tradition, apparently initiated by the Pseudo-Ignatius, Satan inspired the dream, fearing the loss of the souls he held captive:

> Princeps enim mundi in hoc gaudet, quando quis crucem negaverit; interitum enim sibi ipsi esse cognoscit confessionem crucis. hoc est enim trophaeum contra eius virtutem, quod videns expavescit et audiens timet.
> Nam et antequam facta esset crux, festinabat hoc et operari in filiis diffidentiae. operatus est autem in Juda, in Pharisaeis, in Sadducaeis, in senioribus, in iuvenibus et in sacerdotibus. cum autem properaret, ut fieret, conturbatur; et postea immisit proditori et laqueum ei ostendit et suspendium eum docit; et mulieri immisit timorem in somnio, ipse conturbans et compescere temptans patibulum crucis.[74]

St. Gregory the Great,[75] Peter Comestor,[76] Anselm of Laon,[77] and St. Bernard [78] follow this tradition. The venerable Bede, better than anyone else, comments on the devil's fears:

> Haec enim vice non ante se intellexit diabolus, per Christi mortem nudandum, et spolia humani generis sive in mundo sive apud tartaros, amissurum: et ideo satagebat per mulierem, per

quam spolia mortis invaserat, Christum eripere de manibus Judaeorum, ne per illius mortem ipse amitteret mortis imperium.[79]

The Montecassino playwright chose to follow the second tradition, for the devil appears in person to disturb Procula's sleep.

Scene nine shows Pilate's final attempt at freeing Jesus and his invitation to the Jews to choose between Jesus and Barabbas, after which the Roman governor washes his hands of Jesus' blood.

In a most impressive dramatic climax, scene ten takes place in Pilate's *Praetorium*. There Jesus is subjected to invectives and injuries, rid of His clothing, given a reed to hold, clothed in a purple tunic and finally with a crown of thorns placed upon His head, is mocked by the soldiers:

> Ave nunc rex iudeorum
> ave decus [angelorum]
> [dex]tra tenens calamum.[80]

On the soldiers' mocking of Jesus and on the entire *Ecce Homo* scene Anselm of Laon remarks:

> Milites quidem, quia rex Iudaeorum fuerat appelatus; et hoc ei sacerdotes crimen objecerant, quod sibi in populo Israelitico usurparet imperium: illudentes hoc faciunt, ut nudatum pristinis vestibus induant purpura, qua reges veteres utebantur, et pro sceptro regali dant calamum, et adorant quasi regem.[81]

The Crucifixion

In the Crucifixion scene the Montecassino dramatist seems to have been content to illustrate only the most important scriptural details connected with it, although one does not find any reference—the cause being perhaps the incomplete state of the codex—to the important episode of the Centurion. Throughout the scene his perspective is historical, almost academic, and the detail is factual. The scene can be subdivided as follows:

1. Jesus praying for his crucifiers.
2. Deposition on the Cross.
3. The parting of Jesus' clothing.
4. Caiaphas' mocking of Jesus on the Cross.
5. The Thieves.
6. The Virgin's Lament.

1. The detail of Jesus' praying for his crucifiers is found only in Luke's Biblical account: "Iesus autem dicebat: Pater, dimitte illis: non enim sciunt quid faciunt." [82] Once again our author departs from Matthew's account for special dramatic reasons. The detail emphasizes the Redeemer's merciful nature up to the last moment of his life.[83]

2. The Deposition of Jesus on the Cross is recorded by the Montecassino playwright in a most succinct manner: "[po]nant eum in cruce." [84] In this he follows the four Gospel writers who merely record that Jesus was crucified. The complete lack of realistic details in the Gospel accounts seems to have been welcomed by the Montecassino dramatist, who shows little sympathy with the presentation of Jesus on the Cross; this tendency on his part appears to be reinforced by the fact that no reference is made to Jesus' actual death on the Cross, although, of course, it is implied in Jesus' words to the good thief and in Mary's Lament. The lack of vivid details about the Crucifixion is here not particularly surprising, as only in later religious drama was it represented with increased realism and display. Although early medieval commentators and mystics had described at length the method of the Crucifixion,[85] it is only in the eleventh and twelfth centuries that they begin concentrating on Jesus' sufferings. A very detailed and dramatic presentation of the pains and tortures of the Crucifixion, for instance, is that found in St. Anselm's *Dialogus*, one of the most influential Passion treatises of the Middle Ages.[86] The description is related by the Virgin Mary who, as she declares, includes details not recorded by the Gospel writers.[87]

3. The parting of Jesus' clothes seems to have been described by the Montecassino author according to the Gospel account. Matthew states: "Postquam autem crucifixerunt eum, diviserunt vestimenta ejus sortem mittentes." [88] The play's rubric too is very succinct: "Milites dividant vestimenta Christi et [dicant]." And here follows an incomplete stanza:

[V]estes sorte sortiatur
ut in par . . . .
. . . .[89]

Although the *diviserunt vestimenta ejus* does not clearly suggest how the soldiers divided Jesus' clothing, the *vestes sorte sortiatur* implies that they cast lots for his tunic, which remained intact. According to Matthew and John, Jesus' tunic was not divided so that the Scriptural words might be fulfilled: "Diviserunt vestimenta mea et super vestem meam miserunt sortem." [90] The value of Jesus' tunic, according to John, rested in that it was "inconsutilis," that is, "seamless." Medieval exegetes glossed this passage as emphasizing the mystical unity of the Church. This interpretation is already present in St. Cyprian's *De Catholicae Ecclesiae Unitate*, 7:

> Hoc unitatis sacramentum, hoc uinculum concordiae inseparabiliter cohaerentis ostenditur, quando in euangelii tunica Domini Iesu Christi non diuiditur omnino nec scinditur, sed sortientibus de ueste Christi, quis Christum potius indueret, integra uestis accipitur et incorrupta atque indiuidua tunica possidetur.[91]

Bede, too, *In Lucae Evangelium Expositio*, VI, 23, observes that "Tunica vero illa sortita omnium partium significat unitatem, quae charitatis vinculo continetur." [92]

4. The Mocking of Jesus on the Cross is a virtual reproduction of Matthew's account:

Matthew	Montecassino
Vah qui destruis templum Dei, et in triduo illud reaedificas: salva temetipsum: si filius Dei es, descende de cruce.[93]	[Vah qui templum destrueba]s et destructum construebas ipsum die tertio. Se deponat [crucifixum] . . . . [s]alvet semetipsum crucis de supplicio.[94]

The Gospel accounts mention the presence of soldiers and priests at this scene, but they are not identified. The Montecassino Passion clearly indicates that one of them is Caiaphas, thus retaining up to the end a prominent role for the high priest.

5. Considerable attention is given to the episode of the thieves. Although all four Gospel writers indicate that two men were crucified with Jesus, only Luke records the dialogue that took place between them and Jesus' promise to the good thief. Once again our author's choice is dictated by dramatic interest, and consequently he follows Luke's account. In the play the bad thief is portrayed as the traditionally unrepenting sinner who taunts Christ:

> [Tu dixi]sti esse christum
> [fa]c te salvum me et istum
> mergens de supplicio.[95]

The episode of the good thief was extremely popular in the Middle Ages, for it emphasized Jesus' merciful attitude towards those who repented and because through the thief Mankind participated in Jesus' Passion [96] and gave final witness to His Divinity. It is for these reasons that the Montecassino dramatist elaborates on the good thief:

> et alius [latro dicat]:
>
> [Quid dixi]sti miser latro?
> iam nos digni sumus atro
> torqueri iudicio.
> Nonne [times] verum deum?
> non cognoscis esse reum
> eadem sententia?
> Nos dampnati recto [iure?]
> [h]i[c] quid fecit ut tam dure
> subire exitia?
>
> et subsequenter dicat latro ad Iesum:
>
> [Domine] memento mei
> [du]m veneris in regnum dei
> in quo regnas iugiter.

Jesus' promise follows directly:

> Amen dico tibi latro
> mecum hodie in sacro
> paradiso veniens.[97]

Commenting on Jesus' last words St. Augustine observes: "Reddidit Dominus diabolo vicem, ut quem ille de Iuda apostolo fecerat traditorem, Christus de latrone in cruce faceret confessorem." [98] St. Maximus, on the other hand, points out the good thief's participation in Christ's suffering: "et ideo qui consortio passionis utitur, consortio paradisi condonatur. Beatus enim latro, dum supplicium patitur, regnum coeleste consequitur." [99]

Exegetical tradition concerning the Passion was fond of indicating that three crosses were involved with it: that of the bad thief, that of the good thief, and that of Christ. It glossed them as to signify tropologically the cross of the devil, the cross of the penitent, and the cross of Christ. Such is, for instance, the interpretation that Hugo of Folieto offers in his *Claustrum Animae:*

> Tres sunt quidem cruces: prima latronis desperantis, secunda orantis et dicentis: *Memento mei, Domine, cum veneris in regnum tuum* (Luc.), tertia autem Christi. Prima igitur crux diaboli, secunda cujuslibet justi, tertia vero Christi. Prima malitiae, secunda poenitentiae, tertia justitiae. . . . In prima crucior, ad secundam quaero, tertiam desidero. In prima poena tantum, in secunda poena cum venia, in tertia gloria.[100]

Alanus de Insulis offers a more refined moral and theological interpretation of the three crosses by emphasizing the spiritual ascent implicit in them:

> Ascendamus ergo triplicem crucem: poenitentiae, ut libereremur a peccato; crucem compassionis, ut regnemus; crucem passionis, ut glorificemur in Christo.[101]

6. Of the four Gospel writers, only John records the presence of the Virgin at the Crucifixion.[102] Yet this episode was to receive particular attention from the medieval dramatists. They were especially fascinated with the dramatic possibilities inherent in Mary's behavior at the foot of the Cross and invariably gave prominence to her maternal sorrow at the sight of her suffering Son. In this they preferred to follow tradition. Early fathers and theologians, while recognizing that the Virgin did suffer on Calvary, differed widely on the question of her behavior. On the basis of John's account, "Stabant autem iuxta crucem Iesu mater eius, et soror matris eius, Maria Cleophae, et Maria Magdalene," [103] St. Ambrose wrote: "Stabat Sancta Maria iuxta crucem filii et spectabat virgo sui unigeniti passionem; stantem illam lego, flentem non lego." [104]

The vision of an austere and ascetic Virgin seems to have been prevalent in the early years of the Christian era. Her steadfastness at the Crucifixion is commented upon in an Ambrosian *Missale,* for instance, in the preface to the feast of Mary's seven sorrows.[105] Writing on the subject, Lipphardt remarks, "dem ganzen frühen Mittelalter galt Maria unter dem Kreuz als das Vorbild für alle, die einen lieben toten zu betrauern hatten. Wie sie durch Christus gestärkt worden war, so sollten sich alle christen nach ihrem Beispiele verhalten und in der Trauer standhaft bleiben." [106] The Church Fathers, in particular, suggested Mary was aware of the mystery of Redemption and consequently endured her Son's death for the salvation of mankind.[107] A description of her decorous deportment is given by St. Anselm of Lucca:

I

Astat Virgo virginum cruci Salvatoris,
Stat transfixa gladio intimi do-
loris,
Nati paenas intuens, et rivos cruoris
Intus illa sustinet quod hic tulit
foris.

II

Vultu Mater anxio respicit pen-
dentem,
Sanguinem vulneribus largiter fun-
dentem,
Nati cernit faciem in morte pal-
lentem,
Nimirum sic laniat suam dolor
mentem.[108]

A different tradition, however, particularly in the Eastern Church, emphasized Mary's maternal instinct and tears.[109] In the West, too, Mary's anguish is duly articulated by various commentators.[110]

The Montecassino Passion follows the second tradition. As the rubrics suggest, Mary's Lament must have been one of the Passion's dramatic highlights, and thus provisions are made for the Virgin to indulge in histrionic gestures and passionate outbursts before delivering her *planctus:*

. . . mater . . . stans cum I[oanne] et aliis mulieribus ante crucem . . . versus . . . quasi ostendens ei v[entre]m in quo christum portavit. Unde dolens beata vir[go qui]a loquen[do la]troni et matri sue flenti nunquam loquitur cum ingenti cla-[more i]psa bea[ta] vir[g]o vocat filium crucifixum et coram lo[ricatis]. . . . :

. . . . te portai nillu meu ventre
Quando te beio [mo]ro presente
Nillu teu regnu agi me a mmente.[111]

That this *planctus* is in the vernacular and some of its words are accompanied by musical notes seems to suggest that it was chorally sung with the participation of the lay women.[112] A fuller discussion of the *Planctus* and its relation to the Passion plays will be given in the next chapter.

It appears reasonably clear from the analysis of the most prominent scenes of the Montecassino Passion that, although its ultimate basis is the Bible, the immediate sources often lay in the numerous medieval works recounting the story of the Passion. Gospel Harmonies, exegetical commentaries on the Bible, narratives of the Passion, both patristic and apocryphal, sermons, hymns, all were taken into account by the Montecassino dramatist.

The importance of the Montecassino Latin Passion derives not only from its being the earliest extant but also in that it is truly stageworthy. The wealth of rubrics, prescribing movement, gesture, and facial expression, point out our dramatist's concern for the performance of his play. Precise directions are in fact abundant in the play. The soldiers sent to capture Jesus are described as "milites loricati cum lanternis, armis, fustibus, lucernis."

The author pays attention to the most minute particulars. For instance, when Judas and the soldiers find Jesus, Matthew's Gospel narrative reports the incident in a strictly stylized manner, "Ave Rabbi. Et osculatus est eum."[113] The Montecassino author, however, makes sure that Judas speaks "alta voce," in order that the soldiers will hear him when he addresses their common enemy. Also Judas, in kissing Jesus, is made to bow towards Him, "inclinans se ei." When the enraged Caiaphas rends his clothes, the author specifies that he "shall rise from his throne." After Peter's third denial, the cock is actually made to crow: "Ad hec gallus cantet" and Peter goes crying to the disciples "qui stant in abscondito." Having decided to present Peter's denial and Judas' repentance simultaneously, the author sees to it that no confusion arises by writing that "dum Petrus lamentatur," at the same time "Iudas reportet denarios et proiciat in mensa coram Caypha." During Jesus' flagellation, while Pilate's wife is sleeping, the devil is to appear to her, as the rubric shows. When Procula sends her maid to her husband with the message not to harm Jesus, the rubric expressly says that "tamdiu stet Iesus ligatus quo usque ancilla redierit a Pilato." Also Procula directly tells her maid:

> [V]ade sede cum ancillis
> operare iam cum illis
> pleno filans stamine.[114]

When Pilate asks the priests what he is to do with Jesus, the priests are made to point their hands towards the latter, saying "Crucify Him." Just before His crucifixion Jesus is shown praying for His crucifiers while kneeling down with His hands raised towards heaven.

Two other indications of stage movement should be mentioned. When the priests and Caiaphas are presented taunting Jesus on the Cross, the rubric calls for a truly histrionic gesture: "stantes ante crucem moveant capita." Finally, when the Virgin appears at the foot of the Cross "cum Ioanne et aliis mulieribus," she is described as calling her Son "cum ingenti clamore." Clearly, the author uses the loudness of a speaker's voice as a means of dramatic effect or of characterization. Though on several occasions Caiaphas, the priests and the soldiers will speak "alta voce," Jesus and Pilate, in keeping with their more dignified positions, are always made to speak in a regular tone of voice.

The author also provides us with a clear implication of number of *sedes*, such as the Garden of Gethsemane, referred to as "locum ubi orat Iesus"; Caiaphas' house; a place for the disciples to hide; Pilate's house; and the column where Jesus is flagellated. Also there must be Pilate's tribunal, a *Praetorium* called *alium locum*, and the Calvary, referred to as "locum ubi [Jesus] debet crucifigi."

The dramatic suggestions implied or expressed in this play should not surprise us since stage directions for performance existed in the liturgical framework of the twelfth century,[115] and the Montecassino Passion represents an outstanding exemplar of a highly developed complex play requiring a number of stations. Presumably, since it is in Latin, it was presented in church, and although there is no specific indication of a liturgical connection such as the singing of the *Te Deum* at the end, the singing of the *planctus*, perhaps chorally, makes it reasonably sure that it was represented within the sacred walls of the monastic house.

THE SULMONA PASSION

I shall now examine more closely the fourteenth-century Sulmona Passion fragment. Despite the noted textual similarities to and the common origin with the Montecassino Passion, the Sulmona play presents a work greater in scope than the Cassino, for it combines the dramatization of the Passion and of the Resurrection. This fact suggested to Young that possibly

> the Passion play was conceived originally, not as an independent invention, but as an enlargement of the Easter play, composed by way of providing for the latter an appropriate and impressive introduction. Just as the *Peregrinus* served as an epilogue to the *Visitatio Sepulchri* or *Ludus Paschalis*, so the Passion play might be regarded as an avowed prologue.[116]

The discovery of the independent Montecassino Latin Passion permits us now, of course, to dispense with Young's suggestion.

The Sulmona Passion in its fragmentary state offers the following scenes:

I. vv. 1–30.

After the voice of the public crier is heard, the scene begins by presenting two soldiers, who, on observing that two other soldiers are arriving, go to meet them and fight them. The reason given for the struggle is that each group doubted the identity of the other. Presently, however, they are reconciled and together present themselves before Pilate seeking employment in his militia.

II. vv. 31–48.

Scene two abruptly presents Jesus, here referred to as *Persona*, being taken to the *atrium* in Caiaphas' house. After being accused before the priests, Jesus is tied to the column.

III. vv. 49–66.

Scene three shows Jesus before Pilate. The soldiers accuse Jesus before the Roman governor, and reaffirm their allegiance to Pilate.

IV. vv. 67–87.

The meeting with Herod is described in this scene. The soldiers declare that they have been sent by Pilate, accuse Jesus of refusing to pay tribute to Caesar, and, upon Jesus' silent behavior before Herod, return Him to Pilate.

V. vv. 88–126.

Upon being informed by the soldiers that they have just returned from Herod, Pilate asks them whether they want Barabbas or Jesus freed. After the soldiers have decided for Barabbas, Pilate tries to save Jesus by reciting the "hunc non cerno" only alluded to in the rubrics. At the insistence of the soldiers, however, he delivers Jesus to them, after having washed his hands of Jesus' blood as the incipit "Non me tangat" makes us suppose. After this, the soldiers spit on Jesus and crown Him with a crown of thorns.

VI. vv. 127–9.

These few lines present the soldiers on their way to Calvary with Jesus.

VII. vv. 130–2.

This scene gives the incident of the Cyrenean forced to bear the Cross.

VIII. vv. 133–38.

Scene eight shows the soldiers throwing dice for Christ's clothes.

IX. vv. 139–41.

These lines simply tell of Jesus' Crucifixion and the soldiers' taunting of Him.

X. vv. 142–156.

In this scene we are presented with Jesus on the Cross. As He asks for water, one of the soldiers puts a sponge soaked in vinegar to His mouth. Then, Jesus emits the famous cry of "Heli, heli."

XI. vv. 157–165.

These lines concern themselves with the *Planctus* of the Virgin. One of the soldiers, namely *quartus miles*, is disturbed by Mary's lament. A certain *Iosep*, evidently Joseph of Arimathea, tries to come to the aid of the Virgin as is implied by the incipit "O vos viri curiosi." The soldiers answer Joseph harshly, calling him among other things "senex infidelis."

XII. vv. 166–203.

In this scene, after complacently allowing the centurion to take Jesus' body to give to whomever he pleases, the soldiers go to Pilate and ask permission to guard Jesus' sepulcher, for during His life He had promised to rise the third day after His burial. Given permission, the soldiers go to the sepulcher and post guards around it, exhorting each other to keep careful watch to prevent Jesus' followers from removing His body secretly.

XIII. vv. 204–226.

This scene relates Jesus' Resurrection. The first lines present the soldiers greatly excited, evidently after the Resurrection. They hurry to Pilate and tell him their story. Pilate does not believe them as can be inferred by the incipit "Nicil est quod enarratis." The soldiers, however, insist that no matter what Pilate may say or do he will not change their minds. After which, the third and fourth soldier in unison exhort the Jews to believe, for Jesus is truly risen. And here the play ends.

As compared to the Montecassino Passion, the Sulmona fragment in its multiplicity of scenes, in its variety of meters, and in its refined style is truly sophisticated and of large proportions. As Young observes, "the providing of a separate and extensive text for a minor personage indicates that the play itself was very long, and required careful rehearsal." [117]

Structurally considered, the Sulmona Passion is of truly great dimension for it allows us

> to reconstruct the technique of the representation, the distribution of the parts, etc: moreover it makes us perceive an unsuspected amplitude, a plan of a work which extended in many directions, taking care moment after moment of the direct reproduction of what had happened, appealing to the senses and to the curiosity of the spectators, almost cinematographically, without that taste for the stylization and the shortenings of the choral reflection which was the very soul of the liturgical art.[118]

The Sulmona fragment also shows a highly polished and refined technique. Even "for the speeches themselves the writer employs neither liturgical pieces nor Scriptural sentences, but in a variety of meters versifies the Biblical account according to his own rhetorical desire." [119]

The general presentation of the various episodes and certain dramatic and literary allusions suggest that the compiler of the Sulmona fragment possessed both a knowledge of the terminological resources of the religious drama and of literary traditions from which he drew at times in the redaction of the play. In scene two, for instance, Jesus is referred to as *Persona*. Scholars have remarked on the connection existing in the Middle Ages between the classical *persona*, meaning the mask worn by the actor in the theater, and *persona* as human person.[120] In the eleventh and twelfth centuries the term was also used to refer to someone endowed with dignity, such as a priest in the ecclesiastical hierarchy: "Persona dicitur in ecclesia qui dignitatem habet pre ceteris." [121] Some instances are recorded of Jesus being referred to in the Easter plays as "Dominica Persona." [122] Since in the distribution of roles in the Sulmona fragment the word *persona* is not equated with *actor*, but is specifically used to refer to Jesus only, it seems most likely that here too the part of Jesus was taken by a dignified member of the clergy.

The writer combines rhetorical interests and literary reminiscences in one instance to vivify the dramatic action. He is indeed elaborating upon the Biblical account when he names one of the soldiers Tristan:

> Vadat Tristaynus, miles nobiliximus,
> omnium nostrum armorum doctiximus;
> fuit scrimite hic inventor primitus.[123]

Not only is this individual named, but his distinctive qualities are given: he is a very noble soldier, he is well versed in the arts of war, and he is also the inventor of the art of fencing.

Of dramatic significance, too, is the fact that the soldiers in the Sulmona fragment are not part of Pilate's militia, but rather are mercenaries who have come to him seeking employment:

> Fama nunctiavit nobis
> quod prepositum est uobis
>   retinere milites.
> Ideoque famulari
> cupientes voto pari
>   uenimus nos desides.[124]

They assure Pilate that they will be good soldiers; they will even go around the world for him:

> Ergo iube quid agamus
> nil laboris recusamus
>   pro te, uir egregie.
> Orbem totum circuire,
> uel quocumque libet ire
>   cupimus cotidie.[125]

It is obvious, then, that the Sulmona author permitted himself ample liberties throughout the play and that when necessary, he even created new bits of narrative.

Of particular interest in the relationship of the Montecassino and Sulmona Passions is the *Planctus Mariae* that appears in the Passion of Cassino and is alluded to in the Sulmona Passion fragment: "Quando venit Maria ad crucem, quartus milex dicat:

> Solus: Que est mulier que plorat
> et plorando semper orat
>   ut red[d]atur filius? [126]

Since Mary's *Planctus* is not transcribed in the Sulmona fragment, we cannot visualize its dramatic value nor its importance in the fragment itself.

The Montecassino *Planctus* consists, as I have observed, of a few lines in a centro-meridional Italian vernacular:

> . . . . te portai nillu meu ventre
> Quando te beio [mo]ro presente
> Nillu teu regnu agi me a mmente.[127]

It is the Virgin who speaks to her Son; she recalls that she carried Him in her womb and entreats Him to remember her when He reaches His kingdom. A unique feature of the Cassino Passion is that these few lines are in the vernacular, while the rest of the play is in Latin. Francesco Neri believes the Latin text and the lines in the vulgar tongue are productions of two different authors. He affirms that while "the Latin text is in Beneventan handwriting: the verses in vulgar tongue present us a gothic form, which I do not hesitate to attribute to the thirteenth century." [128] C. S. Gutkind, too, thinks the verses in the vernacular are very probably of some decades later and certainly written by another hand.[129] Inguanez, however, although recognizing that the Latin text is in Beneventan script and the lines in the vernacular are in minuscule, thinks various other characteristics of the text indicate that the words in vulgar tongue belong to the same hand that wrote the Latin text.[130]

Toschi does not express any views on the matter but suggests that the *Planctus* is written in the vulgar tongue because it was sung in chorus by the faithful, especially by the women of the people.[131] Upon examining the text I favor the view of Inguanez. To strengthen Toschi's observation, I personally recall that in modern times at Sulmona, Italy, as well as in other towns in Abruzzi, during the night procession on Good Friday, the people would follow the catafalque on which Jesus' body lay, which was followed directly by the statue of the Virgin. Participating in the lament of the Virgin, the people would repeat in the vulgar tongue the verses recited in Latin by the priest. For instance, the people would sing the following verses:

> Santa Madre deh voi fate
> che le piaghe del Signore
> siano impresse nel mio cuore,

which are a word by word translation of the eleventh stanza of Jacopone da Todi's famous *planctus Stabat Mater:*

> Sancta Mater, illud agas:
> Crucifixi fige plagas
> cordi meo valide.[132]

It is indeed regrettable that both the Montecassino and the Sulmona Passions do not give an extended version of the *Planctus*, since, as we shall see, some scholars have suggested that a *Planctus* may have been the germinal point of the Passion play.[133]

Notes to Chapter IV

1 Young, I, 702.
2 Inguanez, (1939 ed.), p. 27.
3 Young, I, 702.
4 Inguanez, (1939 ed.), p. 27.
5 Young, I, 703.
6 Inguanez, (1939 ed.), p. 33.
7 Young, I, 704.
8 Inguanez, (1939 ed.), p. 37.
9 Young, I, 704.
10 Inguanez, (1939 ed.), p. 38.
11 Young, I, 705.
12 Inguanez, (1939 ed.), p. 38.
13 Young, I, 705.
14 Inguanez, (1939 ed.), p. 39.
15 *Ibid.*, p. 12.
16 Inguanez, p. 9.
17 *Ibid.*, p. 16.
18 Neri, p. 130; Toschi, *Archivum*, p. 398; Inguanez, p. 16.
19 Eberhard Nestle, *Novum Testamentum Graece et Latine* (Stuttgart, 1962), Matthew, 26: 52–55.
20 Inguanez, (1939 ed.), p. 28.
21 Matthew, 26: 64–65.
22 Inguanez, (1939 ed.), p. 29.
23 Matthew, 26: 65–66.
24 Inguanez, (1939 ed.), p. 29.
25 Matthew, 26: 68–69.
26 Inguanez, (1939 ed.), p. 30.
27 Matthew, 27: 4.
28 Inguanez, (1939 ed.), p. 31.
29 Inguanez, (1939 ed.), p. 25.
30 Matthew, 26: 48–51. In the betrayal scene early iconographical art gave prominence only to Judas' Kiss without any acts of violence; the fourth and fifth centuries present already the second scene: the Arrest. In the mosaic of S. Apollinare Nuovo at Ravenna (fifth century), one perceives an initial attempt at combining different but still separate actions: Judas' Kiss and the Arrest. On the ciborium of St. Mark in Venice we have an even greater development, for there, while Judas embraces the Lord, a soldier seizes His tunic, and in a second scene appears the Encounter between Peter and Malchus. It was left, however, to Byzantine and Byzantine-influenced art the task of representing simultaneously the three scenes. (On this see Sandberg-Vavalà, *op. cit.*, pp. 233–34; Millet, *op. cit.*, p. 336).

31 Inguanez, (1939 ed.), p. 26.

32 Wilhelm Creizenach, "Judas Ischarioth in Legende und Sage des Mittelalters," *Beiträge zur Geschichte der deutschen Sprache und Literatur*, 2 (1876), 181.

33 *Anselmi Laudunensis Enarrationes in Matthaeum. Cap. XXVI*, col. 1475 in Migne's *P.L.*, CLXII.

34 Anselm's *Dialogus Beatae Mariae et Anselmi de Passione Domini*, II, col. 273 in *P.L.*, CLIX.

35 Jacobus da Voragine, *Legenda Aurea* ed. J. G. Theodor Graesse (Lipsiae, 1850), p. 295.

Evelyn Sandberg-Vavalà, *La croce dipinta italiana e l'iconografia della Passione* (Verona, 1929), pp. 233–4;

36 *St. Birgittas Revelationes* eds., Turrecremata and Duranto (Coloniae Agrippinae, 1628), Rev. 41. chap. 99. Judas' monstrous ingratitude and avarice were stigmatized in the Middle Ages. (See Louis Brau, "Le portrait de Judas d'après la liturgie," *Revue Grégorienne*, 22 (1937), 81–92; 23 (1938), 55–63; also P. F. Baum, "The Mediaeval Legend of Judas Iscarioth," *PMLA*, 31 (1916), p. 62.) St. Ambrose captured the dramatic intensity of Judas' betrayal in the fourth strophe of his hymn *De Passione Domini*:

> Judas mercator pessimus
> Osculo petit Dominum
> Ille, ut agnus innocens,
> Non negat Judae osculum. (*P.L.*, XVII, 1203).

Shortly after its composition, this stanza and the first two verses of the next were incorporated into the liturgy and sung at the second nocturn of Holy Thursday. (Brau, *loc. cit.*, 22 (1937), 87.)

37 F. J. Mone., *Schauspiele des Mittelalters*, 2 vols. (Karlsruhe, 1846), II, 165.

38 Émile Roy, *Le mystère de la Passion en France du XVe au XVIe siècle* (Paris and Dijon, 1903), p. 59.

39 John, 18: 10.

40 Inguanez, (1939 ed.), p. 29. Caiaphas' rending of his clothes was after the traditional Jewish custom, which required such an action when offences were committed against the Divinity, "consuetudinis judaicae est, cum aliquid blasphemiae et quasi contra Deum audierint, scindere vestimenta sua." (Bede's *Paraenetica Sect. I. Homiliae*, col. 401 in *P.L.*, XCIV.)

41 It is interesting to note here the parallel that St. Maximus, in the fifth century, makes between Eve and the maid-servant for "ad similitudinem Evae, Petrum ostiaria mulier quoquo deceperit: et sicut Adam femina circumscripserit, ita et apostolum femina circumvenerit." (*S. Maximi Episcopi Taurinensis Homilia LIII, P.L.*, LVII, col. 349).

42 Inguanez, (1939 ed.), p. 31.

43 Luke, 22: 61. Mystical interpretations suggest that Jesus' glance was meant to fortify Peter spiritually and to induce tears of repentance: "Jesus vero . . . animum trepidantis discipuli foris positi, ut respexit erexit, et ad fletus poenitentiae incitavit." (Anselm of Laon in *Enarrationes in Matthaeum. Cap. XXVII*, col. 1479, in *P.L.*, CLXII; also S. Maximus, *Homilia LIII*, *op. cit.*, col. 351; St. Bernard, *Meditatio in Passionem Domini*, *P.L.*, CLXXXIV, col. 745.

44 Inguanez, (1939 ed.), p. 31.

45 William C. Loerke, "The Miniatures of the Trial in the Rossano Gospels," *Art Bulletin*, 43 (1961), 171–95, p. 171.

46 A. Haseloff, *Codex Purpureus Rossanensis* (Berlin, 1898); Antonio Muñoz, *Il Codice purpureo di Rossano* (Roma, 1907).

47 Muñoz, *op. cit.*, p. 19; N. Kondakoff, *Histoire de l'art byzantin*, 2 vols. (Paris, 1866–1891), I, 120.

48 Charles Rufus Morey, *Early Christian Art* (Princeton, 1953), p. 111.

49 Muñoz, *op. cit.*, p. 2.

50 Loerke, *loc. cit.*, pp. 175–6.

51 Accents do not appear in the Greek passages.

52 Inguanez, (1939 ed.), p. 31.

53 Muñoz, *op. cit.*, p. 27.

54 Russo, *loc. cit.*, p. 466.

55 *Ibid.*, Jules Gay, *L'Italie méridionale et l'empire byzantin* (Paris, 1904), p. 380.

56 Russo, *loc. cit.*, p. 473; Gay, *op. cit.*, p. 597; Antonio Muñoz, *L'art byzantin à l'exposition de Grottaferrata* (Rome, 1906), pp. 88–9.

57 Russo, *loc. cit.*, p. 473; Gay, *op. cit.*, p. 380; D. Mauro Inguanez, "Montecassino e l'Oriente nel Medioevo," in *Atti del IV Congresso Nazionale di Studi Romani*, I, (Roma, 1938), 378.

58 Muñoz, *Il Codice*, pp. 27–30; Russo, *loc. cit.*, p. 473.

59 Francis Wormald, *The Miniatures in the Gospels of St. Augustine* (Cambridge, 1954), p. 1; David Diringer, *The Illuminated Book. Its History and Production* (New York, 1955), p. 72.

60 Inguanez, (1939 ed.), p. 34.

61 *Ibid.*, p. 35.

62 *Ibid.*

63 *Ibid.*, p. 36.

64 *Ibid.*

65 *Ibid.*, p. 34.

66 *Missale Romanum. Feria III post Dominicam Quinquagesimae.*

67 Peter Comestor, *Historia Scholastica* in *P.L.*, CXVIII, col. 1628.

68 Anselm's *Dialogus Beatae Mariae et Anselmi de Passione Domini*, *P.L.*, CLIX, col. 279.

69 Constantinus Tischendorf, *Evangelia Apocrypha* (Lipsiae, 1876), p. 223; also in the *Gesta Pilati*, p. 343.

70 *Origenis in Matthaeum*, col. 1773 in Migne's *P.G.*, XIII.

71 *Expositio Evangelii secundum Lucam, Lib. X. cap. 100*, *P.L.*, XV, col. 1922.

72 *Johannis Chrysostomi in Matthaeum Homilia LXXXXVI*, in *P.G.*, LVIII, col. 764.

73 St. Augustine, *Sermo de Passione*, *P.L.*, XXXIX, col. 2038.

74 Oscar de Gebhardt, Harnack Adolfus, Theodorus Zahn, eds., *Patrum Apostolorum Opera* 2 vols. (Lipsiae, 1876), II, 219.

75 Migne's *P.L.*, LXXIX, col. 1175.

76 *Historia Scholastica*, *P.L.*, CXCVIII, col. 1628.

77 *Enarrationes in Matthaeum*, *P.L.*, CLXII, cols. 1482-3.

78 *In Die Sancto Paschae Sermo*, *P.L.*, CLXXXIII, col. 276.

79 In *Matthaei Evangelium Expositio*, *P.L.*, LXXXXII, col. 121.

80 Inguanez (1939 ed.), p. 39.

81 *Enarrationes in Matthaeum*, col. 1484. The *Ecce Homo* episode appears to be the culmination of various means adopted by Pilate both to safeguard his interests and to appease his conscience.

As a first expedient, Pilate learning that Jesus was a Galilean, despatched him to Herod the Tetrarch of Galilee. This was the son of Herod the Great who had ordered the massacre of the innocents when the Magi announced that the "King of the Jews" had not long been born. Mortified by our Lord's silence, he sought in his turn to humble the Jews by clothing Jesus in the white robe worn by those who laid claim to that royalty which they denied Him. Pilate's second plan was to propose the exchange with Barabbas. This attempt to establish a parallel between Christ and a murderer met with no better success. His third scheme was to order our blessed Lord to be scourged. This was a shameful punishment reserved only for slaves. The culprit, stripped of his garments, had his hands tied to the iron ring attached to a low pillar, while the executioner armed with a scourge of supple thongs with bone tips, with calculated deliberation lashed with it the back of his victim, bent and taut. The thongs bending pliantly about the body passed from shoulder to breast, ploughing deep furrows from which, while the blood gushed forth, pieces of flesh fell away.

In this state our blessed Lord was brought forth to the mob, wearing His crown of thorns and with a reed for His sceptre. The irony of the scene was not lost on the Jews. How dare they pretend any longer to see Caesar's rival in such a king. (Dom Gaspar Lefebvre, *Saint Andrew Daily Missal*, p. 472). The figure of Jesus crowned with thorns was a traditional iconographical theme. The Church commemorated this scene by dedicating the *Feria Sexta Post Dom. in Albis* to the memory of the *SS. Spinae Coronae D.N.J.C.* A prayer for *Lauds* reads: "Praesta quaesumus omnipotens Deus, ut qui in memoriam Passionis Domini nostri Jesu Christi, Coronam ejus spineam veneramur in terris, ab ipso gloria et honore coronari mereamur in coelis." (*Breviarium Romanum*, Mechliniae: H. Deasain, 1859, p. col. xxix).

82 Luke, 23: 34.

83 Christ's compassion and forgiveness of sinners is a cardinal tenet of Christian theology for medieval commentators, as exegetical tradition thoroughly attests. St. Maximus observes in this respect:

Cum enim condemnatus ab impiis penderet Christus in cruce, . . . omnipotentem Patrem pro interfectoribus suis ipsa inter vulnera pius suffragator orabat, dicens: *Pater, dimitte illis: nesciunt quid faciunt;* et cum in manu esset ejus vivorum mortuorumque judicium, veniam tamen pereuntibus precabatur; sed ea, ut arbitror, ratione, ut indubitanter ostenderet, et se ejus tam nefarium relaxare delictum, et a suo illos Patre non esse damnandos, quibus ipse parcebat, si tamen ad nomen Christi, repudiata perfidia, convenirent.

(*Sermo XXXIX, P.L.*, col. 615).

84 Inguanez, (1939 ed.), p. 40.

85 Bede, for example, described the Crucifixion thus:

O quantae voces et ululatus tristes audiuntur ibi ab amicis suis, et precipue a matre ipsius moestissima, quando sic crudeliter elevatur, extenditur, et toto sacro corpore distenditur et dissipatur. Et statim cum clavi grossissimi immittuntur, sanguis incipit manare, et per crucem fluere usque ad terram.

(*Paraenetica. Meditatio Horae Sextae, P.L.*, XCIV, col. 566).

86 Fidèle de Ros, "Le *Planctus Mariae* du pseudo-Anselme," *Revue d'Ascétique et de Mystique*, 25 (1949), 270–83; St. Anselm is usually thought of as the initiator of the Christocentric piety. See Pie Régamey, O.P., *Les plus beaux textes sur la Vierge Marie* (Paris, 1946), pp. 155–6.

87 Anselm's *Dialogus Beatae Mariae et Anselmi de Passione Domini*, cols. 282–3.

88 Matthew, 27: 35.

89 Inguanez, (1939 ed.), p. 40.

90 Matthew, 27: 35–36; John, 19: 23–25.

91 G. Hartel, in *CSEL*, III, i, (Vienna, 1868), p. 215.

92 *P.L.*, XCII, 617 A.

93 Matthew, 27: 40–41.

94 Inguanez, (1939 ed.), p. 40. Jesus' refusal to accomplish a miracle by descending from the Cross was traditionally interpreted as having fulfilled a threefold purpose: it set an example of strict adherence and obedience to divine will, of complete immolation in the carrying out of man's redemption, and it allowed Him to ascertain His power over Death. St. Gregory the Great, for instance, writes:

Qui si de cruce tunc descenderet, nimirum insultantibus cedens, virtutem nobis patientiae non demonstraret. Sed exspectavit paululum, toleravit opprobria, irrisiones sustinuit, servavit patientiam, distulit admirationem; et qui de cruce descendere noluit, de sepulchro surrexit. Plus igitur fuit de sepulchro surgere quam de cruce descendere.

(*P.L.*, LXXVII, *Homilia* 21, col. 1175. See also Peter of Blois in *P.L.*, CCVII, col. 617.)

95 *Ibid.*, p. 41.

96 St. Bernard calls him "socius et comes passionis" in *Meditatio in Passionem*, *P.L.*, CLXXXIV, col. 747. As Ambrose more cogently puts it: "In cruce enim positus in Christum Dominum nostrum credidit crucifixum. Et ideo qui consortio passionis utitur, consortio Paradisi condonatur." (*Homilia S. Ambrosii Episcopi*, *Serm. 49. de S. Latrone* in *Breviarium Romanum*, Mechliniae, H. Dessain: 1859, p. cclxxxj).

97 Inguanez, (1939 ed.), p. 40.

98 St. Augustine, *Sermo de Passione Domini (III)*, *P.L.*, Supplementum *II*, col. 1198.

99 *Homilia LI, De Sancto Latrone I*, *P.L.*, LVII, col. 345.

100 Hugo de Folieto, *Claustrum Animae*, *P.L.*, CLXXVI, 1083.

101 Alanus de Insulis, *De Sancta Cruce*, *P.L.*, CCX, 225. I owe both these references to John Freccero's "The Sign of Satan," *MLN*, 80 (1965), 22. On the whole the two thieves were looked upon as illustrations of man's conflicting tendencies. "The two thieves represent binary symmetry on the moral plane, that is, the two potential attitudes between which Man must choose: penitence leading to salvation and prevarication leading to damnation." (J. C. Cirlot, *A Dictionary of Symbols* (New York, 1962), p. 71.)

102 John, 19: 25–27.

103 *Ibid.*, 19: 25–26.

104 *De Obitu Valentiniani.* Cap. XXXIX, *P.L.*, XVI, col. 1431; also in *Expositio Evangelii Secundum Lucam*, *P.L.*, XV, cols. 1930–31.

105 P. Gabriel M. Roschini, "De modo quo B. Virgo animi dolorem sustinuit," in his *Mariologia* (Romae, 1948), II, 210.

106 Walther Lipphardt, "Studien zu den Marienklagen und Germanische Totenklagen," *Beiträge zur Geschichte der Deutschen Sprache und Literatur*, 58 (1934), 390–444, p. 395.

107 Theo Meier, *Die Gestalt Marias im geistlichen Schauspiel des deutschen Mittelalters* (Berlin, 1959), pp. 147–8.

108 St. Anselm of Lucca, *Meditationes De Gestis D.N. Jesu Christi, P.L.*, CXLIX, col. 598.

109 Filippo Ermini, *Lo Stabat Mater e i pianti della Vergine nella lirica del Medio Evo* (Roma, 1899), p. 13; also E. Cothenet, "Marie dans les Apocryphes de la Passion et de la Résurrection" in Du Manoir's *Maria*, VI (Paris, 1961), 106–13, pp. 111–12.

110 St. Augustine, *Epist.* 149, *P.L.*, XXXIII, col. 644. St. Bernard, *Liber de Passione Christi, P.L.*, CLXXXII, col. 1138. The *Feria Sexta Post Dominicam Passionis* is dedicated to the *Officium Septem Dolorum B.M.V.* A response to the fifth *Lectio* emphasizes her grief: "Passio Domini, ipsam ejus matrem, carnali orbitate graviter percussam, vehementissime contristavit. Ferrum lanceae militaris latus quidem Salvatoris, animam vero transivit Virginis matris." *Breviarium Romanum* (1859), p. 498.

111 Inguanez, (1939 ed.), p. 42.

112 Paolo Toschi, "Narrazione e dramma nel nostro antico teatro religioso," *Rivista Italiana del Dramma*, 2 (1937), 167.

113 Matthew, 26: 49–50.

114 Inguanez, (1939 ed.), p. 36.

115 Gustave Cohen, *Histoire de la mise en scène dans le théâtre religieux français* (Paris, 1926), p. 44; Virginia Galante Garrone, *L'apparato scenico del dramma sacro in Italia* (Torino, 1935), pp. 3–15; Valentino Mancini, "Public et espace scénique dans le théâtre du Moyen Age," *Revue d'Histoire du Théâtre*, 17 (1965), 387–403. The article deals particularly with the Italian theater.

116 Young, I, 537; also Meyer, *op. cit.*, p. 64; Creizenach, I, 91; Frank, *Medieval French Drama*, p. 29.

117 Young, I, 537.

118 Mario Apollonio, *Storia del teatro italiano*, 3 vols. (Firenze, 1943), I, 58.

119 Young, I, 537.

120 Mary H. Marshall, "Boethius' Definition of *Persona* and Mediaeval Understanding of the Roman Theater," *Speculum*, 25, 4 (1950), 471–82.

121 *Ibid.*, p. 477; Hans Rheinfelder, "Das Wort 'Persona': Geschichte seiner Bedeutungen mit besonderer Berucksichtigung des französischen und italienischen Mittelalters," *Beheifte zur Zeitschrift für romanische Philologie*, 77 (Halle, 1928), 95, 104; Joseph de Ghellinck, "L'histoire de 'persona' et d' 'hypostasis' dans un écrit anonyme porrétain du XIIᵉ siècle," *Revue néoscolastique de philosophie*, 36 (1934), 115.

122 Kindermann, *op. cit.*, p. 239. In the thirteenth-century *Ludus de Passione* Jesus is referred to as *Dominica Persona.*

123 Young, I, 707.

124 *Ibid.*, p. 702.

125 *Ibid.*

126 *Ibid.*, p. 706.

127 Inguanez, (1939 ed.), p. 42.

128 Neri, *loc. cit.*, p. 130.

129 Gutkind, p. 14.

130 Inguanez, (1939 ed.), p. 19.

131 Toschi, *Archivum*, p. 398.

132 For text see Brittain, *op. cit.*, p. 207.

133 George C. Taylor, "The English Planctus Mariae," *MP.*, 4 (1906–07), 605–37; Chambers, II, 40; Young, I, 538.

V. The Planctus Mariae and Passion Plays

V IRTUALLY ALL THE EARLIER historians of the medieval religious drama have held that the *Planctus Mariae* was the source of the Passion play. As early as 1893, the German scholar Wechssler stated as a matter of fact that

> In Italien ist das wulgärsprachliche Drama überhaupt aus den Dichtungen der Laudesen und zwar speziell aus den Marienklagen erwachsen. Und in den Ländern, welche ander als Italien schon zuvor ein wulgärsprachliches geistliches Drama entwickelt haben, beruhen wenigsten die Passionsspiele auf unserer Litteraturgattung. Im früheren Mittelalter gab es keine anderen Dramatisierung der Leidengeschichte als die Marienklagen.[1]

The same idea was expressed by the French scholar De Julleville and the German Creizenach.[2] The English medievalist Chambers, too, in his *Medieaval Stage*, declared that "the planctus must be regarded as the starting-point of a drama of the Passion." [3]

A more reserved opinion was expressed by George Coffin Taylor, one of the first English scholars to study the *Planctus*. While recognizing the fact that the theory regarding the *Planctus* as the germ of the Passion play "does not seem to apply to such late compositions as the English plays," [4] Taylor held that it could apply "to early periods of the drama." [5]

Among more recent students of the medieval religious drama, Karl Young concluded, after giving a brilliant examination of the *Planctus*, that "so far as we can tell, the composing of the *planctus Mariae* was the first step taken towards the dramatization of the Passion." [6] Young's conclusion stems from the theory, shared also by earlier medieval scholars,[7] that the use of the *Planctus Mariae* in the drama may have been suggested to ecclesiastical poets by older laments, such as "the laments uttered by the three Marys" [8] and such separate twelfth-century laments of the Virgin as Geoffrey of Breteuil's *Planctus ante nescia*,[9] and a highly dramatic thirteenth-century *Planctus* beginning: "Flete fideles animae." [10] Richard Kienast expresses the same idea when he writes that the laments of Mary are likewise a lyric subspecies in Latin church poetry, which later evolved into dramatic form.[11] These *Planctus*, which according to Young [12] and Kienast [13] were sung on Good Friday, were sometimes transformed into semidramatic representations. For instance, the highly dramatic fourteenth-century *Planctus* preserved at Cividale,[14] with its many rubrics prescribing mimetic gestures for the actors, has some nine of the speeches which are also found, in large part, in the *Planctus* "Flete fideles animae." [15] On the whole, the reasoning of Young and Kienast is the same as that of Creizenach, who suggested the dialogue amplifications of the Sequence of the Good Friday liturgy were transformed (into drama) at a time when there were no true Passion plays, and that the writers of the Passion plays, considered by Creizenach as really amplified Easter plays, utilized them later for their purposes.[16]

Although various arguments have been presented to suggest a possible derivation of the Passion play from the *Planctus*, up to now no real evidence has been offered to prove the origin of a Passion play in a *Planctus*. Even the Cividale lament, though full of realistic movements that approach true drama, does not represent events that precede and follow the Crucifixion itself.

Possibly, as De Vito suggests, the *Planctus* may be taken into consideration as one element of development, though not as a formative starting-point of the Passion drama.[17] We agree with Craig, who observes that "although these *Planctus* are always found in Passion plays, they are not in essence dramatic and are not the seed from which the Passion grew." [18] We agree to this but not for the reason given. Craig observes that in order to be dramatic a piece of writing must have action, impersonation, and dialogue, and adds that it is "in vain for Young to declare as he lingers admiringly over the *Planctus ante nescia*, that 'Were Mary actually impersonated, the composition would instantly become a play.' This is hardly true; the *Planctus* lack action." [19]

On the contrary, a *Planctus* as included in a play may indeed be dramatic with movement and lyric intensification of the dramatic moment. The Montecassino Passion contains at the end a very brief *Planctus* that presents just the three elements Craig considers to be the *sine qua non* of a drama: action, impersonation, and dialogue. Indeed, in our Passion the Virgin is described at the foot of the Cross crying and gesticulating, while she recites a three-line vernacular lament:

> . . . . te portai nillu meu ventre
> Quando te beio [mo]ro presente
> Nillu teu regnu agi me ammente.[20]

But let us return to Young's discussion for a moment. The fundamental reasoning upon which he bases the theory of the derivation of the Passion play from the *Planctus* is expressed in the following paragraph:

> The view that the play is a straightforward development from the *planctus* appears to be supported by certain substantial facts. We have observed, for example, that some of the laments of Mary are in a form fitted for dramatic use, that such compositions were sometimes uttered by impersonated speakers, and that the only comprehensive Passion plays now preserved contain laments of this sort. So far as we can tell, the composing of the

planctus Mariae was the first step taken towards the dramatizing of the Passion. At least one such lament, *Planctus ante nescia*, which was a notable feature of the thirteenth-century plays, arose as early as the twelfth century.[21]

Hence we may deduce that Young's reasons for considering the *Planctus* the germ of the Passion play are the following: that some of the laments are dramatic; and that the *Planctus ante nescia*, which appears in many plays of the thirteenth century, goes back actually to the twelfth century.

Any weight given this time sequence, even in the weak form of a *post hoc, ergo propter hoc*, can now be dispensed with, since the Montecassino play presents a twelfth-century Passion more dramatic and more extensive than any extant formal laments of the twelfth or thirteenth century and contains at the end a very brief *Planctus*, which is as early as the extended lyric *Planctus ante nescia*, if not earlier. The theory, then, that the *Planctus* is the germinal point of the Passion plays falls to pieces, for, as Inguanez observes, since we now have "a text of the Passion, anterior or at least contemporary to the *Planctus*, this [latter] comes to lose its importance as the creative element of the Passion." [22]

Moreover, there seems to be no theoretical reason why the *Planctus* should be supposed to be earlier than the representation of the Passion itself, for, after all, to the faithful the most important liturgical fact to be remembered during Lent was not Mary's lament, but Christ's Passion. The lament of the Virgin was an incidental element in Christ's Passion, and not vice versa, for as Émile Mâle tells us, "the Passion was in fact the one subject of compelling interest to men of the Middle Ages." [23]

The Passion play, as we have indicated, appears to have originated out of the Christocentric mysticism and piety of the eleventh and twelfth centuries, and the *Planctus* seems to have sprung from the Church liturgy and the Gospel readings of Holy Week. Indeed as De Gourmont observes in his examination of the *Planctus Mariae*: "On se souvient des deux versets des Évangiles, point de départ de cette littérature de suprême désolation: 'Stabat autem juxta crucem mater ejus (S. Jean, XIX, 5): Et tuam ipsius animam pertransibit gladius (S. Luc, II, 35).' " [24]

It is true, as Young suggests, that meditations on Mary's suffering appear early in the Western Church,[25] but it is also true that these meditations always appear in connection with the Passion of Jesus. Even in such treatises on Mary's sufferings as the twelfth-century *Liber de Passione* of Bernard,[26] Anselm's *Dialogus Mariae et Anselmi de Passione Domini*,[27] and the fourteenth-century Pseudo-Bonaventure's *Meditationes Vitae Christi*,[28] the Passion of Christ is always the predominant factor. In Bernard's *Liber de Passione*, for instance, we are struck by the feelings given to Mary:

> Aspiciebat et ipse benignissimo vultu me matrem plorantem, et me verbis paucis consolari voluit. Sed ipsis consolari non poteram, sed flebam dicendo, et dicebam plorando: Fili mi, quis mihi dabit, ut ego moriar pro te? Moritur filius, cur nec secum misera moritur mater ejus? Amor unice, fili me dulcissime, noli me derelinquere post te, trade me ad te ipsum, ut ipsa moriar tecum.[29]

But in his *Rhythmica Oratio ad unum quodlibet membrorum Christi patientis et Cruce pendentis*, he pours forth a lament which De Gourmont places "parmi les plus nobles éjaculations sorties du coeur humain": [30]

Ad Faciem
Salve, caput cruentatum,
Totum spinis coronatum,
Conquassatum, vulneratum,
Arundine verberatum,
Facie sputis illita . . .

In hac tua passione
Me agnosce, Pastor bone . . .

Non me reum aspenseris
Nec indignum dedigneris
Morte tibi jam vicina,
Tuum caput hic inclina
In meis pausa brachiis.

Tuae sanctae passioni
Me gauderem interponi
In hac cruce tecum mori:
Praesta crucis amatori
Sub tua cruce moriar.[31]

In the thirteenth century, also, Saint Bonaventure is mainly concerned with "considerations upon the life and Passion of

Jesus in the *Lignum Vitae*, in the *Officium de Passione*, in the *Vitis mystica* and elsewhere." [32] This lingering on the Passion of Christ is to be expected, for "the meditation on the life of Christ was a duty for the Christian and especially for the Franciscan," [33] for whom "the whole religious experience was summed up in the motto of the Order: Mihi absit gloriari nisi in cruce Domini." [34] Indeed the sufferings of the Redeemer upon the Cross are for Bonaventure as for every Franciscan the centre of all man's hope of salvation, his only consolation, his sorrow and his delight.[35] This profound concern for Christ's sufferings and the pathos that meditations on it evoked can best be observed in a few stanzas from Bonaventure's *Laudismus de Sancta Cruce*.[36] Here the faithful are invited to remember Christ's Passion, to meditate upon it, to delight in it:

> Recordare sanctae crucis
> qui perfectam vitam ducis,
> delectare iugiter.
> sanctae crucis recordare,
> et in ipsa meditare,
> insatiabiliter.

As if this were not enough, the faithful are invited to live in the light of the Cross and actually to grow with it:

> estes in Cruce Christo duce
> donec vivas in hac luce,
> moto procul taedio,
> non quiescas nec tepescas,
> in hac crescas et calescas
> cordis desiderio.

It seems evident to me, then, that meditations upon the Passion of Christ in the twelfth and thirteenth centuries are coeval with meditations upon the sufferings of Mary.

We may safely conjecture that when a twelfth-century cleric or monk had drafted a play on the Passion of Christ, he might also incorporate in it the lament of the Virgin. This possibility is strengthened by the fact that the earliest extant Passion play of Montecassino and the two thirteenth-century Benediktbeuern Passion plays present together the Passion and some sort of *Planctus*.

Later, however, with the fuller development of both play and lyric, in Apollonio's words, "the expression of a grief without comfort goes on freeing itself from the sensational encumbrance of the traditional apparatus of the Passion: the multitude of Jews, the soldiers, the thieves, in short the spectacle of the crowd which in the phantasmagoria of the Passion was able to neglect and sometimes to forget completely the humanity of the religious sentiment." [37] Indeed, as Mâle has observed, "de même que l'on dit *Christi Passio* on commence à dire, dès le XIVe siècle, *Mariae Compassio:* cette compassion de la Vierge, c'est l'écho de la Passion dans son coeur." [38] Particularly in England in the fourteenth century the motif of the lamenting mother becomes more and more the subject of forceful sermons. [39] Mâle proposed that this later lingering over Mary's suffering was due to the influence of the *Meditationes Vitae Christi,* [40] now assigned to the early fourteenth century. [41]

The whole of the *Meditationes,* which were written by a cleric for a spiritual daughter of his, although based on the Gospels and the Acts of the Apostles, avoids the parables and the prodigies in them and presents instead human scenes of tender feeling and description with much dialogue. In the *Meditationes Vitae Christi,* in fact, its author differed completely "de tout ce que l'Évangile avait inspiré jusque-là en Occident. Les autres livres s'adressaient à l'intelligence, celui-là parle au coeur." [42] He is not capable of portraying in Christ and the Virgin the divine, but only their humanly affectionate qualities. Mary, for instance, shows these qualities not only at the foot of the Cross, but also in other scenes. After Jesus is laid in the grave, for example, the Virgin goes home; there John bids the Holy Women to leave her because the hour is late and closes the door. Once inside, the Virgin looks around the house ("domum circumspiciens") and utters a most beautiful lament: "Fili mi dulcissime, ubi es quia te non video? Oh Ioannes, ubi est filius meus? O Magdalena, ubi est pater tuus qui te sic tenerissime diligebat? . . ." [43]

On the whole, the *Meditationes,* according to Cellucci, show that the author delights in presenting the pathetic aspect of his subject in order to stir feeling and compassion. [44] The pathos and human detail of the *Meditationes Vitae Christi* fill the Passion plays of the later Middle Ages, whereas in the early Montecassino play the treatment is far simpler.

To conclude, then, the separation of the *Planctus Mariae* from the Passion proper and the fact that numerous *Planctus* have come down to us, have, in general, contributed to the idea that the Passion play may have derived from the *Planctus*. Since, however, no extant *Planctus* precedes the highly developed Passion play of Montecassino, and since this Passion includes only a rudimentary *Planctus* of three lines it seems clear that the *Planctus* is not the germ or stimulus of this Passion play nor probably of others in the twelfth and thirteenth centuries. Rather, it is a lyrical piece which could have been assigned to the intensification of the Crucifixion scene or simply to co-exist with the Passion as a separate type of lyric.

Notes to Chapter V

1 Eduard Wechssler, *Die Romanischen Marienklagen* (Halle, 1893), p. 98.

2 Craig, *English Religious Drama*, p. 46.

3 Chambers, II, 40; more recently W. L. Smoldon, in *Liturgical Drama*, p. 193, writes: "The core of the Passion Play would seem to be the various *planctus* or laments—extra-liturgical compositions represented as being sung by one or another of the mourners at the foot of the Cross."

4 George C. Taylor, "The English Planctus Mariae" in *Modern Philology*, 4 (1906–07), 633

5 *Ibid.*

6 Young, I, 538.

7 Neil C. Brooks, "The Lamentations of Mary in the Frankfurt Group of Passion Plays," *Journal of Germanic Philology*, 3 (1900–01), 416.

8 Young, I, 495.

9 *Ibid.*, p. 496.

10 *Ibid.*, p. 498.

11 Richard Kienast, "Die Deutschsprachige Lyrik des Mittelalters," in Wolfgang Stammler's *Deutsche Philologie Im Aufriss*, II, 774–902, p. 890.

12 Young, I, 503.

13 Kienast, *op. cit.*, p. 890.

14 Young, I, 506; De Bartholomaeis, *Origini*, p. 133.

15 Young, I, 512.

16 Creizenach, *Geschichte des neuren Dramas*, (1911 ed.), I, 248; Theo Meier, *Die Gestalt Marias im geistlichen Schauspiel des deutschen Mittelalters* (Berlin, 1959), pp. 178–9.

17 De Vito, *op. cit.*, p. 164.

18 Craig, *op. cit.*, p. 47; Mrs. Frank, too, in *The Medieval French Drama*, p. 29, maintains that although "potentially dramatic" the *Planctus* "remained lyrical and static."

19 Hardin Craig, "The Origin of the Passion Play: Matters of Theory as Well as Fact," *University of Missouri Studies*, 20 (1946–47), 83–90.

20 Inguanez, (1939 ed.), pp. 41–2.

21 Young, I, 538.

22 Inguanez, (1939 ed.), p. 21.

23 Émile Mâle, *Religious Art in France in the XIII Century* (New York, 1913), p. 222.

24 Remy de Gourmont, *Le Latin mystique* (Paris, 1913), p. 351.

25 Young, I, 494.

26 Migne, P.L., CLXXXII, cols. 1133–1442.

27 *Ibid.*, CLIX, cols. 271–290.

28 Luigi Cellucci, " 'Le Meditationes Vitae Christi' e i poemetti che ne furono ispirati," *Archivum Romanicum*, 22 (1938), 30–98.

29 Migne, P.L., CLXXXII, col. 1135.

30 De Gourmont, p. 235.

31 *Ibid.*, p. 236.

32 Cellucci, p. 36.

33 *Ibid.*, p. 38.

34 Raby, *Christian Latin Poetry, op. cit.*, p. 418. The motto is a paraphrase of St. Paul's "Mihi autem absit gloriari, nisi in cruce Domini nostri Iesu Christi." (*Gal.* 6,14.)

35 *Ibid.*, p. 423.

36 *Ibid.*

37 Mario Apollonio, *Storia del teatro italiano* 2 vols. (Firenze, 1943), I, 190.

38 Émile Mâle, *L'art religieux de la fin du moyen âge* (Paris, 1946), p. 122.

39 Theodor Wolpers, "Englische Marienlyrik im Mittelalter," *Anglia,* 69 (1950), 21.

40 Mâle, *L'art religieux*, p. 122.

41 Cellucci, p. 35.

42 Émile Mâle, *L'art religieux du XIIe au XVIIIe siècles* (Paris, 1946), p. 92.

43 Cellucci, p. 59.

44 *Ibid.*, p. 45.

VI. The Liturgical and Vernacular Tradition

ISTORICAL AND LITERARY research on the relations and influences of one work of art upon another usually tends to be an excursus into daring and abstract generalizations whenever the investigation is not sustained by a critical and objective method that relates all comparative analyses to a cultural and thematic unity existing between the works under consideration. The existence in every epoch of a common cultural denominator would obviously facilitate the undertaking of such a research.

The present investigation into dramatic influences is justifiable by a cultural and thematic unity among the various plays, a unity that we would call Catholic, and by the fact that these productions, at least up to the end of the thirteenth century, generally share a technical-philological medium: the Latin language.[1] In addition, any scholar of the Middle Ages is aware of the conscious transmission and utilization of ancient and contemporary Latin literature from one monastic house to another and of the fact that this dissemination took place throughout Western Europe.[2]

Students of the history of the religious drama have already remarked on its international character and on the fact that it developed more or less contemporaneously in the various nations of the Catholic Western world. A comprehensive study, however, is needed—one such as Edith A. Wright's for France—that would apply the principles of comparative literature to medieval Latin religious drama in order to throw light on the influences of one country upon the other; to investigate the means of communications among the various monastic houses, which were normally the places where the religious dramas were composed and copied; and to determine the extent of the dissemination of the plays among the various countries. Creizenach was aware of the problem of transmission and influences inherent in medieval drama and offered suggestions that are still worth investigation:

> Bei Behandlung der lateinischen Dramen hatten wir es fast immer mit einer Überlieferung zu tun, die einerseits zu spärlich, andererseits zu verworren war, um den Ursprung der einzelnen Denkmaler erkennen zu lassen. Es wäre nicht undenkbar, dass hier noch manche Ergebnisse zu gewissen waren, wenn mann die literarischen Wechselbeziehungen zwischen den Klostern und Stiftern, aus denen die Texte stammen, genauer untersuchen wollte.[3]

We shall attempt to identify the common elements in medieval drama, the scriptural, liturgical, and theological sources, and to show in particular the similarities that exist between the Italian Montecassino play and a French Easter play also in Latin.

LATIN PASSION PLAYS

We shall begin by comparing the Cassino Passion play with the two thirteenth-century Benediktbeuern Latin Passion plays long considered the earliest. The first of the two, the *Ludus*

Breviter de Passione, presents a comprehensive story of the Passion, from the preparations for the Last Supper through the account of the act of Burial. More specifically it presents the following scenes:

1. The Last Supper and Judas' bargain.
2. Judas' Betrayal.
3. Jesus before Pilate.
4. The Crucifixion and Mary's Lament.
5. The Episode of Joseph of Arimathea.

In the incidents represented, the prose *Ludus Breviter* is larger in scope than the verse Montecassino Passion, which also begins with Judas' bargain and ends with the Crucifixion and Mary's lament; the actual text of the *Ludus Breviter,* however, is much shorter. It was composed eclectically from a Gospels harmony. As Young observes "the borrowings are chiefly from Matthew, supplemented freely from John, and, less amply, from Mark and Luke." [4] A few examples will give an idea of how faithful the *Ludus Breviter's* author was to the Gospel narrative. At the beginning of the play, the disciples approach Jesus and ask Him:

Ludus Breviter	Matthew
Ubi vis paremus tibi commedere Pascha? [5]	Ubi vis paremus tibi comedere Pascha? [6]

Christ answers:

Ludus Breviter	Matthew
Ite in civitatem ad quendam et dicite ei: Magister dicit: Tempus meum propre est, apud te facio Pascha cum discipulis meis. [7]	Ite in civitatem ad quendam et dicite ei: Magister dicit: Tempus meum propre est, apud te facio Pascha cum discipulis meis. [8]

When the Jews and the soldiers accuse Jesus before Pilate they exclaim:

Ludus Breviter	Luke
Hunc invenimus subvertentem gentem nostram, et prohibentem tributa dari Cesari, et dicentem se Christum regem esse. [9]	Hunc invenimus subvertentem gentem nostram, et prohibentem tributa dare Caesari, et dicentem se Christum regem esse. [10]

One might expect that in a manuscript belonging to a century later than the Montecassino Passion, the *Ludus Breviter* would show a more advanced form than the Cassino Passion, from both a stylistic and a dramatic point of view. Yet, the *Ludus* follows literally the prose account of the Gospel according to the various Evangelists.

The only novel and striking feature of the *Ludus Breviter* is the rubric for a lament: *Et Maria planctum faciat quantum melius potest.* The dramatic suggestions implied by this rubric, as compared to the strict limitation of the play as a whole, can be explained by the fact that in thirteenth-century Germany the laments of the Virgin were already highly developed. In fact, as Kienast observes,

> one of those, the *Planctus ante nescia*, came from France to Germany in the twelfth century and became the basis of most of the German Mary's laments; in the thirteenth century—more or less enlarged—translated in German, it was sung during the Good Friday Vespers . . . in the choir of many German churches.[11]

German scholars have generally accepted Schönbach's theory that the twelfth-century Latin Sequence *Planctus ante nescia* is the basis of the German Mary's laments, whether they appear as independent lyrics or in relation with the German vernacular Passion plays.[12]

The lament that Mary is to sing in the *Ludus Breviter* is probably just the *Planctus ante nescia*, an abbreviation of which as Young observes "is written out of its appropriate place, upon the page preceding that containing the rubric," in the *Carmina Burana* manuscript.[13] If we exclude this extremely interesting feature, the *Ludus Breviter* shows no dramatic improvement over the Montecassino Passion.

The second of the two Benediktbeuern Latin Passion plays, the *Ludus de Passione* includes a much more extensive and elaborate dramatization of the Passion than the *Ludus Breviter*. It presents events of Christ's life from his calling of Peter and Andrew to his death. The play offers the following main scenes:

> I. vv. 1–35. Jesus' ministry from the calling of Peter and Andrew to the Entry in Jerusalem.

II. vv. 36–152. The Worldly Life and Conversion of Mary
Magdalene. In this scene is included Jesus' supper at the
house of Simon the Pharisee.
III. vv. 50–57. Mary Magdalene at the Merchant's.
IV. vv. 153–247. Jesus' Passion from Judas' bargain to the Cruci-
fixion. The scene begins with the raising of Lazarus.
V. vv. 245–291. Jesus' Crucifixion and the Virgin's Lament.
VI. vv. 306–321. Joseph of Arimathea before Pilate.

Particularly important from a dramatic point of view is the
presentation of the life of Mary Magdalene *in gaudio*, which
together with her later repentance constitutes one third of the
entire play. This has led Meyer to suggest the existence of an
earlier play of which Mary Magdalene was the leading character.[14] Of particular interest is the fact that in the *Ludus de Passione* she utters about ten stanzas in the vernacular. (The other
German passages in this Latin play are the Virgin's lament.)
Since these stanzas do not represent a translation of Mary Magdalene's Latin speeches, and considering that outside of some
sporadic allusions in the Easter cycle no liturgical source treats
her life so extensively, we may infer that these vernacular verses
were invented by the author of the *Ludus de Passione*, or by the
writer of an earlier play, to provide a more vivid representation
of the scene. As in the Montecassino Passion play, the use of the
vernacular by the *Ludus'* author seems to have been motivated
by his desire to secure, in the sacred representation, the greatest
possible participation on the part of the people. The passages in
German clearly separate themselves from the Gospel account,
either as fictional elements or simply as the expression of the
individual characters. They are: the song of Magdalene *in
gaudio*, the dialogue between her and the merchant, her love
songs before and after her conversion, one of the Virgin's
laments at the foot of the Cross, Longinus' words as he strikes
Jesus' side, and the final colloquy between Pilate and Joseph of
Arimathea.

One is struck by the important role played by Mary Magdalene. Needless to say, she was one of the most popular saints of
the Middle Ages.[15] As the prototype of the repentant sinner, the
one who threw herself at the Savior's feet and thus obtained
remission of her sins, she became the patron of all sinners. In

Western tradition, beginning from the time of Gregory the Great she was also identified with the woman who visited Jesus' tomb on Easter morning and the one to whom Jesus first appeared after His resurrection.[16]

Although certain general characteristics about Mary Magdalene were known in the early Middle Ages through homiletic and exegetic literature, the dramatization of her life seems to be traceable to the intensity of the Magdalene cult in the West, which, beginning in the eleventh, found its greatest manifestation in the twelfth century.

Interestingly enough from our point of view is that the lengthy dramatization of Mary Magdalene in the thirteenth-century *Ludus de Passione* coincides with the period of greatest development of the Magdalene cult in Germany.[17] Magdalene's place in liturgical and medieval drama has already been established.[18]

Fruitful and enlightening results in establishing the extent of the Magdalene cult in the Middle Ages have recently been achieved by a thorough study of the medieval hymnody connected with Magdalene.[19] One of the basic types of hymns is the contrasting of Mary Magdalene before and after her conversion.[20] This is particularly germane to our discussion, for indubitably this contrast is exploited by the author of the *Ludus de Passione*. The contrast is further heightened by the *Ludus* dramatist through the intervention of the two spiritually contrasting figures of *Angelus* and *Diabolus*, who obviously represent the forces of good and evil between which Mary is torn. These symbolical figures may be regarded, as Young suggests, "as the precursors of the abstractions of virtue and vice which animate the moral plays of the later Middle Ages." [21] Possible influences from traditional Magdalene hymns on the *Ludus* may be inferred in view of the fact that the Latin stanzas she utters in the play have a hymn or song form, and by the consideration that the Magdalene hymn production is quite intense in the thirteenth century. This possibility is strengthened by the obvious dramatic qualities of some of these Magdalene hymns, such as the one beginning: Flere libet/ac flere debeo.[22] The dramatic connection of the following has already been ascertained:

I. Amoris studio
cuius remedio
en crucifigitur
non mirum igitur

Jesum colueram,
flevi quod feceram
cui me devoveram;
si planctus exeram.

II. Transfixis pedibus
quos ternis crinibus
non his ulterius
Quid infelicius?

quod fletu laveram,
ore lambueram:
hanc eddam operam.
O me, iam miseram.

III. Cruorem fluidum
O nefas (h)orridum,
non dictat aequitas,
virtutum (largitas)

dant quinque vulnera.
o saeva scelera.
non lex, non ratio,
ut ruat gladio.[23]

Dom Wilmart, its discoverer, ascribed this hymn to the twelfth-century poet Walter of Châtillon and indicated that ". . . il a été composé pour un drame sacré, par ailleurs inconnu, un exemplaire de l'*Ordo Passionis* qu'on jouait parfois au cours de la grande semaine liturgique, pour commémorer les souvenirs de la rédemption, et il nous est ici proposé détaché de son cadre, représentant le brief rôle de Madeleine auprès de la Croix." [24]

As to the Cassino Passion play, the *Ludus de Passione* presents scenes that are not to be found in the former, such as Christ's calling of Peter and Andrew, His healing of the blind Bartimaeus, His colloquy with Zacchaeus outside of Jericho, Mary Magdalene's life, the raising of Lazarus, and the colloquy between Pilate and Joseph of Arimathea. Particularly important is the fact that both the Montecassino Passion and the *Ludus de Passione* introduce the Devil, although for different purposes. In the Cassino Passion *diabolus* appears to Pilate's wife while she is sleeping and makes her see strange visions; in the *Ludus*, *diabolus* influences Mary Magdalene to buy cosmetics to entice her lover.

Close consideration must also be given to the speeches in German that are uttered by the Virgin in the form of a *planctus*. That part of Mary's lament is in the German tongue may be because laments of the Virgin in vernacular were so well known and so much part of the Good Friday Church services [25] that the scribe felt the necessity of incorporating them, as they were used in church, in the Latin play. The desire to obtain a greater participation of the people in the drama appears to be responsible for the presence of a vernacular *planctus* in the Monte-cassino Passion too. The entire *Planctus Mariae* in the *Ludus de Passione* is given extensive treatment. Indeed, after the Virgin has uttered a German *planctus* of four stanzas before the Cru-cified,[26] she invites the Holy Women to lament too, in some stanzas of a well known lament written in the thirteenth century:

> Flete, fideles animae
> Flete, sorores optimae
> ut sint multiplices
> doloris indices
> planctus et lacrime . . .[27]

As if to emphasize Mary's grief still more the author makes her utter another stanza of the "Flete fideles animae," with John in her arms: "Mi Iohannes, planctum moue, plange mecum, fili noue . . ."[28] After a pause, the Virgin pronounces the famous *Planctus ante nescia.*[29]

Some scholars attribute this extensive dramatization of Mary's *Compassio* and the very development of the first German Latin Passion plays to the direct influence of the Passion piety of the thirteenth-century flagellant movement of central Italy.[30] It is not too farfetched to suggest here that knowledge of the existence of the Montecassino Passion play may possibly have reached the Benediktbeuern scribe through monastic sources, and could have inspired him to create a Latin Passion. Although we are here postulating a hypothesis, it is an historical fact that close relations were entertained in the Middle Ages between German monastic houses and the Benedictine abbey of southern Italy. The monastery of Fulda and Montecassino from the eighth to the twelfth century, maintained a continuous exchange of ancient, biblical, patristic, and medieval texts.[31] In 748, St. Sturm, Fulda's first abbot, went to the abbey of Montecassino to become familiar with the practice of the Benedictine Rule. Under the administration of St. Sturm, Fulda rose to great splendor and renown and became the mother house of several smaller monasteries. Under Hrabanus Maurus in the ninth century, Fulda became the chief house of learning in Germany and acquired fame throughout Europe. Around 969 John XIII even declared Ful-

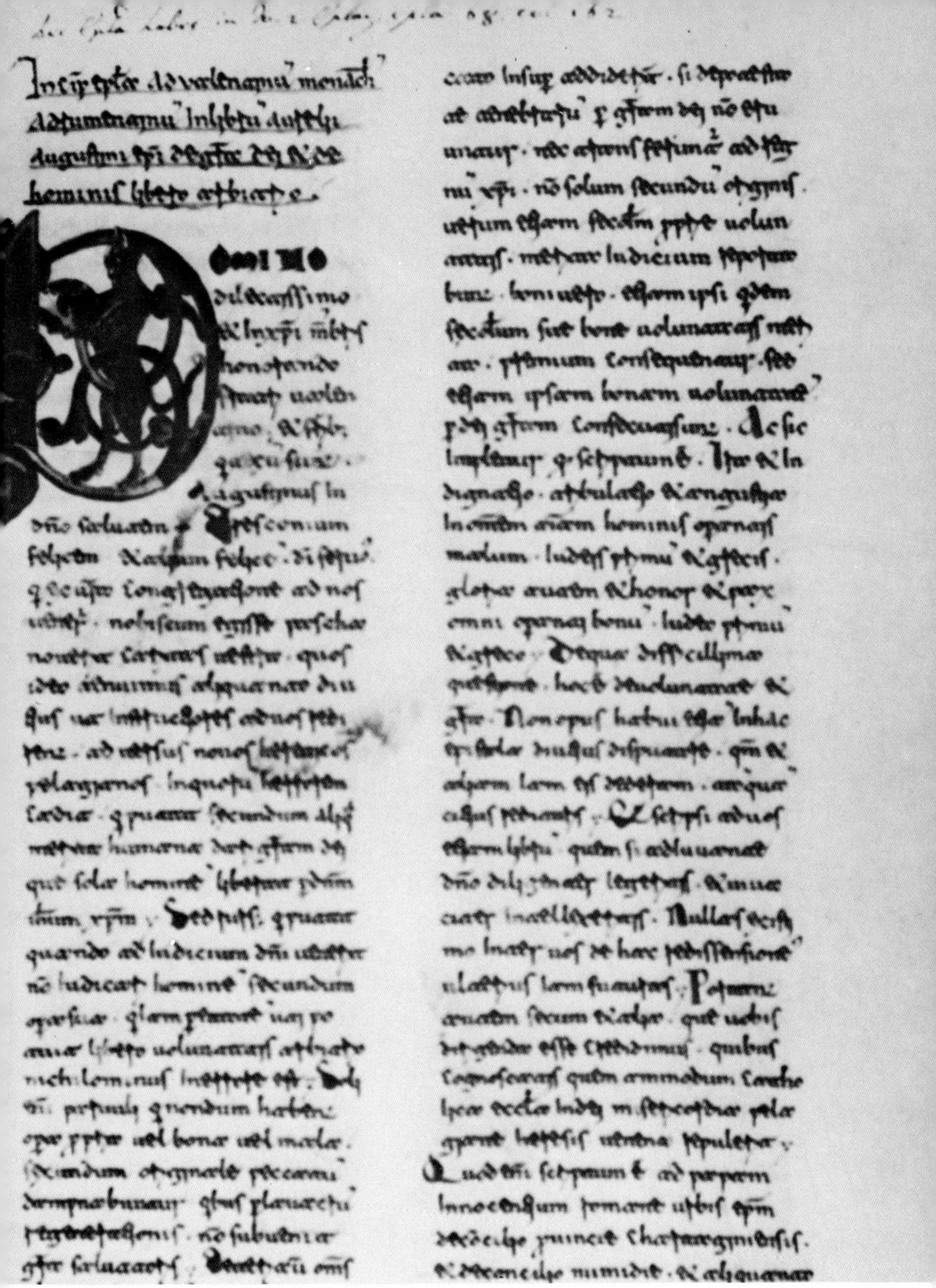

PLATE 1. An Illustration of Beneventan Script

From *Codex 165. P. 155.*

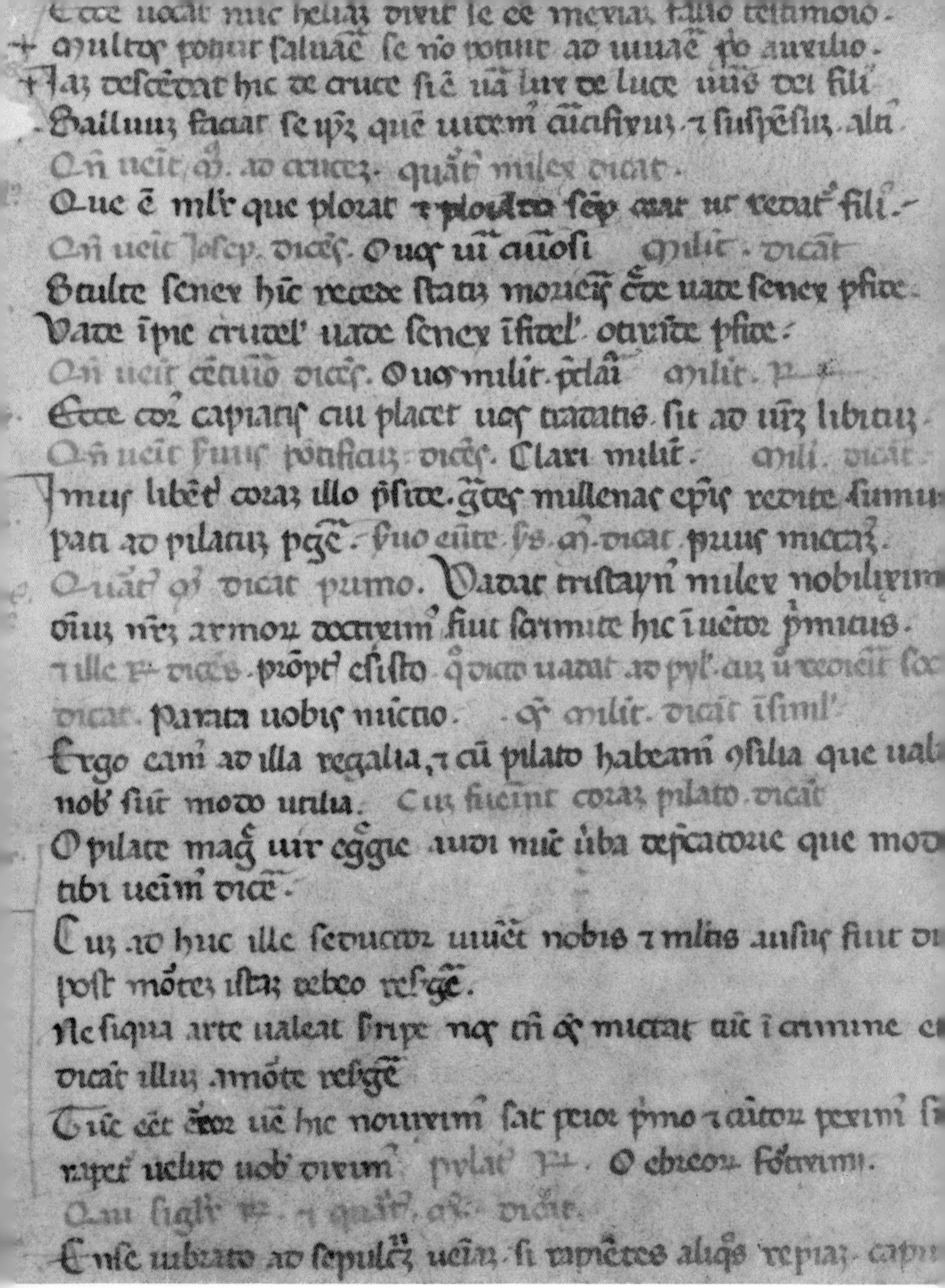

Ecce uocat nuc helias dinit se ee meuiat fillo testimoio

† multoꝛ ponut saluare se no potuit ad uiuare ꝑo auxilio·

† Iaꝣ descendat hic de cruce sic nã lux de luce uiuꝰ dei fili·

Bailluꝛ faciat se uꝑ que uicem aũasturaꝛ · ꞇ suspesuꝛ alii

Cũ ueit cꝰ ꝗ ad cruceꝛ · quaſi miles dicat·

Que ē mlr que ploꝛat ꞇ ploꝛato seꝙ cuꝛ uꝛ ceuat fili·—

Cũ ueit Ioseꝓ dicens · Quoꝙ uꝺ cũosi   milit · dicat

Stulte sener hic recede status moueꝛ ecce uade sener pside·

Vade ipie crucel uade sener isracel· ouꝛide pside·

Cũ ueit cꝰ tũo dicens· Quoꝙ milit· pꝛlaꝛ   milit· ꝑ

Ecce coꝛ capiatuꝼ cui placet uoꝼ tꝛauatis· sit ad uꝛ libituꝛ·

Cũ ueit suuꝼ pontifiꝺ dicens· Clari milit·   milit· dicat

Imuꝼ libeteꝛ coꝛaꝛ illo pside· ꝗtcꝯ millenaꝼ epiꝼ redite sumuꝼ

pati ad pilatuꝛ pꝗe· Suo eũte se ꝗ dicat · primuꝼ mictaꝛ·

Quatꝛ ꝗ dicat pumo· Vadat tristayn miler nobiliꝛim

oiuꝛ uꝛꝣ armoꝛ doctriꝛim siut formite hic iuctoꝛ pmitus·

ꞇ ille ꝑ dicens· ꝓꝓteꝛ eſiſto ꝗoiudo uadat ad pyl· aꝛ uꝛedicit soꝛ

dicat· parata uobiꝼ mictio·   oꝼ milit· dicat isimul·

Ergo cani ad illa regalia · ꞇ cũ pilato habeaꝛ ꝯsilia que ualꝺ

nob sut modo utilia·   Cuꝛ fuerit coꝛaꝛ pilato· dicat

O pilate maꝥ uir eꝗ̃ie audi nuc uꝛba despcatoꝛie que mod

tibi uciꝛ dicaꝛ·

Cuꝛ ad huc ille seruicoꝛ uiuꝺt nobis ꞇ mlꝯs ausiuꝼ siut di

post moꝛtes istaꝛ debeo refuꝥe·

Ne siꝗa arte ualeat suꝛpe noꝼ cũ ꝗ mictat uꝛt icrimine et

dicat illiuꝛ amoꝛe refuꝥe·

True eet eꝛoꝛ uꝺ hic nouirim sat peioꝛ pmo ꞇ cũtoꝛ periui si

rapeꝼ ueluꝺ nob oirim· pylaꝺ ꝑ· O clericoꝛ formiui·

Cui figlꝺ ꝑ· ꞇ quaſi· oꝼ dicat·

Ense iubꝛato ad sepulceꝛ uciaꝛ si rapiētes aliꝗꝼ repiaꝛ· capi

PLATE 2. Passion Fragment from *Officium Quarti Militis*

Archivio Capitolare di San Panfilo, Sulmona. Fasc. 17, n. 9.

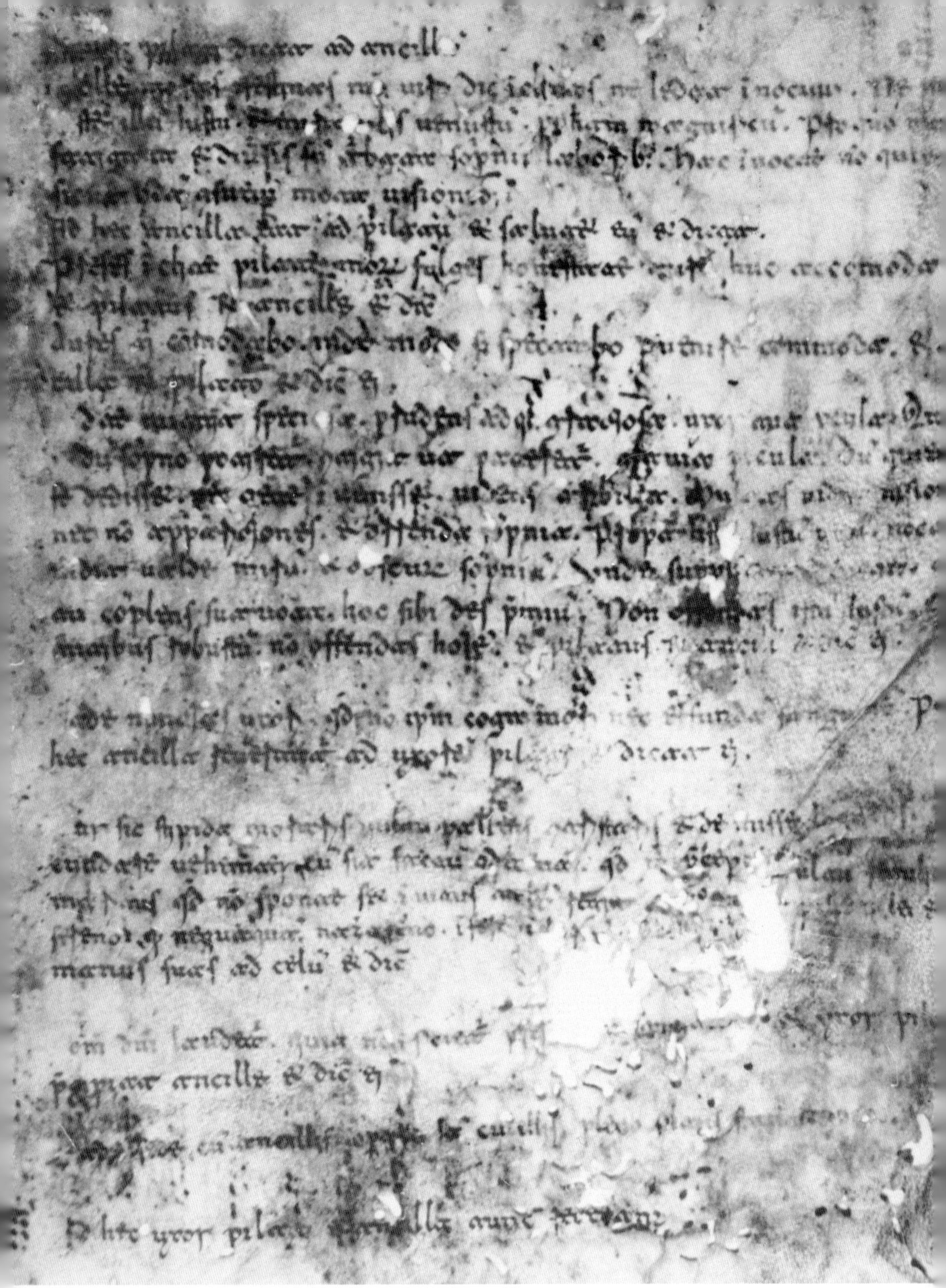

PLATE 4. Page 5 from Montecassino Latin Passion *Compactiones*

da's abbot primate of Germany and Gaul. Possibly in the exchange of liturgical texts between these two famous abbeys, the
Montecassino Passion may have found its way to Germany or
simply may have been made known there by oral transmission
by some of the German monks who could have been present at
one of its performances.

A unique feature of the two Benediktbeuern Passion plays as
compared to the Montecassino Passion is that, although soldiers
appear in both, they do not utter one single line, as the rubrics
show, except for a few lines by Longinus in the *Ludus de Passione*. On approaching Jesus with a lance he exclaims: "Ich wil
im stechen ab das herze sin, das sich ende seiner marter pin." [32]

The Longinus incident must be given a close examination,
since it throws light on the source used by the Benediktbeuern
author. In the canonical Gospels, although both a soldier who
pierced Jesus' side and the Centurion appear, they are not identified as the same person. Matthew and Mark relate the conversion in a closely similar fashion. Matthew writes: "Centurio
autem, et qui cum eo erant, custodientes Jesum, viso terrae motu
et his quae fiebant, timuerant valde, dicentes: Vere Filius Dei
erat iste." [33] John, however, does not report the incident of the
Centurion, but presents the only account of the soldier who
pierced Christ's side: "Sed unus militum lancea latus eius aperuit
et continuo exivit sanguis, et aqua." [34] In the early apocryphal
Gospel of Nicodemus "for the first time appears the name of
Longinus, and here we find it applied to both soldier and centurion." [35] In medieval tradition the Centurion who believed in
Jesus is confused with the soldier who pierced his side. [36] The
text of the *Ludus de Passione* makes it probable that our scribe
went directly to the Gospel of Nicodemus or some derivative
for the Longinus episode. In fact, here Longinus is not only the
soldier who pierces Jesus' side, but he is also identified with the
Centurion, as the words "Vere filius Dei erat iste" amply show. [37]

As regards the mise en scène, the *Ludus de Passione* shows a
highly developed allocation and distribution of parts. At the beginning of the play the rubric makes us aware of the fact that
the various personages are to take their place at the assigned
sedes: "Primitus producatur Pilatus et Uxor sua cum Militibus

in locum suum; deinde Herodes cum Militibus suis; deinde Pontifices; tunc Mercator et Uxor sua; deinde Maria Magdalena." [38] The number of episodes treated suggests that the play must have contained the following *sedes:* a place for the calling of Peter and Andrew, the house of Pilate, and that of Simon and Herod; also *sedes* for the spice merchant, the Last Supper, the Garden of Gethsemane, the Mount of Olives, and Golgotha. The abundance of *sedes* and the presence of eighteen characters besides the crowd of soldiers and Jews makes us conscious of the large proportions of this play.

The main flaw in the *Ludus de Passione* is the disordered way in which some scenes are presented: Peter's denial is placed in the middle of the scene of Christ's capture; the entry into Jerusalem precedes the raising of Lazarus and the supper at Bethany. The *Ludus* gives the impression of being a patchwork of unrelated passages arranged in more or less logical sequence. Its internal disunity has caused some scholars to infer that perhaps it was destined to be read, as a kind of *Lesedrama*, instead of dramatically represented.[39] As Hartl points out:

> It is easy to establish the position of this play within its genre, but more difficult to judge the play correctly as a stage work. The constantly alternating requirements of theatrical style cause the entire work to appear at first sight as dissonant and lacking in uniformity. Latin prose alternates with Latin verses, choral song with solo song, German with Latin, song with spoken text, precise stage directions with quite general ones, content remote from reality together with promixity to life, sections unsuitable for the stage together with those revealing adept stage craft.[40]

Compared to the highly poetical and chronologically perfect Cassino Passion, the *Ludus de Passione* must "be regarded not as an attempt towards a closely knit play, but as an episodic religious opera." [41]

Although the two Benediktbeuern texts are the only other extant Latin Passion plays besides the Montecassino Passion, there are some highly developed Latin Easter plays with scenes involving the soldiers of the grave watch that must be examined because of their striking similarities with the Montecassino Passion in its complete form. These are the two thirteenth-century German Easter plays from Klosterneuburg [42] and Benediktbeuern [43] and the thirteenth-century Tours *Ludus Paschalis*.[44]

The verbal relationship between the two German plays is truly remarkable. Indeed they have sixteen stanzas in common, although with slight textual differences. A few stanzas here will provide an idea of their similarity. At the beginning both plays introduce Pilate being addressed by the high priests, who seek to set a guard at Christ's sepulchre:

Klosterneuburg	*Benediktbeuern*
O Domine, recte meminimus,	O Domine, recte meminimus
quod a turba sepe audivimus,	quod a turba sepe audivimus,
seductorem consuetum dicere:	seductorem consuetum dicere:
Post tres dies uolo resurgere.[45]	Post tres dies uolo resurgere.[46]

Respondeat Pylatus:	Pilatus
Sicut michi dictat discretio	Sicut michi dictat discretio
et astuta vestra cognitio,	et astuta vestra cognitio,
michi crimen vultis imponere	michi crimen vultis imponere
de Iesu, quem fecistis perdere.[47]	de Iesu, quem fecistis perdere.[48]

Of interest in this comparison is the relation borne to the first group of stanzas by some lines of a thirteenth-century medieval Latin poem on the life of Judas Iscarioth:

> Ecce sumus verbi memores memorantque superbi
> Seductor dixit illo quo tempore vixit,
> tertia cum fulget lux, viva caro mea surget.[49]

Written in Leonine hexameters and preserved in the state library of Munich [50] (*Codex lat.* 23490), it is composed of three books. The second of them, bearing the title *De memoria Domini et de Exitu Iude*, offers, in 538 lines, one of the most faithful accounts of Jesus' Passion, from the Supper at Bethany to the setting of the guards at the sepulchre. It is one more example of the intense *Passionsfrömmigkeit*, which characterizes thirteenth-century Germany, and suggests possible relationship between poetry and drama in view of the fact that the two German Latin Passion plays and the two German Easter plays all date from the thirteenth century.

Of the two Easter plays the one from Klosterneuburg is both the more extensive and the more confused. An example of its imperfection is that lines 75–123 are repeated in lines 148–201. The repeated passages include the report of the Marys to the disciples, the episode of Peter and John at the sepulchre, Christ's colloquy with Mary Magdalene, His descent to Hell, and finally the report of the Marys to the disciples concerning Jesus' Resurrection.

However defective this play may be, it presents us for the first time with a fully developed scene of the watch. The scene starts with the Jewish priests asking Pilate's permission to set guards at the sepulchre. Pilate grants their request, and the priests, after giving bribes to the soldiers, take them to the tomb. There the soldiers march around the sepulchre singing the five stanzas that end with the Germanized refrain *Schowa propter insidias.* This is followed by the incident of the Angel with the flaming sword who strikes the soldiers to the earth. After this, they rise, report the happenings to the priests, are corrupted by further bribes, and finally announce to the people that Christ's disciples have stolen His body. Although written in a fairly competent verse form, the scene of the setting of the watch of the Klosterneuburg Easter play lacks individual dramatic characterization, for the speeches are uttered by the soldiers in unison.

A much superior and more elaborate setting of the watch is presented by the Benediktbeuern Easter play. It makes this scene more interesting by the addition of new personages. For instance, when Pilate appoints the guards for the sepulchre, he has among his advisors his wife and characters known as *assessores.* The more striking development, however, is the dramatic handling of the dialogue. While in the Klosterneuburg play both the soldiers and the priests speak in unison, in the Benediktbeuern play Pilate, the priests, his wife, the *assessores,* and the five soldiers, each utter one stanza. In general one may observe that the two German plays have little similarity to the Montecassino Passion either dramatically or poetically.

The Tours *Ludus Paschalis*

Far more significant relationships can be observed between the Montecassino Passion and the thirteenth-century Tours

Ludas Paschalis, through the fourteenth-century Sulmona Passion fragment. The Tours Easter play, probably composed in Normandy,[51] presents us with a large and elaborate composition, 224 lines, although in a fragmentary state. The liturgical pieces in it are scarce and only the presence of the *Te Deum* at the end, suggests a connection with the church services.[52] In view of this, Sepet considers the Tours *Ludus Paschalis* "comme une de ces formes intermédiaires qui ont reçu le nom de mystère semi-liturgique." [53]

Even in its fragmentary form the Tours *Ludus* is the most extensive of the French *Ludi Paschales* and even larger in scope than the Klosterneuburg and Benediktbeuern *Ludi*. It provides scenes for the setting of the watch at Christ's tomb, the merchant episode, the visit of the three Marys to the sepulchre, the soldiers' return to Pilate after Jesus' Resurrection, Christ's appearance to the apostles and then to Thomas. These scenes reveal a sporadic display of literary ability in the presentation of certain incidents, although the entire production is imperfectly articulated. The most important element of this play that concerns us is the brief scene of the setting of the watch, two stanzas long. This scene is important, for it is not preserved in any other French liturgical play. The fifteenth-century Easter plays from St. Chapelle and Coutance provide for the setting of the watch but only in the rubrics.[54] The Easter plays of Benediktbeuern and Klosterneuburg, already discussed, and the Sulmona Passion fragment are the other extant Latin Easter plays where the setting of the watch appears.

The verbal agreement between the partly identical Klosterneuburg and Benediktbeuern Easter plays and the quite different Tours play in the episode of the setting of the watch is limited to just two lines: "ne furentur illum discipuli et dicunt plebi: Surrexit a mortuis." [55] This slight similarity between the three plays can be ascribed to the use of the same Biblical source, the Gospel of Matthew, 27:64. As we have observed, there seems to be no connection between these German Latin plays and the Montecassino-Sulmona play, but a relationship between the Tours play and the Sulmona fragment does exist, for they share a whole stanza:

Tours	*Sulmona*
Ergo eamus	Ergo eamus
et quid dixit, faciamus:	et quod dixit faciamus,
uigilando custodiamus,	vigilando custodiamus
ne sepultum amittamus.	ne sepulchrum admictamus;
Ne forte ueniant eius discipuli	Ne forte veniant eius discipuli
et furando transferant alibi,	rapturi cor[p]us capiantur si[n]-
inuadamos eos cum lanceis	guli,
et uerberemus eos cum gladiis.[56]	ne sint immunis a pena patibuli.
	Cum venerit Pilatus ad sepulchrum
	dicens: Milites clari, Milites cir-
	cumdent sepulchrum dicentes:
	Omnes:
	Ne forte veniant discipuli
	et furando transferant alibi;
	invadamus eos cum lanceis
	et verberemus eos cum gladiis.[57]

Besides this parallel in the two stanzas, the Tours *Ludus* and the Sulmona fragment of the Montecassino Passion offer in the setting of the watch another feature in common. While the soldiers' role in the Klosterneuburg and Benediktbeuern Easter plays is characterized by the readiness with which they accept money from the priests, the soldiers' role in the Tours and Sulmona fragments is characterized by a certain boastfulness: "invadamus eos cum lanceis/et verberemus eos cum gladiis." [58] The difference of treatment here is indicative of the basically dissimilar nature of the German on the one hand, and of the French and Italian dramatists, on the other, in the psychological development of characters. The German dramatists are chiefly concerned with incidents of a moral and liturgical nature, which are usually very simple and consonant with the Gospel accounts; the French and Italian playwrights, however, attach considerable importance to the dramatic aspect of the plays and consequently tend to elaborate on the liturgical texts, exploit details vaguely suggested by the Gospels, and emphasize those of a legendary nature.

The Anglo-Norman *Resurrection*

Both the Sulmona and the Tours plays employ Pilate's soldiers to guard the tomb. In other French plays too, such as the Anglo-Norman *Resurrection* and the Provençal *Passion*, Pilate's soldiers form the guard. However, while in the Tours play Pilate sends the soldiers to guard the tomb,[59] in the Sulmona fragment Pilate's soldiers spontaneously offer their services.[60] This latter feature is also found in the twelfth-century Anglo-Norman *Resurrection* where the first soldier volunteers his services, followed presently by others who assert their willingness to help.[61] As in the Sulmona fragment, the soldiers of the Anglo-Norman play boast of the blows that they will deal to anyone who dares molest the tomb.[62]

Another particular feature shared by the Sulmona fragment and the Anglo-Norman *Resurrection* is the number of guards. While the number of soldiers guarding the tomb is not made clear in the Tours *Ludas Paschalis*, the Anglo-Norman play and the Sulmona fragment present us with four, each one of whom, presumably, takes a station by one of the four sides of the sepulchre. The number of soldiers guarding the tomb is not specified by the Gospel accounts, and early iconographical monuments sometimes show four, more often two, soldiers watching the sepulchre.[63]

The affinities between the Anglo-Norman *Resurrection* and the Sulmona fragment are not restricted, however, to the above similarities. Like the Sulmona Passion, the twelfth-century Anglo-Norman play "reveals considerable freedom from its obvious biblical, apocryphal, and legendary sources. It also combines its material and motivates its scenes with an ingenuity that heightens their dramatic value." [64] As in the Sulmona fragment, the characters of the Anglo-Norman play frequently address each other, adding vivacity and movement to the entire action. The personages also receive adequate characterization. Pilate, for instance, is timorous and cunning at the same time, for he fears to anger Rome and shows craft in suppressing the news of the miraculous healing of the blind Longinus. In general, then, we may say that the Sulmona fragment and the Anglo-Norman *Resurrection* are much superior to the very ambitious but also very defective Tours Easter play.

As to the parallel between the passage of the Tours and the Sulmona fragment, it appears to me that the Tours author fashioned one stanza from two in the Sulmona fragment. Possible plagiarizing by the Tours author is suggested by Young's impression that its compiler "had before him a considerable variety of dramatic material, some highly elaborate." [65] When we also consider that the manuscript of the Tours *Ludus* has been assigned by paleographers to the thirteenth century,[66] and note that the Sulmona fragment, although in a fourteenth-century manuscript, is essentially a part of the twelfth-century Montecassino Passion, it seems permissible to me to infer that possibly the Tours compiler had before him some antecedent of the Sulmona fragment, perhaps the complete Montecassino-Sulmona Passion play or an earlier form of it. In this connection, I would give due consideration to possible intermediaries, since monks and clerics have been known to travel from one religious house to another, and also to the fact that Sulmona had belonged to the Norman kingdom of the two Sicilies.

The hypothesis that the Montecassino-Sulmona play may have influenced the Tours *Ludus* is strengthened by the fact that it is even more extensive than the French text, which has been considered up to now the most complete example of the liturgical drama.[67] Furthermore, the *Planctus* at the end of the Montecassino that is written in the vulgar tongue of south central Italy suggests the drama was actually performed in the area.[68] It should be added that the close relations existing between Sulmona and Cassino [69] "make probable the hypothesis that the drama arrived at Sulmona from Montecassino, which is the most simple, direct and sure road." [70]

VERNACULAR PASSION PLAYS

I shall now explore any possible relation of the Montecassino Passion play to some of the earliest vernacular Passion plays in

Western Europe. It is known that during the twelfth and thirteenth centuries vernacular passages appeared in several Latin plays in Germany and France. The same phenomenon presumably began in England at the same time, although the earliest instances known to us date from the fifteenth century. In Italy, as we have seen, vernacular passages are found in the twelfth-century Montecassino Passion, and the thirteenth century offers complete vernacular Passions with the *Laude*.[71]

The *Lauda*

The presence of a vernacular *Planctus* in the twelfth-century Montecassino Passion permits us to establish with reasonable certainty, although earlier plays may have existed, when the vulgar tongue was first substituted for Latin in the religious drama of Italy—a phenomenon already observable in other religious and secular compositions of the same century.[72] The earliest notable production of vernacular religious plays started, however, in Umbria with the Confraternities of the *Laudesi* and flourished from the second half of the thirteenth to the following century: [73]

> Il nuovo teatro italiano non nasce dall'ufficio drammatico, ma dalla lauda; essa segna l'incontro fra i testi evangelici e il popolo, che in tal modo rivela e attua una più sentita partecipazione religiosa ai misteri della fede. Siamo nei vasti moti eretici o ortodossi del '200. La lingua volgare usata dai laudesi, se è segno del loro salire alla cultura ecclesiastica, d'altra parte è pure la rivelazione d'una liturgia che continua ad esprimersi in una lingua nuova, conforme la novità del tempo.[74]

Like the liturgical drama, the *Lauda* was born out of the people's desire to participate more fully in the church services of the liturgical year. Indeed for the people, as Apollonio notes, the liturgical drama was not enough, for they felt the urgency to retrace all the territory of the religious tradition in their own way, giving vent to their simple emotions.[75] Unconcerned with the subtle and refined forms of the liturgical drama, the brotherhood of the *Laudesi*

> gave employment to those jongleurs and poets who, without desire for more than passing fame, and with more devotion than

art, could frame rude songs or dramatic pieces on the ever-
popular events of the Gospel story, especially on the Passion, the
miracle of the Virgin, and the joys of paradise.[76]

As a dramatic form the *Lauda* began as a lyric chant, sung by
the *flagellanti* through the city streets,[77] or in church and in the
confraternity's oratory.[78] This poetical-musical chant

> transfused in living persons, participated in by the crying and
> singing crowd, gives us the profound reality of the first vernac-
> ular theatre: the dynamic 'humanity' of the Passions, removed
> out of the theological enclosure of the liturgical drama and
> appropriated by the people.[79]

The original nucleus of the *Laude* must be found in the *laude* of
Holy Week, for the Passion of Christ and the laments of the
Virgin were, from the start, the events most intensely felt by the
Umbrian poets.[80] While the liturgical drama found its germinal
point in the dramatic office of Easter, the *Laude* concentrated
their poetical energy on the Passion of Christ, reflecting the pen-
itential and Christocentric spirit of the *flagellanti* and of the spiritual aspirations of the thirteenth-century society, which, perhaps more than any other, accentuated the sorrowful aspect of
the divine mystery.

Extant evidence seems to indicate that the *Laude* passed from
their simple lyrical state to actual dramatic representation towards the middle of the thirteenth century.[81] The early plays
that we possess are mostly of the fourteenth century, but, since
they are not the original ones, we may assign the flourishing of
the dramatic *Laude* to the end of the thirteenth century.

In subject matter, the dramatic *Laude* on the Passion were
similar to the vernacular Passion plays of France and Germany.
Their action centered on the suffering of Christ but presented
also the various other events in His life from the ministry to the
Resurrection.[82] The dramatic *Laude* on the Passion are extensive and interesting, for they reveal a highly developed characterization. Particularly interesting is a short *laus de Passione Iesu
de cruce*. The play presents events in Christ's Passion from the
episode of the believing centurion to the setting of the grave
watch.

At the beginning, we are presented with the centurion in the familiar role of the believing soldier after which Longinus, addressing Christ, repents his cruel act in a most moving stanza:

> O pietoso mio Signore
> Che senza ragione sè morto
> Par che se devida el cuore
> Tanto àie recevuto torto;
> Trista la mia mano esmarrita
> Che t'à fatto tal ferita.[83]

The Jews' taunting of Jesus on the Cross follows soon after. After two characters referred to as *unus* and *alius* gamble for Christ's clothes, a *Planctus* is presented in which participate John, Mary Magdalene, the Virgin, and the other Marys. The stanzas uttered by the Virgin are particularly histrionic. For instance, the Virgin at the foot of the Cross tries to touch Christ's face but she cannot reach it. She therefore entreats the tree on which Christ is crucified to stoop in order that she can reach Him:

Maria

> Figliuolo, io te vorria toccare,
> E apresarme a la tua faccia.
> Croce, volglote pregare
> Dalme un poco ch'io 'l m'abbraccio:
> O arbore alto, enchina 'l ramo,
> Ch'io tocca quil ch'io tanto amo.[84]

Alarmed at the Virgin's profound laments, John begs her to compose herself, for if she were to die, he would remain an orphan.

At this point, Joseph and Nicodemus come to take Jesus from the Cross. Joseph's petition and the subsequent deposition and entombment of Jesus were very popular episodes, for they lent themselves to dramatic elaboration. The meeting between Joseph and Pilate is described by all four Gospel writers.[85] John alone, however, mentions that Nicodemus was present with Joseph and that he brought with him many spices and ointments. Our dramatist seems to follow this account. Joseph meanwhile asks Pilate's permission to take Christ's body; after Pilate is assured by the centurion that Jesus is truly dead, he grants Joseph's request. On approaching the Cross, Joseph hesitates and, addressing the dead Jesus, says "I am not worthy to touch you, my Lord, but I must take you from the Cross to console your mother":

> O Signore, io non só degno
> Mó pertanto de tocarte,
> Ma per levarte d'esto lengno,
> Ond'io volglio esconficcarte,
> Per consolar quista tua mate,
> Che tante pene à già portate.[86]

After Christ is taken from the Cross, He is placed in His mother's arms. Here Mary's lament becomes more intense and pathetic in a crescendo of tears and sighs. All the maternal feelings at the sight of her dead Son are represented with a remarkable psychological and dramatic insight. The Virgin, weeping, looks at Christ's wound; always clinging to Him, she takes His hands in hers, then she cleans His mouth soaked in vinegar. Finally, when the time is come to place Jesus in the sepulchre, stunned and pleading, she entreats Joseph and Nicodemus to place her in the tomb with Him:

> Oimè io c'ò lo core tristo.
> Non cie voie po luie armanere,
> Se voie Cristo me tolglete,
> Me con esso sepelite.[87]

These sorrowful accents are familiar. The *laude*, whether lyrical or dramatic, draw upon traditional Latin features such as the Gospel accounts, other sacred sources, and liturgical works.[88] The Virgin's grief in holding the body of her Son is described, for instance, in this passage from the *Meditationes Vitae Christi:*

> Fili mi in gremio meo te mortuum teneo,
> durum est valde divortium mortis tuae,
> jacunda atque delectabilis fuit inter nos
> conversatio, atque sine querela, atque
> offensa fuit inter alios, quamvis tu
> dulcissime fili mi, ut nocens sis modo
> occisus.[89]

Her desire to die and be entombed with Jesus are expressed in Bernard's *Liber de Passione:*

Noli me derelinquere post te, trahe me
ad te ipsum, ut ipsa moriar tecum . . .
Maria plorabat amare juxta sepulchrum . . .
Volebat mater moesta simul sepeliri cum illo.[90]

At last Jesus is placed in the tomb, while John and Mary
Magdalene accompany the weeping Virgin home. The priests
come to Pilate, asking that the sepulchre of Jesus be guarded
since, while living, He had announced He would rise after the
third day. Pilate offers his own guards, and the Passion ends with
the setting of the watch at the sepulchre. Although limited in
scope, this Passion and similar ones show a dramatic character
that is indeed surprising for such early vernacular compositions.

While no direct and specific influences can be established of
the Montecassino Passion on the dramatic vernacular *Laude*,
they must be presupposed, for it would be inadmissible to think
that the *Laude* dramatists ignored "the ordinaries and the an-
tiphonaries and the dramatic aspects that the Liturgy and the
religious festivities regulated by the Church had been assuming," [91] especially in view of the large proportions of the liturgical drama in Italy. De Bartholomaeis and Toschi have shown
too that the primitive vernacular *Laude* were actually imitations
or reproductions of the liturgical *Laudes,* particularly the canonical *Laudes Matutinae*.[92] The presence, as we have seen, of a
vernacular *Planctus* in the Montecassino Latin Passion indicates
that the vernacular poetry was already connected with the dramatic monastic Easter representation, and some scholars have
seen in that *Planctus* one of the earliest and most important ante-
cedents of the *Lauda*.[93] That the *Laude* dramatists should be
influenced by available religious literature, especially the monastic, is not surprising since, particularly in Italy, one finds in the
monasteries the earliest indefatigable authors and depositaries of
its sacred and profane culture.[94]

French Passion Plays

In France the transition from Latin to vernacular religious
drama was achieved more quickly and completely than in Germany and Italy. Although as early as the ninth century one wit-

nesses in France "un état de bilinguisme véritable" [95] and by
the beginning of the eleventh century "le language courant et
. . . la seule langue vivante est le roman," [96] the French vernacular drama grew out of a distinct liturgical phenomenon called
"farciture." "Cette technique consiste à introduire des parties
romanes, en manière d'interpolation ou de tropes, dans un texte
latin (en principe, liturgique) préexistant." [97] One of the earliest examples of this technique is the twelfth-century *Sponsus*,[98]
a dramatization of the parable of the Wise and Foolish Virgins,
written in the Benedictine abbey of St. Martial of Limoges. That
the vernacular stanzas are mostly translations of, or additions to,
Latin passages suggests they are based on a wholly Latin play.
The "farciture" technique remained liturgical until the middle
of the twelfth century, by which time France offers us an ambitious religious play, the *Mystère* or *Jeu d'Adam*,[99] which is the
first surviving French play almost completely in the vernacular
except for its Latin stage directions, readings, and responsories,
and the Anglo-Norman *Resurrection*, one of the most original
compositions of the vernacular dramatic tradition. Among the
vernacular Passion plays in France, the earliest, the *Palatine Passion*, occupies an important position, for in the tradition of the
medieval drama of France it is completely in the vernacular,
without quotations from the liturgy or liturgical drama, and
because in it are already contained the fundamental themes and
elements of the great *mystères* of the fifteenth century.

On the basis of linguistic evidence, Grace Frank assigns this
play to the beginning of the fourteenth century.[100] In 1,966
lines it provides the events of Christ's life from the preparations
for the Last Supper through Mary Magdalene's announcement
of the Resurrection to Peter. The *Palatine Passion* is most interesting for the realistic conception of well-known characters. For
instance, in the Harrowing of Hell the author presents Satan and
Enfer quarreling as to how best to defend themselves against the
coming of Christ. He also brings in for the first time on the stage
the legendary incident of the forging of the nails, which appears
earlier in the thirteenth-century religious poem, *Passion des jongleurs*.[101] Upon arriving at Calvary the Jews ask the smith to
forge three nails, but he refuses by replying that he has leprosy;
when his hands are miraculously stricken by God's grace, the

smith's wife performs the task while cursing Jesus. We lack precise information about this incident, although it must have been founded on earlier tradition. Pierre Bercheur (1290–1362) seems to refer to it in a Latin passage.[102] Whatever the sources, the fact remains that the author of the *Palatine Passion* was a very conscientious artist who was aware of the dramatic possibilities of various episodes and who tried hard to hold the attention of the spectators.

The only place in which the *Palatine Passion* possibly shows any relation to the Montecassino Passion is in the scenes of the grave watch. The concern of the Jews lest Jesus rise from the dead furnishes the background for the setting of the watch at the tomb. The scriptural source for this scene, found in the Gospel of Matthew, reads:

> Altera autem die, quae est post Parasceven, convenerunt principes sacerdotum, et Pharisaei ad Pilatum, dicentes: Domine, recordati sumus, quia seductor ille dixit adhuc vivens: Post tres dies resurgam. Iube ergo custodiri sepulchrum usque in diem tertium: ne forte veniant discipuli eius, et furentur eum, et dicant plebi: Surrexit a mortuis: et erit novissimus error peior priore. Ait illis Pilatus: Habetis custodiam, ite, custodite sicut scitis. Illi autem abeuntes, munierunt sepulchrum, signantes lapidem, cum custodibus.[103]

Later religious writers interpreted Pilate's statement in two different ways. Some of them presumed that Pilate himself offered his own guards; others assumed that the priests themselves hired militia. The hiring of the soldiers and their identity and their number vary in different plays. In the Tours *Ludus*, Anglo-Norman *Resurrection* and the *Provençal Passion*, as I have observed, Pilate's soldiers form the guard. In plays such as the *Palatine Passion* and the *Passion d'Autun*, Caiaphas and Annas hire soldiers, with Pilate's permission. In this respect the *Palatine Passion* is dissimilar to the Sulmona fragment of the Montecassino Passion, for here Pilate's soldiers offer their services.

The features common to the *Palatine* and the Sulmona Passions are the following: they both have four soldiers and present them as braggarts; and just before Christ's Resurrection the four are mysteriously stunned. There are four guards in the Anglo-

Norman *Resurrection,* the *Palatine* and *Autun* Passions, and we
have the role of the fourth soldier in the Sulmona fragment. A
probable source for their number is the Gospel of Gamaliel,
whose Latin version presents four guards.[104] As I have pointed
out, iconography does not offer any sure suggestion about the
subject, the reason being perhaps that early art was reticent in
representing the mysterious rising from the tomb because it was
not described in the Gospel.[105] Common to both the Sulmona
fragment and the *Palatine Passion* is the soldiers' boasting of the
blows they will deal to anyone attempting to remove Christ's
body.

The waking of the guards and their alarm at the loss of the
body is treated in similar manner in the Sulmona and the *Palatine
Passion.* In this play the first knight awakens the others, inform-
ing them of the loss of the body. In the Sulmona fragment, however, the four soldiers lament their loss in unison.

Even with the similarities noted, clearly no true relationship
can be found between the Palatine and the Montecassino Passions. The reasons may stem from the fact that the authors of
later French Passion plays plundered from various sources other
than their predecessors. The *Provençal Passion,* for instance, particularly in the Resurrection scene, appears to follow sources
closely resembling such liturgical dramas as the Tours *Ludus Paschalis* and the thirteenth-century Latin *Ludus de Passione.*[106]
Yet no close resemblance can be established between the *Palatine*
and *Autun* Passions [107] even though the former precedes the
latter by just a few years. It is apparent, then, that in setting out
to compose a Passion play, medieval dramatists appropriated passages from all sources available to them. This seems to have been
the case of the *Palatine Passion* compiler who "attempted to en-
liven the old text of the narrative *Passion des jongleurs* by cur-
tailing certain scenes, putting others into strophic form, and
adding new realistic details of his own invention." [108]

German Passion Plays

In Germany the transition from Latin to vernacular is slower.
At first, brief vernacular refrains are appended to Latin stanzas

as in the thirteenth-century Klosterneuburg and Benediktbeuern Easter plays, and then entire familiar Latin stanzas are translated into the vernacular as in the thirteenth-century *Ludus de Passione*. It is to be noted, however, that although the penetration of the vulgar tongue in the religious Latin drama occurs somewhat earlier in France, in Germany it is a more representative phenomenon.[109]

Interesting as an early vernacular German Passion is the fourteenth-century *Passion of St. Gall*,[110] which is considered the most complete and typical of early German plays. Its importance derives from its presentation of events of Christ's life from His baptism by John to His ministry, Passion, Resurrection, Harrowing of Hell, and appearance to His followers. This play shows the progress made by the vernacular, for although Latin speeches appear, they perform, as we shall see, a purely symbolical function.

The St. Gall *Passion* closely follows Biblical accounts, particularly those of John and Matthew. Creizenach attributes this to choice by the author.[111] Craig contends, however, that one or more simple Latin originals are behind the St. Gall *Passion*.[112] Miss Marshall also shares this idea, but she restricts the influence of a liturgical model to the last scenes, from the Harrowing of Hell to the end.[113] The St. Gall Passion presents us with a few striking features that it shares with the Montecassino Passion. It utilizes, for dramatic effect, Jesus' tender visual reproach to Peter after the latter's denial, an incident recorded only by Luke:

St. Gall	Montecassino
Tunc cantet gallus, et Dominus respicet Petrum.[114]	Ad hec gallus cantet et Jesus respiciat Petrum.[115]

Both present Judas' suicide and Christ's appearance before Pilate as contemporaneous actions:

St. Gall	Montecassino
Deinde ducant Ihesum ad Pilatum . . . . . , donec Judas suspendatur.[116]	et Iudas exit et suspendit se. Interim loricati ducant Iesum ligatum coram Pilato.[117]

Both plays have the devil appear to Pilate's wife while she is sleeping, causing her to have visions, and both emphasize the state of Pilate's wife after awakening. In the St. Gall *Passion* she has "gedreumet swere," [118] and in the Montecassino Passion she is "turbata sompnii laboribus." [119] Most details shared by the two plays, however, may be ascribed to their having utilized the same Gospel accounts.

Although this play is primarily in the vernacular, definite care is taken to preserve the Latin for the speeches connected with divine characters: God's words during the Baptism, for instance, are in Latin, as are the words of the Angel's choir, and Jesus generally speaks in Latin too, indicating that as late as the fourteenth century the Latin language still retained its function as the speech of sacred characters.

Considered in relation to the Montecassino play, the St. Gall *Passion* offers unusual pieces of dramatization and the introduction of new elements to make the action more vivid. It is interesting, for instance, that St. Augustine is chosen to speak the Prologue, and to comment from time to time during the action. Also the dramatization of the Malchus episode gives the wounded man a lively speech, as the rubric and the stanza show: "et Petrus cum gladio abscindat aurem [Malcho], qui clamet lamentabiliter":

> Owe schanden un schaden,
> bit den bin ich wol beladen!
> ich han hie werlorn min ore:
> dar ume heizet man mich ein dore!
> der groze spot dut mir vil we,
> doch muwet mich der schade me! [120]

Histrionic vigor appears in the extensive speeches given to Rufus, Pilate's servant, who performs the function of a counselor. When a servant announces to Pilate that he should not harm Jesus because his wife had strange dreams, Rufus entreats Pilate not to give much thought to women's dreams: "Herre, des alten wibes draum/ salt du nit nemen grozen gaum." [121] The same Rufus later in the play gives the sponge soaked in vinegar to Jesus on the Cross.

Highly dramatic also is the scene of the blind Longinus. Unable to see, he asks a little boy to get his spear:

> Vil lieber knabe, suche mir das sper:
> an Ihesu siten ist min ger,
> so wil ich in dorchstechen,
> das ime sin herze muz brechen
> sin zauber wil ich so rechen.[122]

After he pierces the side of Christ, the blood runs down the spear into his eyes and he regains his sight. In most of the German plays Longinus thrusts his spear in order to put an end to Jesus' suffering.[123] It is only in the St. Gall and Donaueschingen *Passions*[124] that Longinus' thrusting is motivated simply by a cruel desire, and the motive may have been derived from the *Erlösung*.[125]

The story of Longinus' blindness is still of uncertain origin. "It is to be noted that even so late as the tenth century, the martyrologies give no suggestion of the blindness of Longinus."[126] This may have been due to the fact that early church authorities were not concerned with Longinus himself but with the symbolical importance of the blood and water flowing from Jesus' side. Alcuin, for instance, writing in the ninth century, says that Christ's side was pierced so that

> vitae ostium panderetur, unde sacramenta Ecclesiae manaverunt, sine quibus ad vitam quae vere vita est, non intratur. Ille sanguis in remissionem fusus est peccatorum, aqua illa salutare temperavit paculum: haec et lavacrum praestat et potum.[127]

In the same century Walafrid Strabo comments, "Exivit *sanguis et aqua:* sicut ex latere Adae sumpta est Eva, ita ex latere Christi exivit redemptio Ecclesiae: per sanguinem remissio, per aquam baptismum."[128] One of the first texts to attach any symbolical meaning to Longinus himself is the twelfth-century *Historia Scholastica*. The name of Longinus is here not mentioned, but reference is made to the healing of his blindness: "et qui lanceavit eum, ut tradent quidam, cum fere caligassent oculi ejus, et casu tetigisset oculos sanguine ejus, clare vidit."[129] It is obvious, however, that Peter Comestor doubts the blindness of Longinus, and even the thirteenth-century *Legenda Aurea*, which is usually referred to as the source of the Longinus story, speaks with doubt of it.

The author of the St. Gall *Passion* evidently knew these sources and drew on them to achieve a better dramatic effect.

For this purpose, too, a ladder is used in nailing Jesus on the Cross, as Rufus' command "Stig uf, man muz dich henken!" [130] implies. Its source may have been the pseudo-Bonaventure:

> Ponuntur duae scalae, una retrorsum ad brachium dextrum, alia ad sinistrum brachium, super quas malefici ascendunt cum clavis, atque martellis. Ponitur etiam alia scala ex parte anteriori, attingens usque ad locum ubi debebant pedes affigi . . . Compellitur Dominus Jesus crucem ascendere per hanc scalam parvam.[131]

In keeping with the established German tradition and to dramatically heighten the scene, the St. Gall compiler uses the thirteenth-century "Flete fideles anime" lament for the *Planctus Mariae*.

Even with these sporadic pieces of vivid representation the St. Gall *Passion* remains largely a patchwork of episodes taken from various sources, such as the Gospel, the *Visitatio*, the *Depositio*, the *Elevatio*, the *Victimae paschali*, and possibly an early Passion play such as the Montecassino Passion.

The lack of direct quotations or translations does not allow us to furnish direct evidence of the influence of the Montecassino Latin Passion on the vernacular Passion plays. But it is clear that general similarities of dramatic treatment can be explained in terms of the general imitativeness of the plays, the survival of traditional modes of characterization, and the persistence in the vernacular religious drama of the dramatic tradition of the liturgical drama. The Passion fragment from Sulmona, while attesting to the survival two centuries later of the twelfth-century Montecassino Passion, throws light on the continuity of the liturgical drama and provides a commentary on its dissemination because it shares identical passages with and offers striking similarities to the more comprehensive Latin Easter plays.

1 George R. Coffman, "A New Approach to Medieval Latin Drama" *Modern Philology*, 12 (1924–25), 271.

2 Paul Lehmann, "The Benedictine Order and the Transmission of the Literature of Ancient Rome in the Middle Ages," in *Erforschung des Mittelalters*, 3 (1960), 173–83.

3 Creizenach, *Geschichte des neuren Dramas*, (1911 ed.), p. 101.

4 Young, I, 516–17; Meyer, *op. cit.*, p. 122.

5 Young, I, 514.

6 Matthew, 26: 17–18.

7 Young, I, 514.

8 Matthew, 26: 18–19.

9 Young, I, 511.

10 Luke, 23: 2–3.

11 Kienast, *Die Deutschsprachige Lyrik*, p. 890. W. Lipphardt, "Marienklagen und Liturgie," *Jahrbuch für Liturgiewissenschaft*, 12 (1932), 198.

12 Wolfgang Stammler and K. Langosch, eds., *Die Deutsche Literatur des Mittelalters: Verfasserlexikon* (Berlin, 1933–1955), III, 248; W. Lipphardt, "Studien zu den Marienklagen und Germanische Totenklagen," *Beiträge zur Geschichte der Deutschen Sprache und Literatur*, 58 (1934), 436–7; Manitius, *Geschichte der lateinischen Literatur*, III, 1045.

13 Young, I, 517.

14 Meyer, *op. cit.*, p. 65.

15 Helen Garth, *Mary Magdalene in Medieval Literature* (The Johns Hopkins University Studies in Historical and Political Science, Series 67, no. 3; Baltimore, 1950); H. Hansel, *Die Maria-Magdalena-Legende* (Bottrop, 1957).

16 Victor Saxer, *Le culte de Marie Madeleine en Occident des origines à la fin du moyen âge* 2 vols. (Paris, 1959), I, 2–6; Gustave Cohen, "Le personnage de Marie-Madeleine dans le drame religieux français du Moyen Age," *Convivium*, 25 (1956), 141–3.

17 Saxer, *op. cit.*, II, 184.

18 Young, *The Drama of the Medieval Church*, passim, I and II; N. H. Hoffman, *Die Magdalenenszenen im geistlichen Spiel des Mittelalters* (Wurzburg, 1933); F. O. Knoll, *Die Rolle der Maria Magdalena im geistlichen Spiel des Mittelalters* (Berlin, 1934); Sister Mary John Chauvin, *The Role of Mary Magdalene in Medieval Drama* (Washington: Catholic University, 1951; microcard); Cohen, "Le personnage de Marie-Madeleine"; Omer Jodogne, "Marie-Madeleine pécheresse dans les Passions médiévales," in *Scrinium Lovaniense. Mélanges historiques Etienne Van Cauwenberg* (Louvain, 1961), 272–84.

19 Joseph Szövérffy, " 'Peccatrix Quondam Femina': A Survey of the Mary Magdalen Hymns," *Traditio*, 19 (1963), 79–146.

20 *Ibid.*, p. 123.

21 Young, I, 535.

22 For text see *Analecta Hymnica*, (1961 ed.), XXI, pp. 79–81.

23 Szövérffy, " 'Peccatrix quondam,' " p. 140.

24 A. Wilmart, "Poèmes de Gautier de Châtillon dans un manuscrit de Charleville," *Revue Bénédictine*, 49 (1937), 121–69, 322–65, p. 157.

25 Kienast, *Die Deutschsprachige Lyrik*, p. 890; Lipphardt, *Marienklagen und Liturgie*, p. 198.

26 Young, I, 530.

27 *Ibid.*

28 *Ibid.*, p. 531.

29 *Ibid.*

30 Hennig Brinkmann, "Das religiöse Drama in Mittelalter: Arten und Stufen," *Wirkendes Wort*, 9 (1959), 257–74, p. 271; Kindermann, *op. cit.*, I, 326–8.

31 Paul Lehmann, "Deutschland und die mittelalterliche Überlieferung der Antike" in *Erforschung des Mittelalters*, 3 (Stuttgart, 1960), 163–4. Omer Jodogne, in a learned commentary on my *Latomus* (1961) article, has recently emphasized the necessity of taking into account the transmission of the Latin Passion plays, for "nous ne pouvons pas douter que ces drames ont circulé et, en l'occurence, que les drames decouverts en Italie ou en Germanie aient pénetré en France, d'autant plus qu'ils sont l'oeuvre d'un ordre religieux aussi international que celui de saint Benoît." ("Le plus ancien mystère de la Passion," *Académie Royale de Belge. Classe des lettres et des sciences morales et politiques*. 5 série. Vol. 50 (1964), 282–94, 292.

32 Young, I, 532.

33 Matthew, 27: 54–55.

34 John, 19: 34–35.

35 Rose Jeffries Peébles, *The Legend of Longinus in Ecclesiastical Tradition and in English Literature, and its Connection with the Grail*. (Baltimore, 1911), pp. 7–8.

36 Peebles, p. 20; Wright, *Themes*, p. 4; Carl Kröner, *Die Longinuslegende, ihre Entstehung und Ausbreitung in der französischen Litteratur* (Munster, 1899), p. 16; Caesare Baronio, *Annales Ecclesiastici*, 12 vols. (Romae, 1593), I, 182.

37 Young, I, 532.

38 *Ibid.*, p. 518.

39 Eduard Hartl, "Die Entwicklung des Benediktbeurer Passionsspiels," *Euphorion*, 46 (1952), 113–37, 121.

40 *Ibid.*, p. 127.

41 Young, I, 536.

42 *Ibid.*, I, 421–9.

43 *Ibid.*, pp. 432–7.

44 *Ibid.*, pp. 438–47.

45 *Ibid.*, p. 421.

46 *Ibid.*, p. 433.

47 *Ibid.*, p. 421.

48 *Ibid.*, p. 433.

49 Paul Lehmann, "Judas Iscarioth in der lateinischen Legenden-Überlieferung des Mittelalters," in his *Erforschung des Mittelalters*, II, 229–85, 278.

50 *Ibid.*, p. 242.

51 Chambers, II, 38, 71; Frank, *French Drama*, p. 27.

52 Chambers, II, 39; Young, I, 449.

53 Marius Sepet, *Le drame chrétien au moyen âge* (Paris, 1878), p. 193.

54 Young, I, 288, 408.

55 *Ibid.*, Klosterneuburg, p. 422; Benediktbeuern, p. 433; Tours, pp. 438–9.

56 *Ibid.*, p. 439.

57 Inguanez, (1939 ed.), p. 54.

58 Young, I, Tours, 439; Inguanez, (1939 ed.), p. 54.

59 Young, I, 438.

60 Inguanez, (1939 ed.), p. 53.

61 Mildred K. Pope and Jean G. Wright, *La Seinte Resurrection* (Oxford, 1943), pp. 32–33.

62 *Ibid.*, p. 33.

63 Wessel Klaus, "Das Mailender Passiondiptychon. Ein Werk der Karolingischen Renaissance," *Zeitschrift für Kunstwissenschaft*, Band V (Berlin, 1951), 132–3.

64 Frank, *French Drama*, *pp.* 86–7; Hardison Jr., *Christian Rite and Christian Drama*, p. 254.

65 Young, I, 449.

66 L. Delisle, "Note sur le manuscrit de Tours," *Romania*, 2 (1873), 91–5; Young, I, 438; Frank, *French Drama*, p. 29; also Wright, *The Dissemination*, p. 179.

67 Young, I, 438; Frank, *Medieval French Drama*, p. 29.

68 Toschi, *Narrazione e dramma*, p. 167.

69 See Chapter III, pp. 87.

70 Toschi, *Archivum*, p. 399; also Inguanez, (1936 ed.), p. 15; De Vito, *op. cit.*, p. 58.

71 Paolo Toschi, *L'antico dramma sacro italiano* 2 vols. (Firenze, 1926), I, ix–lxxl. Giulio Bertoni, *Il Duecento* (Milano, 1939), p. 332.

72 Antonio Viscardi, *Le origini* (Milano, 1950), pp. 488–91.

73 Vincenzo de Bartholomaeis, *Laude drammatiche e rappresentazioni sacre* 3 vols. (Firenze, 1943), I, xi–xviii; Toschi, *Antico dramma*, pp. xviii–xix; Apollonio, *Storia del teatro*, I, 149; Toschi, *Le Origini*, p. 676.

74 Ghilardi, *Origini del teatro*, p. 82.

75 Maria Apollonio, *Uomini e forme nella cultura italiana delle origini* (Firenze, 1943), p. 331.

76 Raby, *Christian Poetry*, p. 430.

77 Apollonio, *Teatro italiano*, I, 183.

78 Adolfo Gaspary, *Storia della letteratura italiana* 2 vols. (Torino, 1914), I, 150; De Bartholomaeis, *Origini*, pp. 208–9.

79 Ferdinando Liuzzi, *La Lauda e i primordi della melodia italiana* 2 vols. (Roma, 1934), I, 57.

80 Toschi, *Antico dramma*, I, xliv; also his *Origini*, p. 681; De Bartholomaeis, *Origini*, p. 220.

81 E. Monaci, "Uffizi drammatici dei disciplinati dell'Umbria," *Rivista di Filologia Romanza*, 1 (1872), 235–71; 2 (1873), 29–42, 248; De Bartholomaeis, *Laudi drammatiche*, I, xv.

82 Toschi, *Antico dramma*, I, xxi; Gaspary, *op. cit.*, I, 150.

83 *Ibid.*, pp. 153–4.

84 *Ibid.*, p. 156.

85 Matthew, 27: 57–58; Mark, 15: 43–45; Luke, 23: 50–52; John, 19: 38–39.

86 Toschi, *Antico dramma*, p. 161.

87 *Ibid.*, p. 163.

88 Ignazio Baldelli, "La lauda e i disciplinati," *La Rassegna della Letteratura Italiana*, 65 (1960), 396–418, 413; Toschi, *Origini*, p. 679; De Bartholomaeis, *Origini*, p. 222.

89 A. C. Peltier, ed., *S. Bonaventurae Meditationes Vitae Christi* (Parisiis, 1868), XII, chap. 82, 610.

90 Migne, *P.L.*, CLXXXII, cols. 1135, 1140.

91 Toschi, *Origini*, p. 682.

92 De Bartholomaeis, *Origini*, pp. 206–8; *Origini*, pp. 676–7.

93 Baldelli, *La Lauda*, p. 400; Ugolini, *Testi Abruzzesi*, pp. 23–5; Toschi, *Origini*, pp. 674–6; Benvenuto Terracini, "I mille anni della lingua italiana e il centenario dell'unità," *Lettere Italiane*, 13 (1961), 269.

94 Ruggero M. Ruggeri, *Saggi di linguistica italiana e italo romanzo* (Firenze, 1962), p. 9; Terracini, "I mille anni," 269.

95 Zumthor, *Histoire*, p. 67.

96 *Ibid.*, p. 68.

97 Paul Zumthor, *Langue et techniques poétiques à l'époque romane* (Paris, 1963), pp. 90–93; Toschi, *Origini*, p. 674.

98 On the *Sponsus* see Young, II, 361 foll.; Cohen, *Etudes d'histoire du théâtre en France au moyen âge et à la renaissance* (Paris, 1956), p. 24; Liuzzi, *Studi Medievali*, n.s. III (1930), 82–109; Frank, *French Drama*, pp. 58–64.

99 Gustave Cohen, *Le Jeu d'Adam et Eve* (Paris, 1926); Grace Frank, "Genesis and Staging of the *Jeu d'Adam*," *PMLA*, 59 (1944), 7–17. Paul Aebischer, ed. *Le Mystère d'Adam* (Genève et Paris, 1963).

100 Frank, *Palatinus*, p. x.

101 Frank, *French Drama*, p. 127.

102 Foster, *Northern Passion*, p. 65.

103 Matthew, 27: 62–66.

104 Wright, *Themes*, p. 65.

105 Mâle, *Religious Art in France in the XIII Century* (London, 1913), p. 194.

106 Shepard, *Passion provençale*, pp. xxxvii–xxxviii.

107 Grace Frank, "Palatine Passion and the development of the Passion Play" *PMLA*, 25 (1920), 465–7; Shepard, *op. cit.*, p. xl.

108 Frank, "Palatine Passion," 478; for a more detailed discussion of the subject see Frank's "Vernacular Sources and the Old French Passion Play," *MLN*, 35 (1920), 257–69.

109 Helmut Niedner, "Die deutschen und französischen Osterspiele bis zum 15. Jahrhundert," *Germanische Studien*, 119 (1932) 13–180, 43–44.

110 Eduard Hartl, *Das Benediktbeurer Passionsspiel. Das St. Galler Passionsspiel* (Halle, 1952).

111 Creizenach, I, 122–3.

112 Craig, *English Drama*, p. 105.

113 Mary H. Marshall, *The Relation of the vernacular Religious Plays of the Middle Ages to the Liturgical Drama* Diss. (New Haven, 1932), p. 139.

114 Hartl's text, p. 104.

115 Inguanez, (1939 ed.), p. 31.

116 Hartl's text, p. 104.

117 Inguanez, (1939 ed.), p. 32.

118 Hartl's text, p. 112.

119 Inguanez, (1939 ed.), p. 34.

120 Hartl's text, p. 98.

121 *Ibid.*, p. 113.

122 *Ibid.*, p. 121.

123 *Ludus Breviter*, Young, I, p. 516; *Ludus de Passione*, Young, I, p. 532.

124 Franz J. Mone, *Schauspiele des Mittelalters* (Karlsruhe, 1846), I, p. 121.

125 *Die Erlösung*, ed. Friedrich Maurer in *Deutsche Literatur, Reihe geistliche Dichtung des Mittelalters*, 6 (Leipzig, 1934), vs. 5335–5340, pp. 225–26.

126 Peebles, *op. cit.*, p. 20.

127 Wright, *Themes*, p. 2.

128 *Expositio in quatuor Evangelia. In Ioannem*, Migne, *P.L.*, CXIV, col. 914.

129 Migne, *P.L.*, C, col. 986.

130 Hartl's text, p. 115.

131 Peltier, II, chap. 78, 605–6.

VII. Conclusion

RESEARCH ON THE COMPLEX and vast literary production of the Middle Ages does not permit us to reconstruct with exactness the history of all its genres, the drama, in particular. But the available texts allow us to consider as certainty what some scholars have traditionally regarded as assumptions: the non-existence during the entire Middle Ages of an authentic secular theater either as survival or imitation of the classical one—bearing in mind the true significance of theater which requires scenic action, actually performed by actors impersonating the characters with voice and gestures—and the birth *ex novo* of modern drama from the liturgy of the Church. The inferior modes of representation of the mime and pantomime, the limited and undramatic notions of comedy and tragedy possessed by the Middle Ages and its meager and blurred understanding of the formal drama in the ancient world, suggest the absence, during the Middle Ages, of a secular dramatic tradition. As regards the ecclesiastical role, it has been reaffirmed that the plays of the Church were the product of the growth of the special ceremonies, processions, hymns, and the acts of the ritual that developed within the general framework of Christian worship.

In tracing the origins and development of the Latin Passion, emphasis has been placed both on a reappraisal of certain traditional views regarding the origin of the medieval drama and on the fact that, contrary to widely entertained ideas on the subject, the Church did produce a dramatized Latin version of the Passion before the thirteenth century.

Concerning the first of these two views, it has been indicated that the evolution of the liturgical drama should not be found exclusively in the tropes emanating from the schools of St. Gall and St. Martial of Limoges, but rather in a plurigenetic origin, since primitive types of tropes are found quite early in the various countries of the Western Christian World.

As to the second, the existence of a Latin Passion play as early as the twelfth century clearly indicates that the medieval dramatist did not hesitate to present on the stage the greatest Christian mystery: the Passion of Christ.

As to the tropes, conclusive and irrefutable evidence has marked them as the essential element that engendered the religious theater, for they exhibit all the ingredients of drama: a definite and visible place of action, impersonation by performers of characters, and use of dialogue. An attitude of hostility persists nonetheless in certain scholarly quarters. It is based on the seeming paradox that the trope came into being at a time when the Church was issuing edicts against the secular stage, and on the assumption that the Church, in general, has been antagonistic toward the theater from the earliest beginnings of the Christian era.

Although the irregular and secular additions to religious drama practiced by some communities, particularly in the eleventh and twelfth centuries, brought about the suspicion of the local episcopal authority and its sanctions, it is a fallacy to assume that the Church, as a whole, was hostile to the religious stage. The existence of sporadic ecclesiastical injunctions and restrictions did not hinder the development of the religious drama, for the Church in its official legislation of universal pertinence never condemned the religious stage, which flourished with her approval. With spiritual awareness, St. Ethelwold declared that the liturgical drama was to be directed "ad fidem inducti uulgi ac neofitorum corroborandam." [1] As long as primitive drama was motivated by this catechistic and edifying purpose, it remained an integral part of the Church's service, and it flourished with her apparent blessing and approval. The Church fully realized the utility of a religiously inspired dramatic art. Saint Thomas Aquinas, for instance, wrote about dramaturgy in these terms:

> Sicut dictum est, ludus est necessarius ad conversationem humanae vitae. Ad omnia autem, quae sunt utilia conversationi humanae, deputari possunt aliqua officia licita. Et ideo etiam officium histrionum, quod ordinatur ad solatium hominibus exhibendum, non est secundum se illicitum, nec sunt in statu peccati: dummodo moderate ludo utantur, id est, non utendo aliquibus verbis vel factis ad ludum.[2]

The balanced attitude of the Angelic Doctor is typical of the medieval artist and poet, who, being concerned primarily with the didactic, did not hesitate to make use of pagan culture as long as it was for the greater glory of God and the edification and salvation of His creatures.

The function of the medieval drama is quite clear. It constitutes a powerful dramatic statement on the Christian faith at its richest and most complex. The aim of medieval drama is that which motivated the medieval church as a whole: to express in visible, dramatic terms the facts and values of the accepted body of Scripture and theological belief. Christian art, particularly the dramatic art, is more than a pleasing ornament, it is actually grafted on to the fabric of Christian thought.

As to the Passion of Christ, the central preoccupation of the present study, it has been indicated that, contrary to widely expressed ideas on the subject, medieval dramatists provide an early imaginative visualization of it. Its dramatization, however, does not appear as early as that of the Easter *Quem quaeritis* trope. The explanation lies both in the fact that the celebration of the Mass was itself a highly dramatic event, a reenactment of the shedding of the body and blood of Jesus, and that the Church Easter liturgy gave emphasis to the joyful resolution, the renewal, the spiritual uplifting, the *gaudium*, the theophany incumbent upon Christ's sacrifice on the Cross: *Pascha nostrum immolatus est Christus . . . Qui mortem nostram moriendo destruxit, et vitam resurgendo reparavit.*[3] The Church emphasized the Easter liturgy, for the consecration and sanctification of Christ accomplished in the Resurrection affected all men, and the Christian's ultimate stage of perfection is attained with his bodily resurrection in Christ. Man acquires salvation and regeneration by identifying himself with this passage from death to life.

The stimulus towards the redaction of a Passion play was fostered and provided by a new theology and its commentary on the significance, in the redemptive act, of Christ's human nature. It was felt that the divinity and humanity of Christ were not divided, but rather united within the framework of the divine plan, and that the human nature of Christ was an instrument united in substance to His divinity. The new theology emphasized that although a God with superhuman strength, Christ did acquire human flesh and did suffer as a human being. He carried out mankind's redemption *quasi homo*, and His divinity did not imply the least limitation of His humanity. Honorius of Autun echoes typical medieval exegesis when he states that, although Christ's nature is divine and eternal, *in humanitatae habuit initium nascendo, finem moriendo.*[4] The doctrine of Incarnation and its implication for the salvation of man was, during the Middle Ages, as fundamental a theological tenet as the belief that Christ suffered as a man. The mystic literature of the twelfth century, in particular that of the Victorine school, was fond of pointing out the *sublimitas* and *humilitas* of the God-Man especially in Christ's Incarnation and Passion which realize the two most perfectly. St. Bernard of Clairvaux observes: *Christus enim, cum per naturam divinitatis non haberet quo cresceret vel ascenderet, quia ultra deum nihil est, per descensum quomodo cresceret invenit, veniens incarnari, pati, mori, ne moreremur in aeternum.*[5] Of this great tragic mystery an anonymous twelfth-century medieval dramatist has provided a remarkable dramatization in the Montecassino Latin Passion play.

In relation to early vernacular Passion plays, the Montecassino-Sulmona Latin Passion seems to be a unique and original composition. Essentially different from all the other extant Passion plays, Latin or vernacular, it presents in the Sulmona fragment only one remarkable verbal similarity to another play—to the brief, one-stanza soldiers' scene of the Tours *Ludus Paschalis* discussed above. It also offers a few more general similarities of content to French Easter plays in the motivation of the soldiers and shares with the St. Gall *Passion* similar treatment of certain episodes and the reliance on the Gospel narrative of Matthew. Although the Montecassino Passion itself exhibits an intimate relationship to the Gospel account and a desire to present the essentials of Christian faith and doctrine in a dramatic form, its author, nevertheless, felt the necessity of captivating the imagination of his audience by inserting in the dramatic action details of a realistic and comic nature. The necessity of freeing his work from the stylized solemnity of the liturgical dramatic tradition affords us an insight both into the imaginative creativeness of the author and the increasing secularization of the liturgical dramatic performance through the introduction of extra-liturgical or apocryphal material and the use of the vernacular in the dialogue. This dramatic inventiveness, while it increased the scope of the performance, did not bring about the complete and genuine secularization of the plays, for throughout the period of their effective growth, they remained under the supervision of the Church. It is, rather, indicative of the mundane elements pervading the religious activities of the Church. This peculiar mundaneness in the performance of Church services was part of the *Zeitgeist*. For beginning with the twelfth and thirteenth centuries an atmosphere of worldliness seems to penetrate the various strata of ecclesiastical hierarchy, engendering within it a state of moral laxity and intellectual curiosity which was determined, on one part by the passing of teaching, towards the end of the eleventh century and the beginning of the twelfth, from the monks to the secular clergy,[6] and on the other, by the cultural and artistic revival of the second Latin Renaissance. The flourishing in the twelfth century of the cathedral schools as centers of classical revival; the establishment of the earliest universities with their non-monastic students and Goliard poets; the flowering of vernacular, lyric, epic, and religious poetry; the introduction of Arabic science and the rediscovery of Aristotle, Ptolemy, and Galen; the current Platonism emanating from the humanistic school of Chartres, the scientific study of the Bible by such scholars as Gilbert de la Porrée, Thierry de Chartres and Bernard Silvester; the philosophers of the school of Paris such as Anselm of Laon and Gilbert de la Porrée, who suggested a rational approach to theological doctrine; the humanism of Bologna and Montecassino with their schools of *ars dictaminis* —all infused a definite secular spirit in the ecclesiastical organization, liberalizing traditional Church policies and allowing greater freedom to religious communities in matters involving local customs and usage.

An assessment of medieval religious drama, Latin and vernacular, seems to indicate that in pursuing a rigidly preordained course and indiscriminately borrowing from all available sources the medieval dramatists failed to produce many substantial works of art. Particularly as regards the Passion plays that I have examined, one perceives a lack of logical and of psychological insight, of the architectural order that distinguishes genuine masterpieces. One of the most important reasons for this lack of artistic unity is to be found in the medieval dramatist's tendency to present the entire cosmic drama by bringing on the scene the whole universe: the divinity, the physical world, man, and the devil. He could generally think only in terms of a timeless whole, "one great drama whose beginning is God's creation of the world, whose climax is Christ's Incarnation and Passion, and whose expected conclusion will be Christ's second coming and the Last Judgment." [7] In exploring the possibility of a valuable creative relation of creed and liturgy to an art form, in our case the drama, the medieval artist is concerned with complete vision, embracing all of creation and its relationship to God in a most profound and essential way.

Lyrical and dramatic masterpieces, however few, do exist

within the medieval dramatic corpus from the earliest *Quem quaeritis* to the great Latin and vernacular Passions. Among these, unquestionably, the pre-eminence belongs to the twelfth-century Montecassino Latin Passion. In style, in metrical composition and chronological representation of events, this Passion play is far superior to any extant Passion or Easter play, Latin or vernacular. The highly wrought stanzaic form, the *versus tripartitus caudatus*, makes it indubitable that this is an original artistic composition, a tightly knit work of art, whereas most of the other extant early Passion and Easter plays seem to be mosaic works. The Western Christian drama, born out of the Office of Easter Roman Liturgy, possesses in the Cassinese Passion both the most ancient and ample liturgical drama known up to now.

As a literary form the Latin Passion play appears to me as an artistic product issued from the hands of Montecassino's monastic circle, inspired by the liturgical services of Good Friday, the Gospel accounts, and particularly by the confluence and coexistence, beginning with the eleventh century, of three themes: in liturgy, a concentration on Christocentric piety; in art, a more humanistic treatment of Christ; in literature, a consideration of the scenes of the Passion as dramatic and human episodes.

The *Planctus Mariae*, as I have suggested, could not have been the *causa causans* of the Passion play, since in the only three Latin Passion plays in which it appears in some form, it constitutes only an incident, and the removal of it would not affect at all the action of the plays. Just as the initial impetus to the production of a Latin Passion play was supplied by the intense Christocentric mysticism of the eleventh and twelfth centuries, so too the embryonic nucleus in the redaction of the *Planctus Mariae* sprang out of the meditations on the sorrows of Mary, which, beginning in the eleventh century, reach their climax in the twelfth, and by virtue of their pathetic commentary on the sacrifice on the Cross show the natural ties that exist between the *Passio* and the *Compassio*.[8] Although Patristic writings had commented on Mary's instrumentality in the Passion by indicating that she had cooperated with Christ proximately, directly, and immediately in the achievement of the redemption, eleventh and twelfth-century commentaries emphasized her sorrows and human agony, seeing in the Virgin the figure of the *Mater Dolorosa* experiencing in her heart Christ's suffering.

As to the general subject of the vernacular dramatic tradition, the twelfth-century Montecassino Latin Passion allows us to modify the often expressed theory that it reached a complex level of development before Latin drama.[9] In view of the existence of such other Latin dramas as the twelfth-century *Libellus de Antichristo*, the Hilarius and Beauvais *Daniel* plays, the *Peregrinus*, and the earlier corpus of the liturgical drama, it can indeed be argued that the sophistication attained by vernacular compositions such as the *Mystère d'Adam* and *Resurrection* can best be explained in terms of the dramatic tradition established by the Latin religious drama.

From the evidence provided in the Montecassino Passion it seems reasonable to conclude that this play or some other very much like it provided the germ of later Passion plays. The origin of the Latin Passion play is no longer a moot question and until new material is discovered the Montecassino Latin Passion remains its earliest known form and Italy, its place of origin.

Notes to Chapter VIII

1 Young, I, 133.
2 Aquinas' *Summa Theologiae*, II, 2, *Quaestio*. 168. 3.
3 Preface to the Easter Sunday Mass.
4 Migne, *P.L.*, CLXXII, col. 790.
5 *Ibid.*, CLXXXIII, col. 304.
6 Philippe Delhaye, "L'organisation scolaire au XIIe siècle," *Traditio*, 5 (1947), 211–68.
7 Erich Auerbach, *Mimesis* (New York, 1957), p. 137.
8 Commenting on Mary's role in the Redemption, Arnauld of Bonneval writes:

> Dividunt coram Patre inter se mater et Filius pietatis officia, et miris allegationibus muniunt redemptionis humanae negotium, et condunt inter se reconciliationis nostrae inviolabile testamentum . . . [In Calvario] omnino . . . erat una Christi et Mariae voluntas, unumque holocaustum ambo pariter offerebant Deo: haec in sanguine cordis, hic in sanguine carnis.

(*P.L.*, CLXXXIX, cols. 1726-1727).
9 Hardison, *Christian Rite and Christian Drama*, p. 281.

Bibliography

Abrahams, P. "The Mercator-Scenes in Mediaeval French Passion Plays," *Medium Aevum*, III (1934), 112–23.

Aebischer, Paul. *Le Mystère d'Adam*. Genève et Paris, Droz, 1963.

Ahsmann, Hubertus, Petrus, Johannes, Maria. *Le culte de la sainte Vierge et la littérature française profane du Moyen Age*. Utrecht, Dekker en Van de Vegt, 1930.

Alazard, Jean. *L'art italien des origines à la fin du XIVᵉ siècle*. Paris, Henri Laurens, 1949.

Albers, Bruno. *Consuetudines Monasticae*. I–IV. Mont-Cassin, Typis Montis Casini, 1900–1912.

HUMBERTO LÓPEZ-MORALES' *Tradición y Creación en los orígenes del Teatro Castellano* (MADRID, 1968) REACHED ME TOO LATE FOR INSERTION IN THE DISCUSSION OF THE SPANISH THEATRE.

Allen, Philip Schuyler. "The Mediaeval Mimus. II" *Modern Philology*, VIII (1910–11), 17–60.

——. *The Romanesque Lyric*. Chapel Hill, The University of North Carolina Press, 1928.

Altheim, P. "Persona" *Archiv für Religionswissenschaft*, XXVII (1929), 35–52.

Anastos, V. Milton. "Some Aspects of Byzantine Influence on Latin Thought" in Marshall Clagett, Gaines Post and Robert Reynolds, eds., *Twelfth-Century Europe and the Foundations of Modern Society*. (Madison, 1961), 131–187.

Anderson, M.D. *Drama and Imagery in English Medieval Churches*. Cambridge, At The University Press, 1963.

Apel, Willi. *Gregorian Chant*. Bloomington, Indiana University Press, 1958.

Apollonio, Mario. *Storia del teatro italiano*, Vol. I. Firenze, G. S. Sansoni, 1943.

——. *Uomini e forme nella cultura italiana delle origini*. Firenze, G. S. Sansoni, 1943.

App, A.J. "Roswitha puts love into drama" *The Magnificat*, LXX (1942), 226–231, 281–285.

Atkins, J.W.H. *English Literary Criticism: The Medieval Phase*. Cambridge and New York, At The University Press, 1943.

Auerbach, Erich. *Mimesis*. New York, Doubleday and Company, 1957.

Avalle, D'Arco Silvio. *Cultura e lingua francese delle origini nella "Passion" di Clermont-Ferrand*. Milano, Riccardo Ricciardi, 1962.

Baldelli, Ignazio. "La lauda e i disciplinati" *Rassegna della Letteratura Italiana*, LXIV (1960), 396–418.

——. "Testi poco noti in volgare mediano dei secoli XII e XIII" *Studi di Filologia Italiana*, XVIII (1960).

Baldwin, Charles Sears. *Medieval Rhetoric and Poetic*. New York, The Macmillan Company, 1928.

Baronio, Caesare. *Annales Ecclesiastici*, 12 vols. Romae, Congregationis Oratorij, 1593–1607.

Barré, H. "Le 'Planctus Mariae' attribué à S. Bernard" *Revue d'Ascétique et de Mystique*, XXVIII (1952), 243–266.

Bartsch, Karl. "Das älteste deutsche Passionsspiel" *Germania*, VIII (1863), 273–297.

Bastiaensen, A.A.R. *Observations sur le vocabulaire liturgique dans l'Itinéraire d'Egérie*. Utrecht, Dekker and Van de Vegt, 1962.

Batiffol, Pierre. *L'abbaye de Rossano. Contribution à l'histoire de la Vaticane*. Paris, 1891.

Baum, R.F. "The Mediaeval Legend of Judas Iscarioth" *PMLA*, XXXI (1916), 481–632.

Beddie, James Stuart. "The Ancient Classics in the Medieval Libraries" *Speculum*, V (1930), 3–20.

Bédier, Joseph. "Fragment d'un ancien mystère," *Romania*, XXIV (1895), 86–94.

Beissel, P. Stephan. *Geschichte des Verehrung Marias in Deutschland während des Mittelalters*. Freiburg im Breisgau, Herdersche Verlagshandlung, 1909.

Belvederi, G. "La liturgia della Passione a Gerusalemme e in occidente al secolo IV e al secolo V" *Rivista di Archeologia Cristiana*, VIII (1931), 315–832.

Benda, Julien. "Délice d'Eléuthère" *La Nouvelle Revue Française*, (Juillet-Décembre, 1934), 808–832.

Benton, John F. "Nicolas of Clairvaux and the Twelfth-Century Sequence with special Reference to Adam of St. Victor," *Traditio*, XVIII (1962), 149–79.

Bertaux, Emile. *L'art dans l'Italie méridionale*. Paris, A. Fontemoing, 1904.

Bertoni, Giulio. *Il Duecento*. Milano, Editrice Vallardi, 1939.

Bianchi, Dante. "Per la commedia latina del secolo XII" *Aevum*, XXIX, 2, (1955), 171–178.

Bibli. Vatic., MS lat. 4770, Miss. Benedictinum Sancti Petri in Aprutio saec. X–XI.

Bieber, Margarete. *The History of the Greek and Roman Theater*. Princeton, The Princeton University Press, 1939.

Bigongiari, D. "Were There Theaters in the Twelfth and Thirteenth Centuries?" *Romanic Review*, XXXVII (1946), 201–224.

Billanovich, Giuseppe. "Uffizi drammatici della Chiesa Padovana" *Rivista Italiana del Dramma*, IV (Gennaio, 1940), 72–100.

Bloch, Herbert. "Montecassino, Byzantium and the West in the Earlier Middle Ages" *Dumbarton Oaks Papers*, 3 (1946), 163–224.

Blum, Owen J. "Alberic of Montecassino and the Hymns attributed to Saint Peter Damian" *Traditio*, XII (1956), 87–148.

Blume, Cl. Dreves, G. M. Bannister, H. M. eds. *Analecta Hymnica Medii Aevi*. 55 vols. Leipzig, O.R. Reisland, 1866–1922.

Bonaria, Marius. *Mimorum Romanorum Fragmenta*. 2 vols. Geneva, Istituto di Filologia Classica, 1955.

Bonilla y San Martin, Adolfo. *Las bacantes o del origen del teatro*. Madrid, N. E., 1921.

Borcherdt, Hans Heinrich. *Das europäische Theater im Mittelalter und in der Renaissance.* Leipzig, J.J. Weber, 1935.

——. "Geschichte des deutschen Theaters" in Wolfgang Stammler's *Deutsche Philologie im Aufriss,* III (Berlin, 1957), 417–588.

Borsari, Silvano. *Il monachesimo bizantino nella Sicilia e nell'Italia meridionale prenormanno.* Napoli, Istituto Italiano di Studi Storici, 1963.

Bossuat, Robert. *Manuel bibliographique de la littérature française du Moyen Age.* Paris, Librairie D'Argences, 1951. Suppléments, 1949–53 and 1954–1960.

Bowles, A. Edmunt. "The Role of Musical Instruments in Medieval Sacred Drama" *Musical Quarterly,* XLV (1959), 67–84.

——. "Were Musical Instruments used in the Liturgical Service during the Middle Ages?" *The Galpin Society Journal,* X (1956), 40–56.

Brau, Louis (Dom). "Le portrait de Judas d'après la liturgie" *Revue Grégorienne,* XXII (1937), 81–92; XXIII (1938), 55–63.

Bréhier, Louis. *L'art chrétien.* Paris, Librairie Renouard, H. Laurens, 1918.

——. *Les Origines du crucifix dans l'art religieux.* Paris, Librarie Bloud et Cⁱᵉ, 1904.

Breviarium Romanum. Mechliniae, H. Deasain, 1859.

Bridges-Adams, W. *The Irresistible Theatre.* Vol. I. London, Secker & Warburg, 1957.

Brinkmann, Hennig. "Das religiöse Drama im Mittelalter: Arten und Stufen" *Wirkendes Wort,* IX (1959), 257–274.

——. "Zum Ursprung des liturgischen Spiels" *Xenia Bonnensia* (Bonn, 1929), 106–43.

Brittain, F. *The Medieval Latin and Romance Lyric to A.D. 1300.* Cambridge, At The University Press, 1951.

Bronzini, Giovanni. "Le origini del teatro italiano" *Cultura Neolatina,* XVI–XVII (1956–57), 201–239.

Brooks, Neil C. "The Lamentations of Mary in the Frankfurt Group of Passion Plays" *Journal of Germanic Philology,* III (1900–1), 415–430.

——. "*The Sepulchrum Christi* and its Ceremonies in Late Medieval and Modern Times" *JEGP,* XXVII (1928), 147–161.

Broussolle, J.C. *Etudes sur la sainte Vierge.* Paris, P. Tequi, 1908–1909.

Brown, Beatrice Daw. *The Southern Passion* in *Early English Text Society,* CLXIX. London, Oxford University Press, 1927.

Brugnoli, Giorgio. "Le tragedie di Seneca nei Florilegi medio-evali," *Studi Medievali,* ser. 3, 1 (1960), 138–52.

——. "Note di filologia medievale" *Rivista di Cultura Classica e Medievale,* Anno III, n. 1 (1961), 114–120.

Burdach, Konrad. "Der Longinusspeer in eschatologischen Lichte" in his collected papers, *Vorspiel* (Halle, 1925), I, 217–252.

Butler, Sister Mary Marguerite. *Hrotswita: the Theatricality of Her Plays*. New York, Philosophical Library, 1960.

Cabanis, Allen. "Alleluia: a Word and its Effect" *Studies in English,* V (1964), 67–74.

Cabrol, Fernand et Leclercq, Henri. *Dictionnaire d'archéologie chrétienne et de liturgie.* 15 vols. Paris, Librairie Letouzey et Ané, 1924–1951.

Callewaert, C. "L'oeuvre liturgique de S. Grégoire" *Revue d'histoire ecclésiastique,* XXXIII (1937), 306–326.

Campbell, A.P. "The Mediaeval Mystery Cycle Liturgical in Impulse" *Revue de l'Université d'Ottawa,* XXXIII, 1 (January–March, 1963), 23–27.

Campbell, J.M. "Patristic Studies and the Literature of Medieval England" *Speculum,* VIII (1933), 465–478.

Caravita, Andrea. *I codici e le arti a Montecassino.* 3 vols. Montecassino, Tipi della Badia, 1869.

Cargill, Oscar. *Drama and Liturgy.* New York, Columbia University Press, 1930.

Carré, A.M. *L'église s'est-elle reconciliée avec le théâtre.* Paris, Editions du Cerf, 1956.

Carreter, Fernando Lázaro. *Teatro medieval.* Valencia, Editorial Castalla, 1958.

Carusi, Enrico. "Il 'Memoratorium' dell'abate Bertario sui possessi Cassinesi nell'Abruzzo teatino, e uno sconosciuto vescovo di Chieti del 930" *Casinensia I.* Montecassino, 1929.

Cattaneo, Enrico. "Il dramma liturgico della Settimana Santa nel rito ambrosiano" *Ambrosius,* XXXII (1956), 65–91.

Causa, Raffaello. *Sant'Angelo in Formis.* Milano, Grafiche Ricordi, 1963.

Cecchelli, Carlo. *Il trionfo della croce. La croce e i santi segni prima e dopo Costantino.* Roma, Edizioni Paoline, 1954.

Cellucci, Luigi. "Le 'Meditationes vitae Christi' e i poemetti che ne furono ispirati" *Archivum Romanicum,* XXII (1938), 30–98.

Chailley, Jacques. "Les anciens tropaires et séquentiaires de l'Ecole de Saint-Martial de Limoges (Xe–XIe)" *Etudes Grégoriennes,* II (1957), 163–188.

Chambers, E.K. *English Literature at the Close of the Middle Ages.* Oxford, At The Clarendon Press, 1961.

——. *The Mediaeval Stage,* II. Oxford, At The Clarendon Press, 1903.

Chauvin, Mary John Sister. *The Role of Mary Magdalene in Medieval Drama.* Washington, Catholic University Press, 1951.

Chevalier, Ulysse. *Repertorium Hymnologicum,* 6 vols. Louvain, Imprimerie Lefever, 1892–1921.

Chevallier, Eloi P(ère) O.C.S.O. "Cantus Passionis Antiquior" *Revue Grégorienne,* 39ᵉ année (1960), 150–159.

Chiappini, P. Aniceto. "Codici liturgici di Sulmona e Tagliacozzo" *Collectanea Franciscana,* XXX (1960), 208–218.

Christ, K. "Das altfranzösische Passionsspiel der Palatina" *Zeitschrift für romanische Philologie,* XL (1920), 405–488.

Cilento, Nicola. "Sant'Angelo in Formis nel suo significato storico (1072–1087)" *Studi Medievali,* ser. III, 4² (1963), 799–812.

Cirlot, J.E. *A Dictionary of Symbols.* New York, Philosophical Library, 1962.

Cloetta, W. *Beiträge zur Literaturgeschichte des Mittelalters und der Renaissance.* Halle, Max Niemeyer, 1890.

Coffman, George R. "A New Approach to Medieval Latin Drama" *Modern Philology,* XXII (1924–5), 239–271.

Cohen, Gustave. *Anthologie du drame liturgique en France au Moyen Age.* Paris, Editions du Cerf, 1955.

——. *Etudes d'histoire du théâtre en France au Moyen Age et à la Renaissance.* Paris, Gallimard, 1956.

——. *Histoire de la mise en scène dans le théâtre religieux français du Moyen Age.* Paris, H. Champion, 1951.

——. *La comédie latine en France au XIIᵉ siècle.* 2 vols. Paris, Les Belles-Lettres, 1931.

——. "La 'Comédie' latine en France au XIIᵉ siècle" *Mélanges de linguistique et de littérature, offerts à M. Alfred Jeanroy par ses élèves et ses amis.* (Paris, 1928), 255–263.

——. *La grande clarté du Moyen Age.* Paris, Gallimard, 1945.

——. *La poésie en France au Moyen Age.* Paris, Richard-Masse, 1952.

——. "Le drame liturgique en France" *Rivista di Studi Teatrali,* IX–XII (1954), 13–31.

——. *Le Jeu d'Adam et Eve.* Paris, Librarie Delagrave, 1936.

——. "Le personnage de Marie-Madeleine dans le drame religieux français du Moyen Age" *Convivium,* XXIV (1956), 141–63.

——. *Le théâtre en France au Moyen Age. I. Le théâtre religieux.* Paris, Editions Rieder, 1931.

——. "L'évolution de la mise en scène dans le théâtre français" *Bulletin de la Société de l'Histoire du Théâtre,* (Janvier-avril, 1910), 81–99.

——. "The Influence of the Mysteries on Art in the Middle Ages" *Gazette des Beaux-arts,* s.d., (1943), 327–342.

——. "Un terme de scénologie médiévale: 'lieu' ou 'mansion'?" *Mélanges de philologie et d'histoire littéraire offerts à Edmond Huguet.* (Paris, n.d.), 52–58.

Concasty, M.L. "Manuscrits grecs originaires de l'Italie méridionale conservés à Paris" *Atti dello VIII Congresso Internazionale di Studi Bizantini,* vol. I (Roma, 1953).

Contini, G. *Teatro religioso del Medio Evo fuori d'Italia.* Milano, Bompiani, 1949.

Coosemans, Vincenzo. "Il canto del *Passio*" *Rivista Liturgica,* VI (1919), 49–55.

Coppini, C. "Le crucifix dans l'art" *Illustrazione Vaticana,* Vᵉ, (1934), 230–32.

Corbin, Solange. *La déposition liturgique du Christ au Vendredi Saint.* Paris, Editions Les Belles Lettres, 1960.

——. "Le manuscrit 201 d'Orléans, drames liturgiques dits de Fleury" *Romania,* LXXIV (1953), 1–43.

Cornelius, Brother Luke. *The Role of the Virgin Mary in the Coventry, York, Chester, and Towneley Cycles.* Washington, Catholic University Press, 1933.

Cothenet, E. "Marie dans les Apocryphes de la Passion et de la Résurrection" in Du Manoir's *Maria,* VI. (Paris, 1961), 106–113.

Cottas, Venetia. *Le théâtre à Byzance.* Paris, Paul Geuthner, 1931.

——. *L'influence du drame "Christos Paschon" sur l'art chrétien d'Orient.* Paris, Paul Geuthner, 1931.

Coulter, Cornelia C. "The 'Terentian' Comedies of a Tenth-Century Nun" *Classical Journal,* XXIV (1929), 515–529.

Coulton, G.C. *Art and Reformation.* London, B. Blackwell, 1928.

——. *Ten Medieval Studies.* Boston, Beacon Press, 1959.

Coyle, M.A. *The Attitude of the Early Church toward the Drama.* Diss. Yale, 1928.

Craig, Barbara. "Didactic Elements in Medieval French Drama" *Esprit Créateur,* 2 (1962), 142–48.

Craig, Hardin. *English Religious Drama.* Oxford, At The Clarendon Press, 1955.

——. "The Origin of the Passion Play: Matters of Theory as well as Fact" *University of Missouri Studies,* XXI (1946), 83–90.

Craig, J.D. "Jovialis and the Callopian Text of Terence" (London, 1927), St. Andrew Publications, XXII.

Crawford, J.P. Wickersham. *Spanish Drama Before Lope de Vega.* Philadelphia, The University of Pennsylvania Press, 1922.

Creizenach, Wilhelm. *Geschichte des Neuren Dramas.* 3 vols. Halle, Max Niemeyer, 1893.

——. "Judas Ischarioth in Legende und Sage des Mittelalters" *Beiträge zur Geschichte der Deutschen Sprache und Literatur,* II (1876), 177–207.

Cremaschi, Giovanni. "Planctus Mariae" *Aevum*, Anno XXIX (Settembre-Dicembre, 1955), Fascicolo 5-6, 193-468.

Crosland, Jessie. *Medieval French Literature*. New York, The Macmillan Company, 1956.

Crowne, J. Vincent. "Middle English Poems on the Joys and on the Compassion of the Blessed Virgin Mary" *Catholic University Bulletin*, VIII, N°3 (July, 1902), 304-316.

Cunningham, M.P. "The Place of the Hymns of St. Ambrose in the Latin Poetic Tradition" *Studies in Philology*, LII (1955), 509-14.

D'Amico, Silvio. *Storia del teatro drammatico*. 2 vols. Milano, Grafiche Aldo Garzanti, 1953.

D'Ancona, Alessandro. *Origini del teatro italiano*. 2 vols. Torino, Ermanno Loerscher, 1891.

D'Ancona, Paolo. *La miniatura fiorentina* (secoli XI–XVI). Firenze, Leo S. Olschki, MCMXIV.

——. *La miniature italienne du Xe au XVIe siècle*. Paris, G. Van Oest, 1925.

Dalmais, I.H. "L'adoration de la Croix" *La Maison-Dieu*, XLV (1956), 76-86.

Daniel, Herm. Adalbert. *Thesaurus Hymnologicus*. 5 vols. Hallis, Sumptibus Eduardi Anton, 1841-1846.

Daniel-Rops, Henry. *Mystiques de France*. Paris, Buchet/Chastel, 1941.

Davidson, Charles. *Studies in the English Mystery Plays*. Yale, Yale University Press, 1892.

Davy, M.M. "La présence de la Vierge Marie au XIIe siècle" *La Table Ronde*, 129 (Septembre, 1958), 106-113.

D'Evelyn, Charlotte. *ME Meditations on the Life and Passion of Christ*. (EETS OS No. 158, 1921).

D'Ovidio, Francesco. *Versificazione romanza*. 3 vols. Napoli, Alfredo Guida, 1932.

De Bartholomaeis, Vincenzo. *Il teatro abruzzese del Medio Evo*. Bologna, N. Zanichelli, 1924.

——. *Laude drammatiche e rappresentazioni sacre*. 3 vols. Firenze, Felice Le Monnier, 1943.

——. *Origini della poesia drammatica italiana*. Torino, Società Editrice Internazionale, 1952.

——. *Primordi della lirica d'arte in Italia*. Torino, S.E.I., 1943.

——. "Ricerche abruzzesi" *Bulletino dell'Istituto Storico Italiano*, VIII (1889), 77-173.

De Boor, Helmut. "Die lateinischen Grundlagen der deutschen Osterspiele" *Hessische Blätter für Volkskunde*, LXI (1950), 45-66.

De Coussemaker, E. *Drames liturgiques du Moyen Age*. Rennes, H. Vatar, 1860.

——. *Histoire de l'harmonie au Moyen Age*. Paris, Librairie Victor Didron, 1852.

De Fleury, Rohault. *La sainte Vierge. Etudes archéologiques et iconographiques*. 2 vols. Paris, Librairie Poussielque Frères, 1878.

——. *Mémoire sur les instruments de la Passion de N.-S. J.-C.* Paris, Librairie Liturgique-Catholique, 1870.

De Gebhardt, Oscar, Harnack, Adolphus, Zahn, Theodorus eds. *Patrum Apostolorum Opera*. 2 vols. Lipsiae, J.C. Hinrichs, 1876.

De Ghellinck, J. *L'essor de la littérature latine au XIIᵉ siècle*. 2 vols. Paris, Desclée de Brouwer, 1946.

——. "L'histoire de 'persona' et d' 'hypostasis' dans un écrit anonyme porrétain du XIIᵉ siècle" *Revue néoscolastique de philosophie*, XXXVI (1934), 111–127.

——. *Littérature latine au Moyen Age*. Bruxelles, Bloud et Gay, 1939.

De Gourmont, Remy. *Le latin mystique*. Paris, Georges Crès et Cit., 1913.

De Julleville, Petit. *Les comédiens en France au Moyen Age*. Paris, L. Cerf, 1885.

De Labriolle, Pierre. *Histoire de la littérature latine chrétienne*. 2 vols. Paris, Editions Les Belles Lettres, 1947.

De Lyra, Nicolai. *Postillae super quatuor Evangeliis*. Mantuae, P. Johannis de Putzbach, 1477.

De Vito, Maria Sofia. *Le origini del dramma liturgico*. Milano, Editrice Dante Alighieri, 1938.

Del Valle de Paz, J. *Sulle origini e lo svolgimento del teatro religioso in Italia*. Udine, Stabilimento Tipografico Friulano, 1924.

Dela Vega, Narciso Díaz de Escorar y Francisco de P. Lasso. *Historia del teatro español*. Vol. I. Barcelona, Montaneri Simon, 1924.

Delhaye, Phillipe. "L'organisation scolaire au XIIᵉ siècle" *Traditio*, V (1947), 211–268.

Delisle, L. "Note sur le manuscrit de Tours" *Romania*, II (1873), 91–95.

De Ricaumont, Jacques. "Le théâtre de Hrotsvitha" *La Table Ronde*, 166 (Novembre, 1961), 54–59.

De Ros, Fidèle. "Le *Planctus Mariae* du pseudo-Anselme" *Revue d'Ascétique et de Mystique*, XXV (1949), 270–283.

De Sahus, Jacques. "Les origines du théâtre en France" *Confluences*, V–VI (1941), 604–617, 710–718.

De Saint-Damien, Marie. "L'associée du Christ sauveur" *Etudes Franciscaines*, XI (1961), 17–31; XII (1962), 185–202.

De Zedelgem, P. Amédée. "Aperçu historique sur la Dévotion au Chemin de la Croix" *Collectanea Franciscana*, XVIII–XIX (1948–49), 45–142.

Didron, M. *Iconographie chrétienne*. Paris, Imprimerie Royale, 1843.

Diehl, Charles. *L'art byzantin dans l'Italie méridionale*. Paris, Librairie de l'Art, 1894.

Dill, Samuel. *Roman Society in the Last Century of the Western Empire*. London and New York, Macmillan and Company, 1898.

Diringer, David. *The Illuminated Book. Its History and Production*. London, Faber and Faber, 1958.

Dirks, Walter. *Christi Passion. Farbige Bilder aus dem sechsten bis Zwölften Jahrhundert*. Hamburg, Wittig, 1956.

Dolenz, Sofia. *Le commedie latine di suor Rosvita, poetessa tedesca del secolo X*. Roma, Editrice Esquilina, 1926.

Donovan, Richard B. *The Liturgical Drama in Medieval Spain*. Toronto, Pontifical Institute of Mediaeval Studies, 1958.

Du Cange. *Glossarium Mediae et Infimae Latinitatis*. 10 vols. Niort, L. Favre, 1883–1887.

Du Méril, E. *Les origines latines du théâtre moderne*. Leipzig, H. Welter, 1897.

——. *Poésies populaires latines du Moyen Age*. Paris, Firmin Didot Frères, 1847.

Duchesne, L. "La légende de sainte Marie-Madeleine" *Annales du Midi*, V (1893), 1–33.

Duemmler, Ernestus. *Poetae Latini Aevi Carolini* in *Monumenta Germaniae Historica*, II (Berlin, 1884), 509–515.

Duffield, S. W., *The Latin Hymn-Writers and their Hymns*. New York, Funk & Wagnalls, 1889.

Dunn, Catherine E. "The Miracle Plays as an Art Form" *Catholic Art Quarterly*, (1956), 48–57.

Duriez, George. *La théologie dans le drame religieux en Allemagne au Moyen Age*. Diss. Lille, 1914.

——. *Les apocryphes dans le drame religieux en Allemagne*. Paris, J. Tallendier, 1914.

Dürre, K. *Die Mercatorszene im lateinisch-liturgischen, altdeutschen und altfranzösischen religiösen Drama*. Göttingen, Diss. 1915.

Dziatzko, H. "Zu Terentius in Mittelalter," *Jahrbücher für Klass. Philologie*, (1894), 465–477.

Ebersolt, Jean. *La miniature byzantine*. Paris, G. Vanoest, 1926.

Ebert, Adolf. *Allgemeine Geschichte der Literatur des Mittelalters*. Leipzig, F.C.W. Vogel, 1889.

——. "Die ältesten italienischen Mysterien" *Jahrbuch für Romanische und Englische Literatur*, V (1864), 5–174.

Ekkehardi De Casibus monasterii Sancti Galli in G. Meyer von Knonau, *St. Gallische Geschichtsquellen*. St. Gallen, Huber und Comp., 1877.

Ellespermann, Gerard L. *The Attitude of the Early Christian Latin Writers toward Pagan Literature and Learning.* Washington, The Catholic University of America Press, 1949.

Engels, Joseph, "La portée de l'étymologie isidorienne" *Studi Medievali,* 3a ser. III (1962), 99–128.

Ermini, Filippo. "Adamo da San Vittore" *Medio evo latino,* (Modena, 1938), 289–308.

——. "Hrotsvitha" *Medio evo latino,* (Modena, 1938), 163–181.

——. "Il Babio, commedia latina del secolo XII" *Medio evo latino,* (Modena, 1938), 241–250.

——. Lo *Stabat Mater e i pianti della Vergine nella lirica del Medio Evo.* Città di Castello, 1916.

——. *Storia della letteratura latina medievale.* Spoleto, Panetto e Petrelli, 1960.

Evans, Paul. "Some Reflections on the Origins of the Trope" *Journal of the American Musicological Society,* XIV (1961) 119–131.

Faral, Edmond. "Les conditions générales de la production littéraire en Europe occidentale pendant les IXᵉ et Xᵉ siècles" *I problemi communi dell'Europa post-carolingia,* II (Spoleto, 1955), 247–294.

Faral, Edmond. "Le fabliau latin au Moyen Age," *Romania,* 50, (1924), 321–85.

Fergusson, Francis. *The Idea of a Theater.* Garden City, Doubleday and Company, Inc., 1953.

Ferretti, Paolo. "Il canto della Passione nella Settimana Santa" *Rivista Liturgica,* V (1918), 69–75.

Fortini, Arnaldo. *La lauda in Assisi e le origini del teatro italiano.* Assisi, Tip. Porziuncolai, 1961.

Foster, Frances A. ed. *A Stanzaic Life of Christ* in *Early English Text Society.* vol. CLXVI. London, Oxford University Press, 1926.

——. "The Mystery Plays and *The Northern Passion*" *MLN,* XXVI (1911), 169–71.

——. *The Northern Passion* in *Early English Text Society,* 2 vols. London, Oxford University Press, 1913–16.

Franceschini, Ezio. "Glosse e commenti medievali a Seneca tragico" in *Studi e note di filologia medievale.* (Milano, 1938), 1–105.

——. "Il teatro post-carolingio" *I problemi comuni dell' Europa post-carolingia,* II (Spoleto, 1955), 295–312.

——. "Per una revisione del teatro latino di Rosvita" *Rivista Italiana del Dramma,* I (1938), 300–316.

——. *Teatro latino medievale.* Milano, Nuova Accademia Editrice, 1960.

Frank, Grace. "Genesis and Staging of the *Jeu d'Adam,*" *PMLA,* (1944), 7–17.

——. "Introduction to a Study of the Medieval French Drama" *Essays and Studies in Honor of Carleton Brown,* (New York, New York University Press, 1940), 62–78.

——. *La Passion d'Autun in Société des Anciens Textes Français.* Paris, 1934.

——. *La Passion du Palatinus.* Paris, H. Champion, 1922.

——. *Le livre de la Passion.* Paris, H. Champion, 1930.

——. "Palatine Passion and the Development of the Passion Play" *PMLA,* XXXV (1920), 464–483.

——. *The Medieval French Drama.* Oxford, Clarendon Press, 1954.

——. "Vernacular Sources and an Old French Passion Play" *MLN,* XXXV (1920), 257–269.

Frank, T. ed. *An Economic Survey of Ancient Rome.* Vol. III. Baltimore, The Johns Hopkins Press, 1937.

Frappier, Jean et Gossard, André-Marie. *Le théâtre religieux au Moyen Age.* Paris, Larousse, 1952.

Frappier, Jean. "Châtiments infernaux et peur du diable" *Cahiers de l'Association Internationale des Etudes Françaises,* no 3–4–5 (1953), 87–96.

Freccero, John. "The Sign of Satan" *MLN,* LXXX (1965), 11–26.

Frohlich, Walter. *De Lamentacione Sancte Marie.* Leipzig, Heinrich John, 1902.

Frolow, A. *La relique de la vraie Croix.* Paris, Institut Français d'Etudes Byzantines, 1961.

Froning, Richard. *Das Drama des Mittelalters.* Darmstadt, Wissenschaftliche Buchgesellschaft, 1964.

Frugoni, Arsenio. *Celestiniana.* Roma, G. Bardi, 1954.

Fry, Timothy. "The Alleged Influence of Pagan Ritual on the Formation of the English Mystery Plays" *American Benedictine Review,* IX (1958–59), 187–201.

Gabbrielli, Mariarosa. "Un 'Exultet' cassinese dell'XI secolo" *Bolletino d'Arte,* 3. serie, XXVI (1932–33), 306–313.

Gabotto, F. *Appunti sulla fortuna di alcuni autori romani nel Medio Evo.* Verona, Donato Tedeschi, 1891.

Gamurrini, Johannes Franciscus. *S. Hilarii Tractatus de Mysteriis et Hymni et S. Silviae Aquitanae Peregrinatio ad Loca Sancta.* Romae, Accademia di Conferenze Storico-Giuridiche, 1887.

Gamer, M. Helen. "Mimes, Musicians and the Origin of the Mediaeval Religious Play" *Deutsche Beiträge zur Geistigen Überlieferung,* V (1965), 9–28.

Gardiner, Harold C. *Mysteries' End: An Investigation of the Last Days of the Medieval Religious Stage.* New Haven, Yale, Univ. Press, 1946.

Garrone, Virginia Galante. *L'apparato scenico del dramma sacro in Italia.* Torino, Tipografia Vincenzo Bona, 1935.

Garth, Helen. *Mary Magdalene in Medieval Literature* (The Johns Hopkins University Studies in Historical and Political Science, Series 67, no. 3; Baltimore, The Johns Hopkins University Press, 1950).

Gaselee, Stephen. *The Oxford Book of Medieval Latin Verse.* Oxford, Clarendon Press, 1928.

Gaspary, Adolfo. *Storia della letteratura italiana,* vol. I. Torino, Ermanno Loescher, 1914.

Gassner, John. ed. *Medieval and Tudor Drama.* New York, Bantam Books, 1963.

Gattula, Erasmi. *Historia Abbatiae Cassinensis,* 2 vols. Venetis, Sebastianum Coleti, MDCCXXXIII.

Gaudenzi, A. "Carmi medioevali inediti: II. La vita di S. Pietro per Amato monaco cassinese" *Bulletino dell' Istituto Storico Italiano,* (1899), 46–95.

Gautier, L. "La poésie religieuse dans les cloîtres des IXe–XIe siècles" *Revue du Monde Catholique,* XCI (1887), 221–248.

———. *Les Oeuvres poétiques d'Adam de Saint-Victor,* 2 vols. Paris, Julien, Lanier, Cosnard et Cie., 1858.

Gay, Jules. "Jusqu'où s'étend, à l'époque normande la zone hellenisée de l'Italie méridionale?" *Mélanges Bertaux,* (Paris, 1924), 110–28.

———. *L'Italie méridionale et l'empire byzantin.* Paris, Albert Fontemoing, 1904.

Gennrich, Friedrich. *Grundriss einer Formenlehre des mittelalterlichen Liedes als Grundlage einer musikalischen Formenlehre des Liedes.* Halle, M. Niemeyer, 1932.

Geppert, C.E. "Zur Geschichte des Terentianischen Textskritik" *Neue Jahrbücher für Philologie und Pädogogik,* Supplementband XVIII (1852), 28–87.

Ghéon, Henri. *The Art of the Theatre.* New York, Hill and Wang, 1961.

Gerbert, Martin. *De Cantu et Musica Sacra.* Monast. S. Blasii, Typis San-Blasianis, 1774.

———. *Monumenta Veteris Linguae Alemanicae.* Saint-Blasien, 1790.

Gerson, Jehan. *Les contemplacions hystoriez sur la Passion.* Paris, Anthoine Gerard, 1507.

Gersonii, Joannis. *Opera Omnia,* 5 vols. Antwerpiae, Sumptibus Societatis, 1706.

Ghilardi, Fernando. "Le origini del teatro italiano e San Francesco" *L'Italia Francescana,* XXX (1955), 6, 341–351; XXXI (1956), 2, 81–87.

Giesebrecht, Guliehmus. *De Litterarum Studiis apud Italos Primis Medii Aevi Saeculis.* Berolini, Rudolphi Gaertner, MDCCXLV.

Gilson, Etienne. *The Mystical Theology of St. Bernard* tr. A.H.C. Downes, New York, Sheed and Ward, 1940.

——. "Saint Bonaventure et l'Iconographie de la Passion" *Revue d'Histoire Franciscaine*, I (1924), 405–424.

Gilson, J.P. *British Museum: An Exultet Roll Illuminated in the XIth Century at the Abbey of Monte Cassino*. London, Printed by order of the Trustees, 1929.

Giusti, Davide. *Il teatro drammatico italiano*. Napoli, G. D'agostino, 1959.

Goodman, Hadassah Posey. *Original Elements in the French and German Passion Plays*. Bryn Mawr, Pa., 1951.

Gordziejew, Wlodzimierz. *Ludi scaenici et circenses quid in rebus publicis antiquorum valuerint*. Dissertatio, Warzawa, Universitet Josefa Pilsudskiego, 1936.

Grabar, André. "Un rouleau liturgique Constantinopolitain et ses peintures" *Dumbarton Oaks Papers*, 8 (1954), 163–199.

Gregor, Joseph. "Das mittelalterliche religiöse Theater in Frankreich" *Antares*, 6, (January–June, 1958), 46–51.

Grenier, Albert, "La Gaule Romaine" in T. Frank, ed. *An Economic Survey of Ancient Rome*, III (1937), 381–644.

Grondijs, L.H. *L'iconographie byzantine du Crucifié mort sur la Croix*. Utrecht, Editions Kemink en Zoon, 1947.

Guéranger, Prosper. *L'année liturgique. La Passion et la Semaine Sainte*. Paris, Librairie H. Audin, 1909.

Gutkind, C.S. "Italian Literature to the Renaissance" *Year's Work in Modern Language Studies*, VIII (1938), 13–20.

Hagendahl, Harald. "La comédie latine au XIIe siècle et ses modèles antiques" ΔΡΑΓΜΑ *Martino P. Nilsson dedicatum*. (Lund, 1939), 222–255.

——. *Latin Fathers and the Classics. Studia Graeca et Latina Gothoburgensis*, VI. Goteborg, Elanders Boktryckeri Aktiebolag, 1958.

Haight, Anne Lyon. *Hrotswitha of Gandersheim*. New York, Clarke and Way, Inc., 1965.

Hamelin, Jeanne. *Le théâtre chrétien*. Paris, Librairie Arthème Fayard, 1957.

Handschin, Jacques. "Trope, Sequence, and Conductus" *Early Medieval Music up to 1300*. ed., A. Hughes (New Oxford History of Music, II; Oxford, 1954), 128–174.

Hansel, H. *Die Maria-Magdalena-Legende*. Bottrop, 1957.

Hardison, O.B. Jr. *Christian Rite and Christian Drama in the Middle Ages: Essays in the Origin and Early History of Modern Drama*. Baltimore, The Johns Hopkins University Press, 1965.

Hartl, Eduard. *Das Benediktbeurer Passionsspiel. Das St. Galler Passions-spiel.* Halle, M. Niemeyer, 1952.

——. "Das Drama des Mittelalters" in Wolfgang Stammler's *Deutsche Philologie im Aufriss*, II. (Berlin, 1954), 903–947.

——. "Die Entwicklung des Benediktbeurer Passionsspiels" *Euphorion*, XLVI (1952), 113–137.

——. "Untersuchungen zum St. Galler Passionsspiel" *Festschrift für Wolfgang Stammler.* (Berlin, 1953), 109–129.

Hartel, Guilelmus. ed. *Caecili Cypriani De Catholicae Ecclesiae Unitatae* in *Corpus Scriptorum Ecclesiasticorum Latinorum*, III, i. (Vindobonae, Apud C. Geroldi Filium, 1868), 211–233.

Haseloff, A. *Codex Purpureus Rossanensis.* Berlin, 1898.

Haskins, Charles H. "Albericus Casinensis" *Casinensia*, I (Monte-Cassino, 1929).

——. *The Renaissance of the Twelfth Century.* New York, The World Publishing Company, 1961.

Healy, Emma Therese Sister. *St. Bonaventure's "De Reductione Artium ad Theologiam".* St. Bonaventure, St. Bonaventure College Press, 1939.

Heard, John. "Hrotsvitha, the Nun of Gandersheim" *Poet-Lore*, XLII (1933–35), 291–328.

Heer, Friederich. *The Medieval World.* New York, Mentor Books, 1963.

Heitz, Carol. *Recherches sur les rapports entre architecture et liturgie à l'époque carolingienne.* Paris, S.E.V.P.E.N., 1963.

Helin, Maurice. *Medieval Latin Literature.* New York, William Salloch, 1949.

Henshaw, M. "The Attitude of the Church toward the Stage to the end of the Middle Ages" *Medievalia et Humanistica*, VII, 3–17.

Heyse, Paul. *Romanische Inedita auf italienischen Bibliotheken.* Berlin, Wilhelm Hertz, 1856.

Hildburgh, W.L. "English Alabaster Carvings as Records of the Medieval Religious Drama" *Archaeologia*, XCIII (1949), 51–101.

Hoffman, M.N. *Die Magdalenenszenen im geistlichen Spiel des Mittelalters.* Diss. Münster, 1933.

Hopper, Vincent F. and Lahey, Gerald B. *Medieval Mysteries, Moralities, and Interludes.* New York, Barron Educational Series, 1962.

Hunningher, Benjamin. *The Origin of the Theater.* New York, Hill and Wang, 1961.

Hurrell, John Dennis. "The Figural Approach to Medieval Drama" *College English*, XXVI, (May, 1965), 598–604.

Husmann, Heinrich. "Die älteste erreichbare Gestalt des St. Galler Tropariums" *Archiv für Musikwissenschaft*, XIII (1956), 25–41.

——. "Die St. Galler Sequenz-tradition bei Notker und Ekkehard" *Acta Musicologica*, XXVI (1954), 6–18.

——. "Sequenz und Prosa" *Annales Musicologiques*, II (1954), 61–91.

Inguanez, D.M. and Willard, H.M. *Alberici Casinensis Flores Rhetorici, Miscellanea Cassinese*, XIV (1938), 9–59.

Inguanez, D.M. "Il 'Quem quaeritis' pasquale nei codici Cassinesi," *Studi Medievali*, 14 (1941), 142–49.

——. "La lettura ed il canto della Passione nel Medioevo" *Pax* (Sorrento), IV (1938), 5–8.

——. "Montecassino e l'Oriente nel Medioevo" *Atti del IV Congresso Nazionale di Studi Romani, I* (Roma, 1938), 377–384.

——. "Reliquie della Passione a Montecassino" *Illustrazione Vaticana*, anno V, numero 7 (1934), 315–316.

——. "Un dramma della Passione del secolo XII" *Miscellanea Cassinese*, XII (1936), 7–36.

——. "Un dramma della Passione del secolo XII" with preface by Giulio Bertoni *Miscellanea Cassinese*, XVII (1939), 7–55.

Jackson, W.T.H. *The Literature of the Middle Ages*. New York, Columbia University Press, 1960.

Jacobsen, J.P. "La comédie en France au Moyen Age" *Revue de Philologie Française et de Littérature*, XXIII (1909), 1–22, 81–106, 161–196.

Jacquot, Jean. "Théâtre médiéval et tragédie Elisabéthaine" *Le théâtre tragique*, (Paris, 1962), 89–105.

James, Stanley B. "A Study in Passion Plays" *Month*, CXLV (1927), 309–315.

Jannini, Aniel Pasquale. *Guida al teatro medievale francese*. Milano, La Goliardica, n.d.

Jeanroy, Alfred. *Le Théâtre religieux en langue française jusqu'à la fin du XIVᵉ siècle*. Paris, Imprimerie Nationale, 1959.

——. *Le théâtre religieux en France du XIᵉ au XIIIᵉ siècles*. Paris, E. de Boccard, 1924.

——. "Le mystère de la Passion en France" *JS*, n.s., IV (1906), 476–492.

——. "Sur quelques sources des mystères de la Passion" *Romania*, XXXV (1906), 365–378.

De Jerphanion, G. "La représentation de la Croix et du Crucifix aux origines de l'art chrétien" in his *La voix des monuments*, (Paris, 1930), 138–164.

——. "Le cycle iconographique de Sant'Angelo in Formis" *La voix des monuments*, (Paris, 1930), 260–280.

Jodogne, Omer. "La tonalité des Mystères français" in *Studi in Onore di Italo Siciliano*, Vol. I (Firenze, 1966), 581–592.

——. "Le plus ancien mystère de la Passion" *Académie Royale de Belgique. Classe des lettres et des sciences morales et politiques* 5, serie. vol. 50 (1964), 282–294.

——. "Le théâtre médiéval et sa transmission par le livre" *Research Studies,* XXXII (1964), 63–75.

——. "Marie-Madeleine pécheresse dans les Passions médiévales" *Scrinium Lovaniense,* (Louvain, 1961), 272–284.

——. "Recherches sur les débuts du théâtre religieux en France" *Cahiers de Civilisation Médiévale,* I (1965), 1–24; II (1965), 179–189.

Jones, Charles W. *The Saint Nicholas Liturgy and its Literary Relationship.* Berkeley, The University of California Press, 1963.

Journel, P. "Le culte de la Croix dans la liturgie romaine" *La Maison-Dieu,* LXXV (1963), 68–91.

Jungmann, Joseph A. *The Mass of the Roman Rite: Its Origin and Development.* 2 vols. New York, Bonziger Brothers, 1950.

Jusserand, Jules Jean. *Le théâtre en Angleterre.* Paris, Ernest Leroux, 1881.

Kaff, Ludwig. *Mittelalterliche Oster und Passionsspiele aus Oberösterreich im Spiegel musikwissenschaftlicher Betrachtung.* Linz, Oberösterreichischer Landesverl, 1956.

Kehrein, Joseph. *Lateinische Sequenzen des Mittelalters.* Mainz, Florian Kupferberg, 1873.

Kemmer, Alfons. "Christ in the Rule of St. Benedict" *Monastic Studies,* no. 3 (1965), 87–98.

Keppler, P. "Zur Passionspredigt des Mittelalters" *Historisches Jahrbuch,* III (1882), 285–315; IV (1883), 161–188.

Kesting, Marianne. *Das Epische Theater.* Stuttgart, Kohlhammer, 1969.

Kienast, Richard. "Die Deutschsprachige Lyrik des Mittelalters" in Wolfgang Stammler's *Deutsche Philologie im Aufriss,* II (Berlin, 1954), 772–902.

Kindermann, Heinz. *TheaterGeschichte Europas I. Antike und Mittelalter.* Salzburg, Otto Müller, 1957.

Kirsch, J.P. "L'origine des stations liturgiques du missel romain" *Ephemerides Liturgicae,* XLI (1927), 137–150.

——. "Origini e carattere primitivo delle stazioni liturgiche di Roma" *Atti della Pontificia Accademia di Archeologia. serie III, Rendiconti,* v. III (1925), 123–141.

Klapper, Joseph. "Der Ursprung der lateinischen Osterfeiern" *Zeitschrift für deutsche Philologie,* L (1923), 46–58.

Klaus, Wessel. "Das Mailender Passiondiptychon. Ein Werk der Karolingischen Renaissance" *Zeitschrift für Kunstwissenschaft,* Band V (Berlin, 1951), 125–138.

Knight, Wilson G. *The Christian Renaissance*. New York, W.W. Norton and Company, 1962.

Knoll, F.O. *Die Rolle der Maria Magdalena in geistlichen Spiel des Mittelalters. Ein Beiträge zur Kultur und Theatergeschichte Deutschlands*. Berlin, Leipzig, de Gruyter, 1934.

Knudsen, Hans. *Deutsche TheaterGeschichte*. Stuttgart, Alfred Kröner, 1959.

Kondakoff, N. *Histoire de l'art byzantin*. 2 vols. Paris, Jules Rouam, 1886–1891.

Kraus, Franz Xaver. "Der Heilige Nagel in der Domkirche zu Trier" Erster Band of *Beiträge zur Trierschen Archaelogie und Geschichte*. (Trier, 1868), 1–179.

Kretzmann, Paul Edward. "The Liturgical Element in the Earliest Forms of the Medieval Drama" *Studies in Languages and Literature of the University of Minnesota*, I–IV (1916), 1–170.

Kröner, Carl. *Die Longinuslegende, ihre Entstehung und Ausbreitung in der Französischen Litteratur*. Inaugural Dissertation. Münster, Theissing, 1899.

Kronenberg, Kirt. *Roswitha von Gandersheim: Leben und Werk*. (Aus Gandersheims grosser Vergangenheit, 4), (Bad Gandersheim, Hertel, 1962).

Krumbacher, Karl. *Geschichte der Byzantinischen Litteratur* in Handbuch der klassischen Altertumswissenchaft series. München, Beck'sche Verlag-Buchhandlung, 1897.

Kuhn, Hugo. "Hrotsviths von Gandersheim Dichterisches Programm" in *Dichtung und Welt in Mittelalter* (Stuttgart, 1959), 91–104.

Langfors, Artur. "Contribution à la bibliographie des plaintes de la Vierge" *Revue des Langues Romanes*, LIII (1910), 58–69.

Langosch, Karl. *Geistliche Spiele*. Stuttgart, Benno Schwabe and Co., 1957.

Latil, Maria Agostino (Dom). *Le miniature nei rotoli dell'Exultet*. Montecassino, Litografia di Montecassino, 1899.

Lauchert, Friedrich. "Ueber das Englische Marienlied im 13. Jahrhundert" *Englische Studien*, vols. 15–16 (1891–1892), 124–142.

Laurion, Gaston. "Essai de groupement des hymnes médiévales à la Croix" *Cahiers de Civilisation Médiévale*, VI (1963), 327–331.

Lawrence, Natalie Grimes. "Quem quaeritis" *A Chaucerian Puzzle and Other Medieval Essays*. Natalie Grimes Lawrence and Jack E. Reynolds, eds. (Miami, 1961), 47–61.

Lebègue, Raimond. "La Passion d'Arnould Greban" *Romania*, LX (1934), 218–231.

——. "La vie d'un ancien genre dramatique: le mystère" *Helicon, Revue Internationale des Problèmes Generaux de la Littérature*, II (1939), 216-224.

——. "Le diable dans l'ancien théâtre religieux" *Cahiers de l'Association Internationale des Etudes Françaises* N. 3-4-5 (1953), 97-105.

——. "Le problème du salut dans les mystères et dans les tragédies protestantes" *Le théâtre tragique*, (Paris, 1962), 77-87.

LeClerq, Jean Dom. "Aspects de la dévotion mariale au Moyen-Age" *Cahiers de la Vie Spirituelle*, VII-VIII (1946), 242-249.

——. *L'amour des lettres et le désir de Dieu: initiation aux auteurs monastiques du Moyen Age*. Paris, Editions du Cerf, 1957.

——. "Dévotion et théologie mariales dans le monachisme bénédictin" in Du Manoir's eds. *Maria*, II (Paris, 1952), 547-577.

——. "L'humanisme bénédictin du VIIᵉ siècle" *Studia Anselmiana*, XX (1948), 1-20.

Leclercq, H. "Tutilo, Notker, Ratpert," *Dictionnaire d'Archéologie Chrétienne*, XV (1950), 2848-2884.

——. "Les collections de sermons de Nicolas de Clairvoux" *Revue Bénédictine*, 66 (1956), 269-320.

Lefebvre, Gaspar Dom. *Saint Andrew Daily Missal*. St. Paul, Minnesota, The E.M. Lohmann Company, 1945.

Lehmann, Paul. "The Benedictine Order and the Transmission of the Literature of Ancient Rome in the Middle Ages" in *Erforschung des Mittelalters*, (Stuttgart, 1960), 173-183.

——. "Deutschland und die mittelalterliche Überlieferung der Antike" in *Erforschung des Mittelalters*, Band, III (Stuttgart, 1960), 149-172.

——. "Judas Iscarioth in der Lateinischen Legenden-Überlieferung des Mittelalters" in *Erforschung des Mittelalters*, Band, II (Stuttgart, 1959), 229-285.

Leon, Harry J. "A Medieval Nun's Diary" *The Classical Journal*, LIX (1963), 121-127.

Leonardi, Claudio. "Nuove voci poetiche tra secolo IX e XI" *Studi Medievali*, ser. 3, Anno II, (June, 1961), 139-168.

Lepitre, A. "La Vierge Marie dans la littérature française et provençale du Moyen Age" *L'Université Catholique*, nouv. série, L (Sept.-Dec., 1905), 51-91.

Leroquais, Victor (Abbé). *Les Bréviaires manuscrits des bibliothèques publiques de France*. I. Paris, 1938, XXXV-LXII.

——. *Les sacramentaires et les missels manuscrits des bibliothèques publiques de France*. 3 vols. Paris, Macon, 1924.

Leutermann, Teodoro (Dom). *Ordo Casinensis Hebdomadae Maioris Saec. XII* in *Miscellanea Cassinese*, 20 (Montecassino, 1941).

Liegey, Gabriel M. "Faith and the Origin of Liturgical Art" *Thought*, XXII (1947), 126–138.

Lindsay, W. M. ed. *Isidori Etymologiae* 2 vols. Oxonii, Clarendoniano, 1911.

Lipphardt, Walther. *Die Weisen der lateinischen osterspiele des 12. und 13. Jahrhunderts*. Kassel, Im Bärenreiter, 1948.

———. "Marienklagen und Liturgie" *Jahrbuch für Liturgiewissenschaft*, XII (1932), 198–205.

———. "Studien zu den Marienklagen und Germanische Totenklagen" *Beiträge zur Geschichte der Deutschen Sprache und Literatur*, LVIII (1934), 390–444.

Liuzzi, Ferdinando. *La lauda e i primordi della melodia italiana*. 2 vols. Roma, Libreria dello Stato, 1934.

———. "L'espressione musicale nel dramma liturgico" *Studi Medievali*, II (1929), 74–109.

Loerke, William C. "The Miniatures of the Trial in the Rossano Gospels" *Art Bulletin*, XLIII (1961), 171–195.

Lombardo, Agostino. *Teatro inglese del medioevo e del rinascimento*. Firenze, Sansoni, 1963.

Loomis, R.S. and G. Cohen. "Were There Theatres in the Twelfth and Thirteenth Centuries?" *Speculum*, XX (1945), 92–98.

Loomis, R.S. "Some Evidence for Secular Theatres in the Twelfth and Thirteenth Centuries" *Theatre Annual*, (1945), 33–43.

Lowe, E.A. *The Beneventan Script*. Oxford, The University Press, 1914.

———. *Codici Latini Antiquiores*. IX vols. Oxford, The Clarendon Press, 1934–1953.

———. *Scriptura Beneventana*. II vols. Oxford, The Clarendon Press, 1929.

Luis, A. "Evolutio historica doctrinae Compassione B. Mariae Virginis" *Marianum*, V (1943), 261–285.

Lutz, J. and Perdrizet, P. eds. *Speculum Humanae Salvationis*. 4 vols. Leipzig, Ernest Meininger, 1907.

McKean, Mary Faith (Sister). *The Interplay of Realistic and Flamboyant Art Elements in the French Mysteres*. Washington, The Catholic University of America Press, 1959.

Maas, P.M. *Etude sur les sources de la Passion du Palatinus*. Drukkerij en Boekhandel. "St. Maarten." Tiel, 1942.

Mabillon, Johannis. *De Re Diplomatica*. Luteciae Parisiorum, Sumtibus Ludovici Billaine, 1681.

Magnin, C. *Les origines du théâtre moderne*. Paris, L. Hachette, 1838.

Maguire, Alban A. *Blood and Water. The Wounded Side of Christ in Early Christian Literature.* Washington, The Catholic University of America Press, 1958.

Mâle, Emile. *L'art religieux de la fin du Moyen Age.* Paris, Armand Colin, 1946.

——. *L'art religieux du XIIe au XVIIIe siècle.* Paris, Armand Colin, 1946.

——. *L'art religieux en France.* Paris, Armand Colin, 1908.

——. *Religious Art in France in the XIII Century.* New York, E.P. Dutton and Co., 1913.

Mancini, Valentino. "Public et espace scénique dans le théâtre du Moyen Age" *Revue d'Histoire du Théâtre,* XVII (1965), 387–403.

Mandel, Oscar. *A Definition of Tragedy.* New York, The New York University Press, 1961.

Manitius, Max. "Beiträge zur Geschichte des Ovidius und anderer romischer Schriftsteller im Mittelalter" *Philologus,* Suppl. 7, (1899), 723–767.

——. *Geschichte der lateinischen Literatur des Mittelalters.* 3 vols. München, Beck'sche Verlagsbuchhandlung, 1911–1931.

Manly, J.M. "Literary Forms and a New Theory of the Origin of Species" *MP,* IV (1906–07), 577–595.

Manoir, D'Hubert ed. *Maria* (Etudes sur la Sainte Vierge). 6 vols. Paris, Beauchesne et Fils, 1949–1961.

Marcel, Gabriel. *Théâtre et religion.* Lyon, Emmanuel Vitte, 1958.

Marshall, Mary H. "Aesthetic Values of the Liturgical Drama" *English Institute Essays,* (1950), 89–115.

——. "Boethius' Definition of *Persona* and Mediaeval Understanding of the Roman Theater" *Speculum,* XXV (October, 1950), 471–482.

——. "The Dramatic Tradition Established by the Liturgical Plays" *PMLA,* LVI (1941), 962–991.

——. "The Relation of the Vernacular Religious Plays of the Middle Ages to the Liturgical Drama." Diss. Yale, 1932.

——. "Theatre in the Middle Ages: Evidence from Dictionaries and Glosses" *Symposium,* IV (1950), 1–39.

Martene, Edmund. *De Antiquis Monachorum Ritibus.* 5 bks. Lugduni, Sumptibus Anisson, Posuel, et Rigaud, MDCLXXXX.

Martin, F. (Abbé). *Etude historique et archéologique sur les reliques de la Passion.* Paris, P. Lethielleux, 1897.

Martin, J.R. "The Dead Christ on the Cross in Byzantine Art" in *Late Classical and Mediaeval Studies in Honor of Albert Mathias Friend, Jr.* (Princeton, 1955), 189–196.

Maurer, Friedrich. ed. *Die Erlösung* in *Deutsche Literatur, Reihe geistliche Dichtung des Mittelalters,* VI (Leipzig, Wissenschaftliche Buchgesellschaft, 1934).

Mason-Vest, Eva. *Prolog, Epilog und Zwischenrede im deutschen Schauspiel des Mittelalters*. Basel, Dr. J. Weiss, 1949.

Mathieu, M. "Le personnage du marchand de parfums dans le théâtre médiéval en France" *Le Moyen Age*, LXXIV (1968), 39-71.

Mattfeld, Jacquelyn A. "Some Relationship between Texts and *Cantus Firmi* in the Liturgical Motets of Josquin des Pres" *Journal of the American Musicological Society*, XIV (1961), 159-183.

Meier, Theo. *Die Gestalt Marias im geistlichen Schauspiel des deutschen Mittelalters*. Berlin, E. Schmidt, 1959.

Mélanges d'histoire du théâtre du Moyen Age et de la Renaissance offerts à Gustave Cohen. Paris, Librairie Nizet, 1950.

Menager, L.R. "La 'byzantinisation' religieuse de l'Italie méridionale (IXᵉ-XIIᵉ siècles) et la politique monastique des normands d'Italie" *Revue d'Histoire Ecclésiastique*, LIII, no. 4 (1958), 747-774, LIV (1959), no. 1, 5-40.

Menut, Albert Douglas. ed. *Maistre Nicole Oreseme. Le livre de éthiques d'Aristote*. New York, G.E. Stechert and Co., 1940.

Mercati, Giovanni. "Antiche omilie e sacre rappresentazioni medievali" *Rassegna Gregoriana*, IV (1905), 15-20.

———. *Per la storia dei manoscritti greci*. Città del Vaticano, Biblioteca Apostolica Vaticana, 1935.

Messenger, Ruth Ellis. *Christian Hymns of the First Three Centuries*. New York, The Hymn Society of America, 1942.

———. *The Medieval Latin Hymn*. Washington, Capital Press, 1953.

Meyer, Wilhelm. *Fragmenta Burana* in Festschrift zur Feier des Hundertfünfzigjahrigen Bestehens der Koniglichen Gesellschaft der Wissenschaften zu Göttingen, Philologisch-Historischen Klasse Abhandlungen der Philologisch-Historischen Klasse. Berlin, Weidmannsche Buchhandlung, 1901.

———. *Gesammelte Abhandlungen zur Mittelateinischen Rythmik*. Berlin, Weidmannsche Buchhandlung, 1905.

Michael, Wolfgang F. "Das deutsche Drama und Theater vor der Reformation" *Deutsche Viertljahrsschrift*, XXXI (1957), 106-153.

Migne. *Patrologia Latina*.

Millet, Gabriel. *L'iconographie de l'évangile*. Paris, Fontemoing et Cie., 1916.

Mishrahi, Jean. "A *Vita Sanctae Mariae Magdalenae* in an Eleventh-Century Manuscript" *Speculum*, XVIII (1943), 335-339.

Misset, E. *Les proses d'Adam de Saint-Victor*. Paris, H. Welter, 1900.

Mohrmann, Christine. "*Pascha, Passio, Transitus*" in her *Etudes sur le latin des chrétiens*. (Roma, 1961), 205-222.

Monaci, E. "Uffizi drammatici dei disciplinati dell'Umbria" *Rivista di Filologia Romanza*, I (1872), 235–271, II (1873), 29–42.

Mone, F.J. *Lateinische Hymnen des Mittelalters*. 3 vols. Freiburg, Herder'sche Verlagshandlung, 1853–55.

——. *Schauspiele des Mittelalters*. 2 vols. Karlsruhe, C. Macklot, 1846.

Morey, Charles Rufus. *Early Christian Art*. Princeton, University Press, 1953.

Morisani, O. "La pittura cassinese e gli affreschi di S. Angelo in Formis" in *Atti dello VIII Congresso Internazionale di Studi Bizantini*, Vol. II (Roma, 1953), 220–22.

Morris, Richard. ed. *Cursor Mundi* in *Early English Text Society*. London, N. Turner and Co., 1874.

Moussinac, Léon. *Le théâtre des origines à nos jours*. Paris, Amiot-Dumont, 1957.

Muller, A. "Das Buhnenwesen in der Zeit von Constantin d. Gr. bis Justinian," *Neue Jahrbücher für das Klassische Altertum; Geschichte und deutsche Literatur*, XXIII (1909), 36–55.

Müller, H.F. "Pre-History of the Medieval Drama" *Zeitschrift für Romanische Philologie*, XLIV (1914), 544–577.

Muñoz, Antonio. *I codici greci miniati delle minori biblioteche di Roma*. Firenze, Alfani e Venturi, 1905.

——. *Il codice purpureo di Rossano*. Roma, Danesi, 1907.

——. *L'art byzantin à l'exposition de Grottaferrata*. Rome, Danesi, 1906.

Mushacke, W. "Tractatus Beati Bernhardi de Planctu Beate Marie" *Romanische Bibliothek*, III (1890), 41–50.

Neri, F. "Un dramma della Passione del secolo XII" *Giornale Storico della Letteratura Italiana*, CIX (1937), 129–30.

Nestle, Eberhard. *Novum Testamentum Graece et Latine*. Stuttgart, Wüttembergische Bibelanstald, 1910.

Nicoll, Allardyce. *Masks, Mimes and Miracles*. New York, Cooper Square Publishers, Inc., 1931.

Nicomediensis, Georgii. "In SS. Mariam Assistentem Cruci" *Patrologia Graeca*, C, 1457–1490.

Niedner, Helmut. "Die deutschen und französischen Osterspiele bis zum 15. Jahrhundert" *Germanische Studien*, 119 (1932), 13–180.

Nilson, M.P. "Zur Geschichte des Bühnenspiels in der römischen Kaiserzeit" *Acta Universitatis Lundensis*, XL, 3 (1904), printed 1906, 3–29.

Nitto de Rossi, B.G. e Nitti di Vito, Francesco. *Codice diplomatico barese*. 2 vols. Bari, V. Vecchi, 1897–1899.

Noomen, W. "Passages narratifs dans les drames médiévaux français: essai d'interprétation" *Revue Belge de Philologie et d'Histoire*, XXXVI (1958), 761–785.

Norberg, Dag. *Introduction à l'étude de la versification latine médiévale* Stockholm, Almquist et Wiksell, 1958.

Ogilvy, J.D.A. *"Mimi, Scurrae, Histriones:* Entertainers of the Middle Ages" *Speculum*, XXXVIII, 4 (1963), 603–619.

Oliger, Livario. P. "Le *Meditationes Vitae Christi* dello pseudo-Bonaventura" *Studi Francescani*, VII (1921), 143–183; VIII (1922), 18–47.

Omont, Henri. *Evangiles avec peintures byzantines du XIe siècle*. 2 vols. Paris, Imprimerie Berthaud Frères, n.d.

Owst, G.R. *Literature and Pulpit in Medieval England*. Cambridge, University Press, 1933.

Otto, R. "Der Planctus Mariae" *MLN*, (1899), 210–15.

P, M. "Drammatica liturgica" *Studi Romanzi*, XXVII–XXX (1937–43), 147–48.

Pacetto, G. *La fortuna di Terenzio nel medio evo e nel rinascimento*. Catania, Viaggio-Campo, 1918.

Paratore, Ettore. *Storia del teatro latino*. Milano, F. Vallardi, 1957.

Paré, G., Brunet, A., Tremblay, P. *La renaissance du XIIe siècle: les écoles et l'enseignement*. Paris, J. Vrin, 1933.

Paris. Bibli. Nat. *MS lat. 1240, Trop. Sancti Martialis Lemovicensis saec.* X, fol. 30^v.

Paris, Gaston. *La littérature française au Moyen Age*. Paris, Hachette, 1890.

——. "Origines du Théâtre italien" *Journal des Savants*, (1892), 670-685.

Parker, A. Alexander. "Notes on the Religious Drama in Medieval Spain and the Origin of the 'Auto Sacramental' " *MLR*, XXX (1935), 170–182.

Pascal, R. "On the Origins of the Liturgical Drama of the Middle Ages" *MLR*, XXXVI (1941), 369–387.

Pearson, Karl. *The Chances of Death*. 2 vols. London, E. Arnold, 1897.

Peebles, Rose Jeffries. *The Legend of Longinus in Ecclesiastical Tradition and English Literature, and its Connection with the Grail*. Baltimore, J.H. Furst Company, 1911.

Peltier, A. C. ed. *S. Bonaventurae Meditationes Vitae Christi* in *Opera Omnia*, XII. Parisiis, 1868.

Pétré, Hélène. *Ethérie. Journal de Voyage*. Paris, Editions du Cerf, 1948.

Petrocchi, G. *Ascesi e mistica trecentesca*. Firenze, F. Le Monnier, 1957.

——. "Sulla composizione e data delle *Meditationes Vitae Christi*" *Convivium*, XX (1952), 757–778.

Pignarre, Robert. *Histoire du théâtre*. Paris, Presses Universitaires, 1957.

Pietresson de Saint-Aubain, P. "La Passion de notre Seigneur Jésus Christ" *Bibliothèque de l'Ecole de Chatres*, LXXXV (1924), 310–322.

Pittaluga, Mary. *Arte italiana.* 3 vols. Firenze, F. Le Monnier, 1955.

Pope, Mildred and Wright, Jean G. *La Seinte Resurrection.* Oxford, Anglo-Norman Text Society, 1943.

Porcher, Jean. *French Miniatures from Illuminated Manuscripts.* London, Collins, 1960.

Pourrat, P. *La spiritualité chrétienne.* 2 vols. Paris, Victor Lecoffre, 1918–1921.

Prat, Angel Valbuena. *Historia del teatro español.* Barcelona, Editorial Noquer, 1956.

Prediche Quaresimali del padre F. Emmanuele Orchi. Venetia, 1650.

Prosser, Eleanor. *Drama and Religion in the English Mystery Plays.* Stanford, University Press, 1961.

Raby, F.J.E. *Christian Latin Poetry.* Oxford, Clarendon Press, 1927.

——. *Secular Latin Poetry in the Middle Ages.* Oxford, Clarendon Press, 1934.

Rand, Edward Kennert. "Early Mediaeval Commentaries on Terence" *Classical Philology*, IV (1909), 359–389.

——. "Sermo de Confusione Diaboli" *Modern Philology*, II (1904–05), 261–278.

Réau, Louis. *Iconographie de l'art chrétien.* Vol. I. Paris, Presses Universitaires, 1953.

Reese, Gustave. *Music in the Middle Ages.* New York, W.W. Norton and Co., 1940.

Reich, Hermann. *Der Mimus.* Berlin, Weidmannsche, 1903.

Reyal, Albert. *L'église, la comédie et les comédiens.* Paris, Editions Spes, 1953.

Rheinfelder, Hans. "Das Wort 'Persona': Geschichte seiner Bedeutungen mit besonderer Berucksichtigung des französischen und italienischen Mittelalters" *Beheifte zur Zeitschrift für romanische Philologie*, LXXVII, Halle, 1928.

Reinhardt, Heinz. "Uber den Ursprung des Dramas" *Die Pforte*, III (1951–2), 339–347.

Reichert, George. "Strukturprobleme der alteren Sequenz" *Deutsche Viertljahrschrift für Literaturwissenschaft und Geistsgeschichte*, XXIII (1949), 227–251.

Riché, P. "Recherche sur l'instruction des laïcs du XIe au XIIe siècle" *Cahiers de Civilisation Médiévale*, V (1962), 180–82.

Rigobon, Marcella. *Il teatro e la latinità di Hrotsvitha.* Padova, Milani, 1932.

Roberts, P. "A Christian Theory of Dramatic Tragedy" *Journal of Religion*, XXXI (1951), 1–20.

Robertson, W.A.S. "The Passion Play and Interludes at New Romney" *AC*, XIII (1888), 216–226.

Robinson, J.W. "The Late Medieval Cult of Jesus and the Mystery Plays" *PMLA*, LXXX, 5 (1965), 508–514.

Rohde, A. *Passionsbild und Passionsbühne*. Berlin, Furche, 1926.

Rolfe, C.C. *The Ancient Use of Liturgical Colors*. London, Parker and Co., 1879.

Rolland, Joachim. *Essai paléographique et bibliographique sur le théâtre profane en France avant le XVᵉ siècle*. Paris, Bibliothèque d'histoire littéraire, 1945.

Römer, G. "Die Liturgie des Karfreitags" *Zeitschrift für Katolische Theologie*, LXXVII (1955), 39–93.

Roschini, P. Gabriel M. "De Modo quo B. Virgo animi dolorem sustinuit" in his *Mariologia*, II (Romae, 1948), 208–213.

Rossiter, A.P. *English Drama from Early Times to the Elizabethans*. London, Hutchinson and Co., 1950.

Roy, Emile. "Le mystère de la Passion en France" *Revue Bourguignonne*, XIII (1903), 3–121; XIV (1904), 203–512.

Rudwin, M.J. *A Historical and Bibliographical Survey of the German Religious Drama*. Pittsburgh, University Press, 1924.

——. *Der Teufel in den deutschen geistlichen Spielen des Mittelalters und der Reformationszeit*. Göttingen, Vandehoeck and Ruprecht, 1915.

Ruggieri, Ruggero M. *Saggi di linguistica italiana e italo romanza*. Firenze, L.S. Olschki, 1962.

Rushton, Gerald Wynne. "Passion Plays and their Origin" *CW*, CXXXIX (1934), 40–46.

Russo, Luigi. "La letteratura religiosa nel Duecento" *Romana*, 3 (1939), 483–497, 542–559, 611–643.

Russo, P.F. "Attività artistico-culturale del monachesimo calabro-greco anteriormente all'epoca normanna" in *Atti dello VIII Congresso Internazionale di Studi Bizantini*, Vol. I. (Roma, 1953), 463–475.

——. *Il codice purpureo di Rossano*. Roma, Oreste Rossi, 1952.

Sabbadini, R. "Biografi e commentatori di Terenzio" *Studi Italiani di Filologia Classica*, V (1897), 289–327.

Salmi, Mario. *L'enluminure italienne*. Milano, Electa Editrice S.p.A., 1954.

Salter, F.M. *The Trial and Flagellation with Other Studies in the Chester Cycle*. London, Oxford University Press, 1935.

Salzer, Anselm. *Die Sinnbilder und Beiworte Mariens in der deutschen Literatur und lateinischen Hymnenpoesie des Mittelalters*. Linz, Jos. Feichtingers Erben, 1893.

Saxer, Victor. "Les saintes Marie Madeleine et Marie de Béthanie dans la tradition liturgique et homilétique orientale" *Revue des Sciences Religieuses*, XXXII, 1 (1958), 1–37.

——. *Le culte de Marie Madeleine en Occident des origines à la fin du Moyen Age.* 2 vols. Paris, Clavreuil, 1959.

Sandberg-Vavalà, Evelyn. *La croce dipinta italiana e l'iconografia della Passione.* Verona, Casa Editrice Apollo, 1929.

Sandys, John Edwin. *A History of Classical Scholarship.* Cambridge, University Press, 1906.

Sapegno, Natalino. *Storia letteraria d'Italia.* Milano, Vallardi, 1938.

Sauro, Antoine. *Le théâtre en France au Moyen Age.* Napoli, L. Lepre, 1953.

Salvioni, Carlo. "Il Pianto delle Marie in antico volgare Marchigiano" *Rendiconti della R. Accademia dei Lincei* (Classe di scienze morali, storiche, filologiche.), serie V, VIII (1900).

Schäfer, Thomas. *Die Fusswaschung in monastischen Brauchtum und in der lateinischen Liturgie.* Beuron, Beuroner, 1956.

Schmidt, Hermanus A.P. *Hebdomada Sancta.* 2 vols. Romae, Pontificiae Universitatae Gregorianae, 1956–57.

Schmitz, Kenneth L. "A Sermon of Thomas of York on the Passion" *Franciscan Studies*, XXIV, 2 (1964), 205–222.

Schnürer, Gustave. *L'église et la civilisation au Moyen Age.* 3 vols. Paris, Payot, 1933–1938.

Schönbach, Anton. *Die Marienklagen.* Graz, Universitäts Buchhandlung, 1874.

Schreiber, Cécile. "L'Univers compartimenté du théâtre médiéval" *French Review*, XLI (1968), 468–478.

Schumacher, Fr. "Les éléments narratifs de la Passion d'Autun" *Romania*, XXVII (1908), 570–593.

Schwietering, J. "Uber den liturgischen Ursprung des mittelalterlichen geistlichen Spiels" *Zeitschrift für deutschen Altertum und deutsche Literatur*, LXII (1925), 1–20.

Sepet, Marius. *Le drame chrétien au Moyen Age.* Paris, Didier et Cie., 1876.

——. *Le drame religieux au Moyen Age.* Paris, Bloud et Cie., 1903.

——. *Origines catholiques du théâtre moderne.* Paris, P. Lethielleux, 1901.

Sesini, Ugo. *Poesia e musica nella latinità cristiana dal III al X secolo.* Torino, Società Editrice Internazionale, 1949.

Shepard, William P. *La passion provençale du manuscrit Didot.* Paris, SATF, 1928.

Simonetti, Manlio. "Studi sull'innologia popolare cristiana dei primi secoli" in *Atti della Accademia Nazionale dei Lincei* anno CCCXLIX

(Roma, 1952), Memorie, Classe di Scienze morali, storiche e filologiche, Serie VIII, vol. IV, fasc. 6, 341–484.

Sletsjöe, Leif. "Quelques Réflexions sur la Naissance du Théâtre Religieux" *Actes du Xe Congrès International de Linguistique et Philologie Romanes* (Strasbourg, 1962; published at Paris, 1965), II, 667–675.

Smalley, Beryl. *The Study of the Bible in the Middle Ages.* Oxford, Clarendon Press, 1952.

Smoldon, W.L. "Liturgical Drama" in *Early Medieval Music up to 1300* edited by Dom Anselm Hughes (New Oxford History of Music, II, (London, New York, 1954), 176–219.

——. "The Easter Sepulchre Music-Drama" *Music and Letters,* XXVII (1946), 1–17.

Southern, R.W. *The Making of the Middle Ages.* New Haven, Yale University Press, 1959.

——. *Saint Anselm and His Biographer: A Study of Monastic Life and Thought 1059– c. 1130.* Cambridge and New York, Cambridge University Press, 1963.

Spanke, H. "Die KompositionsKunst der Sequenzen Adams von St. Victor" *Studi Medievali,* N.S. Anno XIV (1941), 1–29.

Speaight, Robert. *Christian Theatre.* New York, Hawthorn Books, 1960.

Speirs, John. *Medieval English Poetry.* London, Faber and Faber, 1957.

Sprague, Rosemary. "Hrotswitha-Tenth-Century Margaret Webster" *The Theatre Annual,* XIII (1955), 16–31.

Stäblein, Bruno. "Zur Frühgeschichte der Sequenz" *Archiv für Musikwissenschaft,* XVIII (1961), 1–33.

Stammler, Wolfgang. *Das religiöse drama im deutschen Mittelalter.* Leipzig, Quelle and Mener, 1925.

——. ed. *Deutsche Literatur des Mittelalters: Verfasserlexikon.* 5 vols. Berlin, Walter de Gruyter und Co., 1933–1955.

——. *Deutsche Philologie im Aufriss.* 3 vols. Berlin, Erich Schmidt, 1954–1959.

——. *Kleine Schriften zur Litteraturgeschichte des Mittelalters.* Berline, Erich Schmidt, 1953.

Steidle, Basilius (Dom). "Abba, Vater" *Benediktinische Monatschrift,* 16 (1934), 89–101.

Sticca, Sandro. "The Priority of the Montecassino Passion Play," *Latomus. Revue d'Etudes Latines,* XX (1961), 381–391, 568–574, 827–839.

Strecker, Karl. *Hrotsvithae Opera.* Leipzig, B. G. Teubueri, 1906.

——. *Poetae Latini Aevi Carolini* in *Monumenta Germaniae Historica,* IV (Berlin, 1914–1923).

Stuart, Donald Clive. *The Development of Dramatic Art.* New York, Dover Publications, 1960.

Stubbe, A. *La Madone dans l'art.* Bruxelles, Editions et Ateliers d'art graphique Elsevier, 1958.

Stumpfl, Robert. *Kultspiele der Germanen als Ursprung des Mittelalterlichen Dramas.* Berlin, Junker und Dünnhaupt, 1936.

Sullivan, John (Sister). *A Study of the Themes of the Sacred Passion in the Medieval Cycle Plays.* Washington, The Catholic University Press, 1942.

Symonds, Th. "Sources of the Regularis Concordia" *Downside Review,* LIX (1941), 14–30, 143–170, 204-289.

Szövérffy, Joseph. "Kreislauf von Ideen und Bildern: Randbemerkungen zum mittelalterlichen Drama, zur Hymnendichtung und Ikonographie" *Zeitschrift für romanische Philologie,* LXXVII (1961), 289–298.

——. "L'hymnologie médiévale: recherches et méthodes" *Cahiers de Civilisation Médiévale,* IVᵉ Année n. 4, (October–Décembre, 1961), 389-422.

——. " 'Peccatrix Quondam Femina': A Survey of the Mary Magdalene Hymns" *Traditio,* XIX (1963), 79–146.

——. "Tuba Mirum Spargens Sonum . . . Some Peculiarities of a Holy Cross Hymn" *Aevum,* XXXII (1958), 37–50.

Taylor, George C. "The English Planctus Mariae" *MP,* IV (1906–07), 605–637.

——. "The Relation of the English Corpus Christi Play To the English Religious Lyric" *MP,* IV (1906–08), 1–38.

Terracini, Benvenuto A. "I mille anni della lingua italiana e il centenario dell 'unità" *Lettere Italiane,* XIII (1961), 265–285.

——. "Un dramma della Passione del secolo XXII" *Archivio Glottologico Italiano,* XXIX (1937), 92–94.

Teyssèdre, Bernard. *Le sacramentaire de Gellone.* Paris, E. Privat, 1959.

Thibaut, J.B. *Ordre des offices de la Semaine Sainte à Jerusalem du IVᵉ au Xᵉ siècle.* Paris, 5 Rue Bayard, 1926.

Thien, Hormann. *Uber die englischen Marienklagen.* Kiel, Druck von H. Fiencke, 1906.

Thilo, G. and Hagen, H. eds. *Servii Grammatici in Virgilii Bucolica Commentarii,* III. Lipsiae, 1887.

Thiry, Paul. *Le théâtre français au Moyen Age.* Bruxelles, Office de publicité, 1944.

Thoby, Paul. *Le crucifix des origines au Concile de Trente.* Nantes, Bellanger, 1959.

Thomas, R.G. ed. *Ten Miracle Plays.* Evanston, Northwestern University Press, 1966.

Tischendorf, Constantinus. *Evangelia Apocrypha.* Lipsia, 1876.

Tonelli, Luigi. *Il teatro italiano.* Monza, Arti grafiche Monza, 1924.

Toschi, Paolo. "D.M. Inguanez: Un dramma della Passione del secolo XII" *Archivum Romanicum,* XXI (1937), 397–400.

——. *L'antico dramma sacro italiano.* 2 vols. Firenze, Libraria Editrice Fiorentina, 1927.

——. "L'origine romana del dramma liturgico" *Rivista Italiana del Dramma,* II (1938), 257–268.

——. *Le origini del teatro italiano.* Torino, Edizioni Scientifiche Einaudi, 1955.

——. "Narrazione e dramma nel nostro antico teatro religioso" *Rivista Italiana del Dramma,* 2 (1937), 159–180.

Tosti, Luigi. *Storia della badia di Montecassino.* 3 vols. Napoli, Filippo Cirelli, 1842.

Trench, Richard Chenevix. *Sacred Latin Poetry.* London, Kegan Paul, Trench and Co., 1886.

Trens, Manuel. *El arte en la Pasion de nuestro Señor.* Barcelona, Catálogo de la Exposición, 1945.

Tunison, Joseph S. *Dramatic Traditions of the Dark Ages.* Chicago, University Press, 1907.

Turrecremata and Duranto. eds. *St. Birgittae Revelationes.* Coloniae, 1628.

Ugolini, Francesco A. *Testi volgari abruzzesi del Duecento.* Torino, Rosenberg e Sellier, 1959.

Van der Veken, B.J. "De Primordiis Liturgiae Paschalis" *Sacris Erudiri,* XIII (1962), 461–501.

Van Wageningen, Jacobus. *Scaenica Romana.* Groningae, In aedibus P. Noordhoff, 1907.

Vale, G. "Le lamentazioni di Geremia ad Aquileia" *Rassegna Gregoriana,* VIII–IX (1909–10), 105–116.

Vecchi, Giuseppe. "Innodia e dramma sacro" *Studi Mediolatini e Volgari,* I (Università di Pisa, 1953), 225–237.

Venturi, A. *Storia dell'arte italiana.* 9 vols. Milano, Ulrico Hoepli, 1901–1933.

Verdevoye, Paul. *Nacimiento del teatro francés.* Santa Fe, Publication de "Extensión Universitaria", 1954.

Vernet, Felix. *La spiritualité médiévale.* Paris, Bloud et Gay, 1929.

Vev, Rudolf. *Christliches Theater in Mittelalter und Neuzeit.* Zurich, Christiana-Verl, 1960.

Vinay, Gustavo. "La commedia latina del secolo XII" *Studi Medievali,* II (1954), 209–271.

Viscardi, Antonio. "Appunti per la storia della religiosità e della letteratura religiosa in Italia nei secoli XIII e XIV" *Studi Medievali,* I (1928), 438-455.

———. *Le origini.* Milano, F. Vallardi, 1950.

———. *Saggio sulla letteratura religiosa del Medio Evo romanzo.* Padova, Antonio Milani, 1932.

Vogel, C. "Introduction aux sources de l'histoire du culte chrétien au Moyen Age" *Studi Medievali,* Ser. 3. 3, (1962), 1-92.

———. "Les échanges liturgiques entre Rome et les pays francs jusqu'à l'époque de Charlemagne" *Le Chiese nei Regni dell'Europa occidentale e i loro Rapporti con Roma sino all'800* in *Settimane di Studio del Centro Italiano di Studi sull'alto Medioevo,* VII (7-13 April, 1959), 185-295, 326-330.

Von Rieden, Oktavian P. "Das Leiden Christi im Leben des Hl. Franziskus von Assisi. Eine Quellenvergleichende Untersuchung im Lichte der Zeitgenossischen Passionfrömmigkeit" *Collectanea Franciscana,* XXX (1960), 5-30, 129-145, 241-263, 353-397.

Von Simon, Otto Georg. "Das abendländische Vermächtnis der Liturgie," *Deutsche Beiträge zur geistigen Überlieferung,* I (1947), 1-57.

Von den Steinen, W. "Die Anfange der Sequenze-dichtung" *Zeitschrift für schweizeren Kirchengeschichte,* XL (1946), 190-212.

Von Stoephasius, Renata. *Die Gestalt des Pilatus in den mittelalterlichen Passionsspielen.* Wurzburg, Konrad Triltsch, 1938.

Von Winterfeld, Paul. "Der Mimus in Mittelalter" *Herrig's Archiv,* CXIV, 48-75, 293-324.

Voragine, Jacobus da. *Legenda Aurea.* ed. J.G. Theodor Graesse. Lipsiae, 1850.

Wagenaar-Nolthenius, Hélène. "Sur la construction musicale du drame liturgique" *Cahiers de Civilisation Médiévale,* III (1960), 449-456.

Wallach, Luitpold. "Education and Culture in the Tenth Century" *Medievalia et Humanistica,* IX (1955), 18-22.

Walpole, A.S. *Early Latin Hymns.* Cambridge, University Press, 1922.

Walshe, M. O'C. *Medieval German Literature.* Cambridge, The Harvard University Press, 1962.

Walther, Hans. *Carmina Medii Aevi Posterioris Latina.* Göttingen, Vandenhoeck and Ruprecht, 1959.

Watson, John Calvin. "The Relation of the Scene-headings to the Miniatures in Manuscripts of Terence" *Harvard Studies in Classical Philology,* XIV (1903), 37-54.

Wattenbach, W. ed. *Leonis Marsicani et Petri Diaconi Chronica Monasterii Casinensis* in *Monumenta Germaniae Historica,* Fol. seria Scriptorum, VII (Hannoverae, Aulici Hahniani, 1846), 551-844.

Weakland, Rembert, O.S.B. "The Beginning of Troping" *Musical Quarterly*, XLIV (1958), 477–488.

——. "The Rhythmic Modes and Medieval Latin Drama" *Journal of the American Musicological Society*, XIV (1961), 131–146.

Weber, Paul. *Geistliches Schauspiel und Kirchliche Kunst.* Stuttgart, Ebner und Seubert, 1894.

Wechssler, Eduard. *Die Romanische Marienklagen.* Halle, Ehrhardt Karras, 1893.

Wellesz, Egon. "The Origin of Sequences and Tropes" in his *Eastern Elements in Western Chant.* (Oxford, 1947), 153–174.

Wellington, St. Paul Sister. *The Influence of the Medieval Hymn on Medieval Drama.* Diss. University of Southern California, 1930.

Wells, John Edwin. *A Manual of the Writings in Middle English.* 1050–1400. (Yale, University Press, 1926), 539–543.

Werner, Wilfred. *Studien zu den Passions und Osterspielen des deutschen Mittelalters in ihrem Ubergang vom Latein zur Volkssprache.* Berlin, Erich Schmidt Verlag, 1963.

Wessel, Klaus. "Das mailander Passionsdiptychon. Ein Werk der Karolingischen Renaissance" *Zeitschrift für Kunstwissenschaft*, Band V (Berlin, 1951), 125–138.

Weston, Karl E. "The Illustrated Terence Manuscripts" *Harvard Studies in Classical Philology*, XIV (1903), 37–54.

Wetzer und Welte. *Kirchenlexicon.* 12 vols. Freiburg im Breisgau, Herder'sche, 1882–1901.

Wickham, Glynne. *Early English Stages 1300 to 1660.* Vol. I, 1300–1576 London, Routledge and Paul, 1959.

Wilmart, A. (Dom). *Auteurs spirituels et textes dévots du Moyen Age latin.* Paris, Bloud et Gay, 1932.

——. "Poèmes de Gautier de Châtillon dans un manuscrit de Charleville" *Revue Bénédictine*, XLIX (1937), 121–169, 322–365.

Williams, Arnold. "The English Moral Play before 1500" *Annuale Mediaevale*, IV (1963), 5–22.

Wilmotte, M. "Les origines du drame liturgique" *Académie Royale de Belgique. Bulletin de la Classe des Lettres et des Sciences Morales et Politiques et de la Classe des Beaux-Arts*, VII (1901), 715–749.

Woerdeman, J. "Source of the Easter Play" *Orate Fratres*, XX (1945-46), 262–272.

Wolf, Ferdinand. *Uber die Lais, Sequenzen und Leiche.* Heidelberg, C.F. Winter, 1841.

Wolff, Erwin. "Die Terminologie des Mittelalterlichen Dramas in Bedeutungsgeschichtlicher Sicht" *Anglia*, LXVIII, 1 (1960), 1–27.

Wolpers, Theodor. "Englische Marienlyrik im Mittelalter" *Anglia*, LXIX (1950), 3–88.

Wormald, Francis. *The Benedictional of St. Ethelwold*. London, Faber and Faber, 1960.

——. *The Miniatures in the Gospels of St. Augustine. Corpus Christi College M.S. 286*. Cambridge, University Press, 1954.

Wrangham, Digby S. *The Liturgical Poetry of Adam of St. Victor*. 3 vols. London, Kegan Paul, Trench and Co., 1881.

Wright, F. A. and Sinclair, T. A. *A History of Later Latin Literature*. New York, The Macmillan Company, 1931.

Wright, Jean Gray. *A Study of the Themes of the Resurrection in the Medieval French Drama*. Menasha, George Banta, 1935.

Wright, Edith A. *The Dissemination of the Liturgical Drama in France*. Bryn Mawr, Pa., 1936.

——. *Ystoire de la Passion, The Johns Hopkins Studies in Romance Literatures and Languages*, XLV. Baltimore, Johns Hopkins University Press, 1944.

Wülcher, Richard Paul. *Das Evangelium Nicodemi in der Abendländischen Literatur*. Paderborn, Ferdinand Schöningh, 1872.

Young, Karl. "Concerning the Origin of Miracle Plays" in *The Manley Anniversary Studies*, (1923), 254–68.

——. "Observations on the Origin of the Medieval Passion Play" *PMLA*, XXV (1910), 309–54.

——. *The Drama of the Medieval Church*. 2 vols. Oxford, Clarendon Press, 1933.

Young, W. D. *Devices and "feintes" of Medieval Religious Theatre in England and France*. Dissertation. Stanford, 1960.

Zesmer, David M. *Guide to English Literature*. New York, Barnes and Noble, Inc., 1961.

Zeeman, Elizabeth. "Continuity and Change in Middle English Versions of the *Meditationes Vitae Christi*" *Medium Aevum*, XXVI (1957)

Zeydel, H. Edwin. "The Authenticity of Hrotswitha's Works" *Modern Language Notes*, LXI (1946), 50–55.

——. "Were Hrotswitha's Dramas performed during her lifetime?" *Speculum*, XX, 4 (1945), 443–456.

Zumthor, Paul. *Histoire littéraire de la France médiévale. VIᵉ–XIVᵉ siècles*. Paris, Presses Universitaires, 1954.

——. *Langue et technique poétiques à l'époque romane (XIᵉ–XIIIᵉ siècles)*. Paris. Librairie C. Klincksieck, 1963.

Index